NCAER 1956 2016 QUALITY. RELEVANCE. IMPACT

INDIA POLICY FORUM 2015|16

VOLUME 12

EDITED BY

Shekhar Shah
Subir Gokarn
Karthik Muralidharan

NATIONAL COUNCIL OF APPLIED
ECONOMIC RESEARCH
New Delhi

NCAER 60

SAGE

Los Angeles | London | New Delhi
Singapore | Washington DC | Melbourne

First published in 2016 by

SAGE Publications India Pvt Ltd
B1/I-1 Mohan Cooperative Industrial Area
Mathura Road, New Delhi 110 044, India
www.sagepub.in

SAGE Publications Inc
2455 Teller Road
Thousand Oaks, California 91320, USA

SAGE Publications Ltd
1 Oliver's Yard, 55 City Road
London EC1Y 1SP, United Kingdom

SAGE Publications Asia-Pacific Pte Ltd
3 Church Street
#10-04 Samsung Hub
Singapore 049483

Library of Congress Serial Publication Data applied for

ISSN: 0973-4805
ISBN: 978-93-860-6208-6 (PB)

Published by Vivek Mehra for SAGE Publications India Pvt Ltd, typeset in 10.5/13 pt Times by RECTO Graphics, Delhi, and printed at Avantika Printers, New Delhi.

INDIA POLICY FORUM 2015|16

VOLUME 12

PURPOSE AND ORGANIZATION

This 12th *India Policy Forum 2015–16 Volume* comprises papers and highlights of the discussions at the India Policy Forum (IPF) held in New Delhi on July 14–15, 2015. The IPF promotes original policy and empirical research on India, providing a unique combination of intense scholarship and policymaker engagement at the annual IPF conference for commenting on the research, and the eventual publication of the revised work in this international journal. The IPF invites both original empirical research and policy-focused expert reviews that define the best policy advice based on robust, empirical research.

The IPF is now sponsored and organized by NCAER, the National Council of Applied Economic Research in New Delhi. It started in 2004 as a collaborative endeavor between NCAER and the Brookings Institution in Washington D.C.

An international Research Panel of India-based and overseas scholars with an abiding interest in India supports this initiative through advice, active participation at the IPF, and the search for innovative papers that promise fresh insights. An international advisory panel of distinguished economists provides overall guidance. Members of the two IPF panels are listed below.

Papers appear in the annual *IPF Volume* after revisions based on IPF discussants' comments, a usually lively floor discussion, and the guidance provided by the IPF editors. To allow readers to get a sense of the richness of the conversations that happen at the IPF, discussants' comments are included here as delivered at the IPF, as is a brief summary of the floor discussion on each paper. The papers and the associated comments represent the views of the individual authors and do not imply agreement by the Governing Body, officers, or staff of NCAER or members of the IPF panels.

The *Annual IPF Lecture* for 2015 was delivered on July 14th to a packed audience by Professor Arvind Panagariya, Vice Chairman of NITI Aayog, and, before he assumed office, a Non-Resident Senior Fellow at NCAER. Panagariya spoke on "Economic Policies and Outcomes in India: A Retrospective." The 2015 IPF Lecture can be viewed on www.ncaer.org.

True to its name, in recent years the IPF has also featured an *IPF Policy Roundtable* that allows a deeper, timely, and energetic discussion of policy and political issues around topics of current policy relevance. The 2015 IPF Roundtable on "The Challenge of Financing Infrastructure in India" was expertly chaired by Mr Suresh Prabhu, Union Minister for Railways in the Government of India. The names of the Roundtable panelists can be found at the end of the Editors' Summary.

PARTNERS

NCAER gratefully acknowledges the generous support for IPF 2015 from HDFC Ltd, Reliance Industries Ltd, IDFC Ltd, State Bank of India, and Citibank N.A. Their support reflects the deep commitment of the enlightened leadership of these organizations to rigorous, independent, economic policy research that helps promote more informed policy debates and evidence-based policymaking in India.

CORRESPONDENCE

Correspondence about papers in this *IPF Volume* should be addressed directly to the authors (each paper contains the email address(es) of the corresponding author(s)). All author affiliations in the papers are as of the IPF Conference. Manuscripts are not accepted for review because the *IPF Volume* is devoted exclusively to invited contributions. Feedback on the *IPF Volume* itself may be sent to: The Editor, India Policy Forum, NCAER, 11 Indraprastha Estate, New Delhi 110002, or by email to ipf@ncaer.org. More information on the IPF is available on www.ncaer.org.

THE IPF TEAM

NCAER is responsible for the development, planning, organization, publication, and fund-raising for the India Policy Forum. The Editors and IPF Panels are deeply grateful to the following NCAER staff for their dedication and hard work on the 2015 IPF:

Sudesh Bala and Geetu Makhija	*Team leads and overall coordination*
Akansha Dubey	*Coordination, Director-General's Office*
Anupma Mehta	*Editing*
Jagbir Singh Punia	*Publication*
Sangita Chaudhary	*Team assistance*
P. P. Joshi	*Hospitality and logistics*
Praveen Sachdeva	*Conference production and graphics*

Editors' Summary

The India Policy Forum (IPF) crossed its dozen-year mark in New Delhi on July 14–15, 2015. The IPF has come a long way from the first conference in March 2004, hosted by NCAER jointly with the Washington DC-based Brookings Institute. The goal then was very much promoting original policy and empirical research on India, providing a unique combination of intense scholarship and policymaker engagement at the IPF conference for commenting on the research, and finally publishing the revised work in an international journal.

Over the ensuing years, interest in India has grown, to the point where there is now much more original research on India appearing in international economic journals. The IPF has also changed, making room for more policy-focused review articles that seek to define the best policy advice based on robust, empirical research. It has also added more roundtable discussions of key policy issues dominating the discussion of Indian economic policy-making and the economy in recent years. This 12th edition of the *India Policy Forum* journal volume contains the five 2015 IPF conference papers, the comments of the formal paper discussants, and a summary of the floor discussion of each paper.

Understanding Inflation in India

Inflation has emerged as a leading concern in India. The inflation rate measured by the consumer price index (CPI) rose from 3.7 percent to 12.1 percent per year over 2001 to 2010. By early 2015, the inflation rate had fallen to 5.2 percent, leading to questions both about how to explain movements in India's inflation, and whether this more recent moderation under the Reserve Bank of India (RBI) led by Raghuram Rajan was likely to endure.

Economists, policymakers, and journalists have proposed a variety of answers. Some of these emphasize the impact of food inflation—especially for non-cereals such as pulses, milk, fruits, and vegetables—shifting dietary patterns, rising rural wages, government policies including the minimum support price used for public procurement, and India's rural unemployment guarantee scheme. Others have blamed India's monetary and fiscal stimulus following the 2008 global financial crisis for inflation, while the rest have cited supply-side constraints arising from policymaking failures and India's huge infrastructure deficits. Many have feared that high inflation may become embedded in price expectations, creating a classic, self-sustaining inflationary spiral. The role of monetary policy has remained controversial, with analysts and the financial media still debating the impact of interest-rate increases in explaining recent declines in inflation, and, more generally, the RBI's mandate to control inflation versus the need to loosen monetary policy to promote economic growth.

To address some of these questions, the paper by Laurence Ball, Anusha Chari, and Prachi Mishra examines the behavior of quarterly inflation in India since 1994, particularly as revealed by looking at headline versus core inflation. Core inflation is intended to capture the underlying relatively smooth trend in the inflation rate determined by inflation expectations and the level of economic activity. Headline inflation is the sum of core inflation and price shocks coming from particular industries, particularly in the relative prices of food and energy and is, therefore, usually more volatile than core inflation. Core inflation is often measured by the inflation rate excluding food and energy prices. This practice is motivated by the fact that food and energy prices are volatile, and excluding them produces a much smoother inflation series.

The authors follow an approach to measuring core inflation, originally developed by the Federal Reserve Bank of Cleveland, using the weighted median of price changes across industries. Research on the US finds that median inflation, with all large price changes removed, has less short-term volatility than inflation leaving out food and energy. For India, the authors use monthly Indian Wholesale Price Index (WPI) data from 1994 to 2014 aggregated to quarters (as we know, the WPI is really not a measure of wholesale prices but measures prices at various stages of the value chain). The highly disaggregated sector data are available only for the WPI, allowing the creation of a historical series for median inflation. The headline WPI inflation rate is the mean inflation rate across industries weighted by their importance as supplied by the official statistics. For core inflation, the weighted median inflation rate is the rate at which industries with 50 percent of the total weight have higher inflation and the others have lower inflation.

The authors find that core inflation, as measured by weighted, quarterly median WPI inflation, is substantially less volatile than headline inflation, a result found for many other countries. But the authors also find that on average core inflation measured by the weighted median inflation (about 3.4 percent over the period) is substantially lower than the average level of headline inflation (about 5.6 percent). This difference arises because the distribution of price changes across industries is often skewed to the right—there is a tail of large price increases that raise headline inflation, but are filtered out of the median—and rarely to the left. Many of the large price increases that raise headline WPI inflation, but far from all of them, occur for different types of food and fuel. The role of food prices is consistent with the common view that these prices strongly influence aggregate inflation.

The paper then explores the determinants of Indian core inflation by estimating a version of a Phillips curve seeking to explain inflation with expected inflation and the level of economic activity relative to the economy's long-run potential. The authors' estimates of the Phillips curve are somewhat imprecise compared to estimates for advanced economies, reflecting the fact that the necessary data are available only since 1996, and that they are noisy, with substantial quarter-to-quarter movements in the weighted median inflation. Nonetheless, the data point to two conclusions about India's Phillips curve.

First, current core inflation seems to depend on many lags of past inflation with weights that decline slowly. The authors interpret this as reflecting a very slow adjustment of expected inflation: a one-percentage-point deviation of inflation from its expected level changes the expected inflation in the next quarter by only 0.1 percentage points, and once a high level of inflation becomes embedded in expectations, this does not change easily.

Second, for a given level of expected inflation, there is a positive relationship between inflation and the deviation of output from trend. This effect is central to the textbook Phillips curve, but some previous work has questioned it for India. Along with the finding about the slow adjustment of inflation expectations, the estimated effect of the output gap implies that monetary policy can reduce inflation, but with a short-run cost in output. The authors estimate a sacrifice ratio of approximately 2.7—a permanent one-percentage-point reduction in WPI core inflation is likely to reduce the annual output by 2.7 percentage points. This estimate is the same order of magnitude as sacrifice ratios for other economies and previous estimates for India, the latter despite using different methodologies. Since the RBI is targeting CPI inflation, whereas the authors are working with WPI inflation, they suggest that future work should examine whether the relationship of output to core CPI inflation is similar.

The paper also studies dynamic interactions among core inflation, headline inflation, and supply shocks. One finding is that movements in headline inflation appear to influence expected inflation, and hence future levels of core inflation. As a result, a one-time supply shock, such as a large spike in food prices, can have a persistent effect on inflation. Like other aspects of India's inflation, this finding is reminiscent of inflation in advanced economies in the 1970s and 1980s.

The authors' findings have implications for the role of different measures of inflation in monetary policy, and for the tradeoffs facing policymakers. Although they have emphasized the usefulness of the weighted median inflation rate as a measure of core inflation, nonetheless they believe that conventional measures of headline inflation should still have a central role in monetary policy. One reason is communication with the public, which inevitably relates more easily to news on headline inflation. Headline inflation appears to feed into expected inflation and, hence, into future core inflation. At the same time, the authors suggest further work on core inflation to understand the policy tradeoffs. Understanding the Phillips curve for India better seems essential for more effective policies to control inflation. We hope that the RBI will take heed of these recommendations.

Reforming India's Tax System

Govinda Rao in his paper on India's tax system revisits a topic he addressed in a joint paper in the very first IPF in 2004. It reviews tax policy and reforms at the Union and State levels to identify why India's tax to GDP ratio still remains so low. How has the Indian tax system done on the best-practice goals of broadening the tax base, lowering rates and reducing their spread, and achieving a transparent and predictable tax regime that has high revenue productivity and minimizes the costs of compliance, administration, and resource distortions?

This review is timely for a number of reasons. First, despite 24 years of tax reform beginning with the recommendations of the 1992 Chelliah Committee, India's ratio of tax to GDP has remained remarkably stagnant, even showing a decline in recent years. Improving allocations to health and education and strengthening physical infrastructure crucially depend on increasing tax revenues. This is all the more important if the fiscal deficit targets set by India's Fiscal Responsibility and Budget Management Act are to be met.

Second, without an efficient tax regime, India cannot be globally competitive. Third, India has not been able to evolve harmonious, coordinated, broad-based direct and indirect tax systems covering the Union and States. The fragmented constitutional assignment of income tax and poor coordination in calibrating internal and external indirect taxes have posed difficulties in getting to a good income and consumption tax system. Finally, widespread frustration among both foreign and multinational companies doing business in India and among tax collectors is bringing greater attention to the complexities in taxing international capital set against the legal and administrative ambiguities in India's tax system.

The paper first cites a number of tax successes. These include the simplification of the personal income tax by reducing rates and tax brackets, the introduction of the taxpayer identity number (TIN), value-added tax at the State level and service tax, and the establishment of large taxpayer units. The introduction of the TIN in 2004 sharply increased direct tax revenue by almost two percentage points of GDP between 2004 and 2008, showing the potential from the appropriate application of technology to tax administration.

What continues to ail the Indian tax system? Among the factors the paper cites are: the fragmented assignment of income tax on agriculture between the Union and States in the Indian Constitution, the plethora of tax exemptions, concessions, and deductions that raise tax expenditure very substantially, lopsided indirect tax revenue concentration in petroleum products and basic metals, the low yield of property taxes, tax avoidance by multinational corporations against the backdrop of ambiguities in tax provisions and collection practices, and underlying many of these problems, the low capacity of tax administrations.

One sign of these systemic weaknesses is the huge amount of tax arrears amounting to some 5.1 percent of GDP in 2013–14. Some 76 percent of this is held up in disputes of up to 5 years old. Less than 3.4 percent of the population pays individual income tax. The fragmented Constitutional assignment of tax on agricultural and non-agricultural incomes to Union and State governments makes it difficult to levy a comprehensive income tax and opens up an easy avenue for avoidance and evasion.

The lack of coordination among the Union and the States in indirect taxes has been a major impediment. As a result, the biggest item in the reform agenda is the introduction of the goods and services tax (GST). There is no doubt that the GST's replacing a plethora of Union and State indirect taxes will be an important reform. This is expected to improve the ease of doing business, enhance efficiency in supply chains by obviating the need to have branch offices (created to avoid inter-states sales tax), reduce transaction costs by ensuring seamless trade in commodities and services across the country, and improve export competitiveness by providing comprehensive relief from domestic taxes. The extent to which these objectives can be accomplished will depend upon the ultimate structure and operational details that will emerge. The author feels that the contentious nature of the Indian polity is such that the interests of the Union and States and of the producing and consuming States are not likely to converge any time soon. The initial GST implementation should, therefore, be seen as one more step in consumption tax reform, with more to follow as the GST is fine tuned.

The paper is critical of the multiple objectives imposed on the tax system, resulting in India's multiple exemptions, concessions, and preferences that cause significant revenue loss and create distortions. Besides raising revenues equitably, the tax system, for example, is expected to promote regional development, protect small scale industry, promote infrastructure development and employment, and make special economic zones attractive. These enormously complicate the tax system and create avenues for tax evasion and avoidance. The government tends to tax those sectors where it can raise revenues easily in an ad hoc manner, and this causes additional distortions. The difficulty in taxing India's very large unorganized sector further narrows the tax base. Finally, poor tax administration capacity underlies many of these problems.

In ending, the paper notes that the Indian tax system truly suffers from "the tyranny of the status quo" in tax reforms because those who gain from reforms tend to be ungrateful and those who lose tend to be vengeful. This situation invites the influence of special interest groups. Though the most important constraint is tax administration, not enough has been done to make it more efficient through capacity building. Reaching political consensus even when there is broad agreement, such as on GST, remains difficult, but is vital for rapid progress on a large reform agenda that remains to be tackled.

India's Energy Future

In their paper, Kaushik Deb and Paul Appleby assess consumption and production changes in India's primary energy mix and their likely economic and emissions impacts. Faster GDP growth and the economy's changing structure over the past three decades have resulted in a significant growth in energy consumption, but with little impact on the domination of coal and oil in the primary energy mix.

Energy consumption has grown by 5.5 percent per annum since 1980, on par with the fastest growing economies in the world, particularly in Asia. Of the total increase in consumption between 1980 and 2014, 93 percent was met by fossil fuels, with coal contributing the largest at 57 percent of the total increase, followed by oil at 28 percent and gas at 8 percent. Non-fossil fuels together contributed just 7 percent of the consumption increase during this period. India's share of global energy demand during this period rose from 1.5 percent of global energy consumption in 1980 to 4.9 percent by 2014, from being the tenth largest energy consumer globally in 1980 to becoming the fourth largest by 2014.

Domestic production has been sluggish in responding to energy demand growth, and imports have been high and are likely to continue rising. The authors share their concern about this increased share of energy imports as a percentage of GDP placing a significant burden on the macro economy.

Going forward, the authors estimate in their forecasts that India's primary energy consumption will grow faster than China's. Industrialization and urbanization are other key factors that would influence the growth in India's energy demand, as also the energy mix. Coal will continue to dominate the energy mix, though with some loss of market share to gas and renewables. Slow change in the energy mix will have implications for the overall energy intensity (the amount of energy consumed per unit of GDP) and carbon emissions. Declines in India's energy and emissions intensity have mostly been due to improving energy efficiency. According to the authors, with the energy mix not shifting, the gains from improving the share of more energy and carbon efficient fuels will remain limited.

Based on their elasticity and other assumptions, including an assumed average per capita GDP growth rate of 4.6 percent over 2013–35, India's primary energy consumption is expected by the authors to grow at an average growth rate of 3.8 percent per annum over this period, that is, almost double the average rate of growth for non-OECD energy markets. India's share of global energy demand would rise to 8 percent in 2035, still some way behind China (at 26 percent), but ahead of Russia (5 percent), and Brazil (3 percent).

Despite the rapid growth in total energy consumption, India's per capita consumption of energy will remain relatively low, at less than half the global average in 2035. To put this in perspective, India's per capita energy use in 2035 will be roughly where South Korea's was in 1978, or Thailand's in 1995. India's energy intensity will also remain low, declining by 1.6 percent per annum. India's economic development is expected to be much less energy-intensive than China's recent experience.

The authors develop two other growth scenarios. A higher GDP growth of 7.5 percent per annum over 2013–35 with unchanged sectoral demand elasticities and fossil fuel production levels would result in energy imports rising from 40 percent of energy consumption currently to 54 percent by 2035, with some 16 percent of global oil exports going to India. In this high growth case for India, China and India together would be importing around a quarter of the world's oil production and more than 40 percent of the world's liquid natural gas.

Their second "green" scenario has carbon emissions in 2035 remaining at the same level as in 2015, requiring significantly more rapid declines in energy intensity, which will not be easy since India already has low energy intensity levels. This green scenario also requires a decline in coal's share in consumption to 20 percent in 2035 from its current share of about 55 percent. Gas and renewables would have to grow much more rapidly. This would also have significant implications for import dependency and domestic production. The authors compare the challenge this green scenario would pose for India with the policy interventions and their cost that the European Union (EU) pursued to obtain the rapid and sustained growth of renewables in the EU.

Regulating Foreign Currency Borrowing by Indian Firms

India's policy framework regulating commercial foreign debt is premised on the notion that a large foreign debt can make the country vulnerable and exchange rate management difficult, that long-term debt is better than short-term debt, that it is more dangerous for the economy for smaller companies to borrow, that some sectors need lower cost finance more than others, and that when India wishes to increase or reduce capital inflows it can do so by easing and tightening restrictions on such debt flows.

Consequently, India's capital controls on foreign currency borrowing have multiple restrictions. Firms and banks can borrow but households cannot, so most of what is called External Commercial Borrowing (ECB, with maturity greater than three years) is by companies. Rules restrict who can borrow, who can lend, how much can be borrowed, at what cost, what end use the borrowed resources can be applied to, who can offer credit guarantees, when borrowed proceeds must be brought into India, when loans can be prepaid, and when loans can be refinanced; and there are procedural rules for these activities and rules for banks to force all borrowers to hedge currency exposure. Loans above a certain amount require approval, and while there is no stated limit on the stock of India's foreign currency borrowing through ECB, on a flow basis there is an unstated cap at USD 30 billion per year.

The ECB policy has become highly complex and uncertain, and, as suggested by the Government of India's 2014 Sahoo Committee Report, now fails to address several key concerns about the level of unhedged foreign corresponding reduction in allocations to Centrally-sponsored schemes—especially in the social sectors—provide an excellent opportunity for states to use these additional resources to innovate and experiment with more effective ways of delivering services.

The Annual 2015 IPF Lecture and IPF Policy Roundtable

Though not included in this volume, the 2015 IPF featured the *2015 Annual IPF Lecture* delivered by Arvind Panagariya, Vice Chairman of the NITI Aayog, and until he assumed office, a Non-resident Senior Fellow at NCAER. Panagariya spoke on "Economic Policies and Outcomes in India: A Retrospective," focusing on how India's economic policy framework has evolved over several decades and the outcomes it has produced in the process. He also highlighted the massive differences in economic outcomes before and after the advent of economic reforms in 1990–91, the reasons why India lost out in the early decades post Independence, and what has led to its rise in recent decades.

Also not reported in this volume, another key part of the 2015 IPF was the *IPF Policy Roundtable* on "The Challenge of Financing Infrastructure in India." The roundtable was expertly chaired by Suresh Prabhu, Union Minister for Railways in the Government of India, with the other eminent panelists being Urjit Patel, RBI; Rajiv Lall, IDFC Bank; Amit Kapur, J. Sagar & Associates; and Tarun Ramadorai, Oxford University and NCAER.

Materials on both the IPF 2015 Lecture and Policy Roundtable are available on NCAER's website, www.ncaer.org. A video recording of the 2015 IPF Lecture by Arvind Panagariya can be viewed there.

LAURENCE BALL*
Johns Hopkins University and *NBER*

ANUSHA CHARI†
University of North Carolina at Chapel Hill and *NBER*

PRACHI MISHRA‡
Reserve Bank of India

Understanding Inflation in India§

ABSTRACT This paper examines the behavior of quarterly inflation in India since 1994, both headline inflation and core inflation, as measured by the weighted median of price changes across industries. We explain core inflation with a Phillips curve in which the inflation rate depends on a slow-moving average of past inflation and on the deviation of output from its long-run trend. Headline inflation is more volatile than core: it fluctuates due to large changes in the relative prices of certain industries, which are largely but not exclusively industries that produce food and energy. There is some evidence that changes in headline inflation feed into expected inflation and future core inflation. Several aspects of India's inflation process are similar to inflation in advanced economies in the 1970s and 1980s.

Keywords: *Inflation, Phillips Curve, India*

JEL Classification: *E31, E37, E52*

1. Introduction

"Inflation poses a serious threat to the growth momentum. Whatever be the cause, the fact remains that inflation is something which needs to be tackled with great urgency ..."
[Dr Manmohan Singh, Then Prime Minister of India, February 4, 2011, New Delhi]

* *lball@jhu.edu*
† *achari@unc.edu*
‡ *prachimishra@rbi.org.in*

§ Prepared for the NCAER India Policy Forum. We would like to thank Pami Dua, Subir Gokarn, Ken Kletzer, and participants at the India Policy Forum conference for comments, and Edmund Crawley, Manzoor Gill, Jianhui Li, Wasin Siwasarit, and Ray Wang for excellent research assistance. The views presented are those of the authors and not of the Reserve Bank of India, or any of the institutions to which the authors belong.

Over the last decade, inflation has emerged as a leading concern for India's economic policymakers and citizens. Worries grew as the inflation rate (measured as the 12-month change in the consumer price index [CPI]) rose from 3.7 percent to 12.1 percent over 2001–10. The inflation rate fell to 5.2 percent in early 2015, leading to a debate about whether this moderation was likely to endure or inflation would rise again.

What explains the movements in India's inflation rate? Economists, policymakers, and journalists have proposed a variety of answers to this question. Many emphasize the effects of rises and falls in food price inflation, especially for certain staples such as pulses, milk, fruits, and vegetables.[1] These price increases are, in turn, explained by factors including shifting dietary patterns, rising rural wages, and a myriad of government policies such as price supports and the rural unemployment guarantee scheme (Rajan 2014). Some suggest that the monetary and fiscal stimulus following the 2008 financial crisis led to higher inflation, while others cite supply side constraints arising from policy bottlenecks (Government of India 2014).

Many, including the Reserve Bank of India (RBI) Governor, Raghuram Rajan, fear that high levels of inflation may become embedded in the expectations of price setters, creating a self-sustaining "inflationary spiral" (Rajan 2014). The role of monetary policy is controversial, with media reports and analysts debating the role of interest rate increases in explaining the recent fall in inflation, and more generally the RBI's ability to control inflation and the effects on the real economy (Bhalla 2014a and 2014b; Lahiri 2014).

The debates about inflation in India are reminiscent of debates that have been going on for decades in advanced economies, especially debates about the 1970s and 1980s, when inflation in the United States and Europe reached double-digit rates, similar to the inflation rate in India more recently. These debates have spurred a large body of research on inflation, especially in the United States. We draw on this literature to explore inflation in India. One broad theme is that, despite the differences between the Indian and US economies, the factors driving inflation fluctuations are similar in many respects.

Section 2 of this paper explores a central issue in discussions of inflation: the distinction between headline and core inflation. Core inflation captures the underlying trend in inflation, and headline inflation fluctuates around core because of large changes in the relative prices of certain

1. Gokarn (2011), for example, analyzes the microlevel price dynamics of the major dietary sources of protein in India.

goods—price changes that are often called "supply shocks." We follow an approach to measuring core inflation developed by the Federal Reserve Bank of Cleveland: core inflation is measured by the weighted median of price changes across industries. To implement this approach for India, we examine the inflation rate in the wholesale price index (WPI). WPI inflation is highly disaggregated by sector, allowing us to compute a historical series for median inflation.

We find that weighted median inflation is substantially less volatile at the quarterly frequency than headline inflation, a result that researchers have found for many other countries. We also have a finding that is not typical of other countries: the average level of median inflation (about 3.4 percent per year since 1994) is substantially lower than the average level of headline inflation (5.6 percent). This difference arises because the distribution of price changes across industries is often skewed to the right—there is a tail of large price increases that raise headline inflation, but are filtered out of the median—and the distribution is rarely skewed to the left. Many of the large price increases that raise headline WPI inflation—but far from all of them—occur for different types of food products and fuels. The role of food prices is consistent with the common view that these prices strongly influence aggregate inflation.

Section 3 explores the determinants of core inflation. We estimate a version of a standard inflation equation in textbooks and in a large body of empirical research, a Phillips curve. In this equation, core inflation at the quarterly frequency depends on expected inflation, which is determined by past levels of inflation, and by the level of economic activity, as captured by the deviation of output from its long-run trend. Our estimates of the Phillips curve are somewhat imprecise compared to estimates for advanced economies, reflecting the fact that the necessary data are available only since 1996, and that they are noisy, with substantial quarter-to-quarter movements in weighted median inflation. Nonetheless, the data point to the following two conclusions about India's Phillips curve.

First, current core inflation depends on many lags of past inflation with weights that decline slowly. We interpret this finding as reflecting the slow adjustment of expected inflation. In particular, we estimate that a one-percentage-point deviation of inflation from its expected level changes expected inflation in the next quarter by only 0.1 percentage points. This inertia in expectations is consistent with the view that, once a high level of inflation becomes embedded in expectations, it is not easy to reduce.

Second, for a given level of expected inflation, there is a positive relationship between inflation and the deviation of output from its long-run trend. This effect is central to the textbook Phillips curve, but some previous work has questioned it for India.[2] Along with our finding about the slow adjustment of expectations, the estimated effect of output implies that the monetary policy can reduce inflation, but with a short-run cost in output. In particular, we estimate a sacrifice ratio—the loss in percentage points of annual output needed for a permanent one-point fall in inflation—of approximately 2.7. This estimate is of the same order of magnitude as sacrifice ratios for other economies.

Section 4 studies the dynamic interactions among core inflation, headline inflation, and supply shocks. One finding is that movements in headline inflation appear to influence expected inflation and, hence, future levels of core inflation. As a result, a one-time supply shock, such as a large spike in food prices, can have a persistent effect on inflation. Like other aspects of India's inflation, this finding is reminiscent of inflation in advanced economies in the 1970s and 1980s.

Section 5 discusses some policy implications of our study. Although we have emphasized the usefulness of the weighted median inflation rate as a measure of core inflation, we, nonetheless, believe that conventional measures of headline inflation should still have a central role in monetary policy. One reason is communication with the public. Another reason is our finding that headline inflation feeds into expected inflation, and, hence, future core inflation. At the same time, it is vital for the RBI to examine core inflation to understand policy tradeoffs. We have used data on weighted median inflation to find a Phillips curve for India and estimate its slope, which we cannot do with headline inflation because of its quarterly volatility. Understanding the Phillips curve is essential for effective policies to control inflation.

2. There is a significant body of literature going back at least to Rangarajan (1983) and Dholakia (1990) that estimates the Phillips curve for India. Most of the early literature uses annual data and does not find much evidence for the existence of a short-run trade-off between inflation and output. See also Chatterji (1989), Rangarajan and Arif (1990), Das (2003), Virmani (2004), Bhattacharya and Lodh (1990), Balakrishnan (1991), Callen and Chang (1999), Nachane and Laxmi (2002), Brahmananda and Nagaraju (2002), and Srinivasan et al. (2006). However, more recently, several studies have used quarterly data and demonstrated the existence of a positive relationship between the output gap and inflation. Dua and Gaur (2009), Mazumder (2011), Patra and Kapur (2012), Kapur (2013), Kotia (2016), and Das (2014) are recent studies on the topic.

2. Core Inflation and Supply Shocks

Here we discuss the decomposition of headline inflation into core inflation and supply shocks, which is common in studies of inflation, and apply these concepts to quarterly data for India since 1994.

2.1. Background

By "core inflation," economists and central bankers mean an underlying trend in the inflation rate determined by inflation expectations and the level of economic activity, a trend that follows a relatively smooth path. The headline inflation rate is the sum of core inflation and "supply shocks," which reflect large changes in the prices of particular industries. Headline inflation is more volatile than core inflation.

The most common measure of supply shocks in empirical work is the change in the relative prices of food and energy. Consistent with this practice, core inflation is often measured by the inflation rate excluding the prices of food and energy. This practice is motivated by the fact that food and energy prices are volatile and that excluding them produces a much smoother inflation series.

However, from a theoretical point of view, it is arbitrary to choose certain industries as the source of supply shocks and to exclude from the measures of core inflation. Ball and Mankiw (1995) define supply shocks as unusually large changes in the prices of *any* industries. They suggest that supply shocks be measured by the degree of asymmetry in the distribution of price changes across industries. If there is a tail of unusually large price increases, skewing the distribution to the right, that is, a supply shock that raises inflation, a tail of unusually large price decreases has the opposite effect. Ball and Mankiw motivate this view of supply shocks with models of costly price adjustment, in which large changes in firms' desired relative prices have disproportionately large effects on inflation, because they trigger price adjustment while other prices are sticky.[3]

3. Although the unusually large changes in the prices are assumed to be caused by "supply shocks" in Ball and Mankiw (1995), a tail of unusually large price increases, in our framework, has the same effect on the price change distribution and, hence, on inflation, regardless of whether it is determined by demand or supply factors. Gokarn (1997), for example, also examines the behavior of the skewness of the distribution of relative price changes in India over the period from 1982–1996 and interprets the skewness to be caused by supply shocks. See more below on this later.

If supply shocks reflect asymmetries in the distribution of price changes, then a measure of core inflation should strip away the effects of these asymmetries—it should eliminate the effects of the tails of the price distribution. A simple measure that does that is the weighted median of price changes across industries. This measure of core inflation is proposed by Bryan and Cecchetti (1994), and the Federal Reserve Bank of Cleveland maintains a measure of weighted median inflation for the United States.

Figure 1 (based on Ball and Mazumder 2014) illustrates these ideas for the United States by comparing headline CPI inflation to the weighted median of price changes across US industries for the period 1985–2014. We see that the weighted median filters out much of the quarter-to-quarter volatility in headline inflation, suggesting that it is a good measure of core inflation.

FIGURE 1. Headline CPI and Weighted Median Inflation: United States

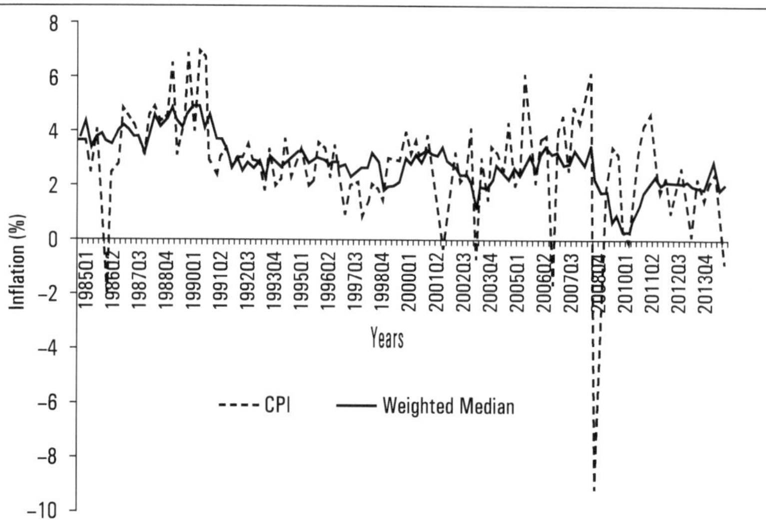

Source: Authors' computation.

In US data, there is a strong correlation between median inflation and the common core measure of inflation excluding food and energy—but far from a perfect correlation. These findings reflect the fact that many of the large price increases filtered out by the median occur in the food and energy industries, but not all. Research on the United States finds that median inflation, with all large price changes removed, has less short-term volatility than inflation less food and energy.

In our following analysis, we find that in India, as in the United States, median inflation is substantially less volatile than headline inflation. Once again, the large price changes filtered out by the median occur largely but not entirely in food and energy industries.

We note that the traditional measure of core inflation, inflation less food and energy, is particularly unattractive for India. Given India's level of development, food is a large share of the aggregate economy, and its relative price has increased or decreased substantially for sustained periods. Thus, stripping out food prices leaves an inflation series that wanders far away from the headline inflation rate that is the ultimate concern of policymakers; it does not just dampen quarterly fluctuations in inflation.

2.2. Application to India

Here we begin to describe our empirical analysis for India. For some aspects of our approach, we outline what we do and provide details in the Appendix to the paper. The measures of inflation that we study are the rate of change in the headline WPI and core inflation in the WPI as measured by the weighted median inflation rate. We study the WPI because, starting in 1994, it has a relatively high level of disaggregation into industry inflation rates, which is critical for measuring median inflation. We note that the Central Statistical Organization (CSO) began releasing disaggregated CPI data in 2014. In future, these data could be used to compare headline and median inflation based on the CPI.

Historically, the WPI has been the most commonly used price index for measuring inflation in India.[4] Our raw data are monthly WPI prices disaggregated by industry from April 1994 through December 2014. We aggregate across three-month periods to create quarterly series from 1994Q2 through 2014Q4.

For each quarter, the headline inflation rate for the WPI is approximately the mean of inflation rates across industries, weighted by the importance of the industries.[5] We compare this inflation rate, as reported in official statistics, to the weighted median of inflation rates across industries—the inflation rate such that industries with 50 percent of the total weights have higher inflation rates and the others have lower rates. The set of industries

4. The term "wholesale" in the index is, however, misleading as the index does not necessarily measure prices in the wholesale market. In practice, the WPI in India measures prices at different stages of the value chain. As discussed in Srinivasan (2008), according to the National Statistical Commission, "in many cases, these prices correspond to farm-gate, factory-gate or mine-head prices; and in many other cases, they refer to prices at the level of primary markets, secondary markets or other wholesale or retail markets" (NSC 2001).

5. We computed the weighted mean of price changes across industries. As one would expect, this series closely follows the inflation rate calculated from the official series for the WPI.

and weights in the WPI are revised every decade, so our sample comprises one subsample from 1994Q3 through 2004Q1 with 61 industries and one from 2004Q2 through 2014Q4 with 81 industries. Given the discontinuity in the series, an approximation is needed to compute the inflation rate in 2004Q2, the first quarter with the revised set of industries (see Appendix for details). We use the second level of disaggregation that is available. Examples of industries include primary articles such as food (grains: cereals) and minerals (metallic) as well as manufacturing such as textiles (cotton: yarn) and electrical apparatus and appliances.

Figure 2 shows the series for official WPI inflation and weighted median inflation, with all quarterly inflation rates annualized by multiplying by 4. Panel A shows the series we construct from our raw data, which is not seasonally adjusted, and Panel B shows the series that are seasonally adjusted with the X-13 Arima-Seats procedure from the US Census Bureau. The seasonally adjusted and unadjusted series are highly correlated (correlation = 0.9 for median inflation), but the seasonally adjusted series are somewhat less volatile.

As expected, weighted median inflation is substantially less volatile than headline WPI inflation. For our seasonally adjusted series, the standard deviation of WPI inflation is 3.93 percent, while the standard deviation of the weighted median is 2.62 percent between 1994Q2 and 2014Q4.

We also find that the average level of median inflation over the sample, 3.43 percent, is substantially lower than the average level of WPI inflation, 5.56 percent. As we see in the figure, this result reflects the fact that WPI inflation often spikes up above median inflation, whereas median inflation is almost never substantially above WPI inflation (with only a few exceptions, for example, 2008Q4 and 2009Q1). This result is surprising, because in other economies, median inflation fluctuates fairly symmetrically around headline inflation and the average levels are similar, as shown for the United States in Figure 1.

Mechanically, WPI inflation exceeds median inflation when the distribution of industry price changes is skewed to the right—in other words, when there is a thick tail of large price increases. Figure 3 illustrates this fact with some examples of the cross-sectional distribution of industry price changes, based on the seasonally unadjusted series that we use initially to compute weighted medians. Panels A and B show the distribution of inflation rates for 2008Q2 and 2000Q2, two quarters in which WPI inflation is substantially greater than median inflation. In 2008Q2, industries including fruits and vegetables, fibers, other minerals, tea and coffee, and ferrous

FIGURE 2A. Quarterly WPI Inflation: Weighted Mean and Weighted Median

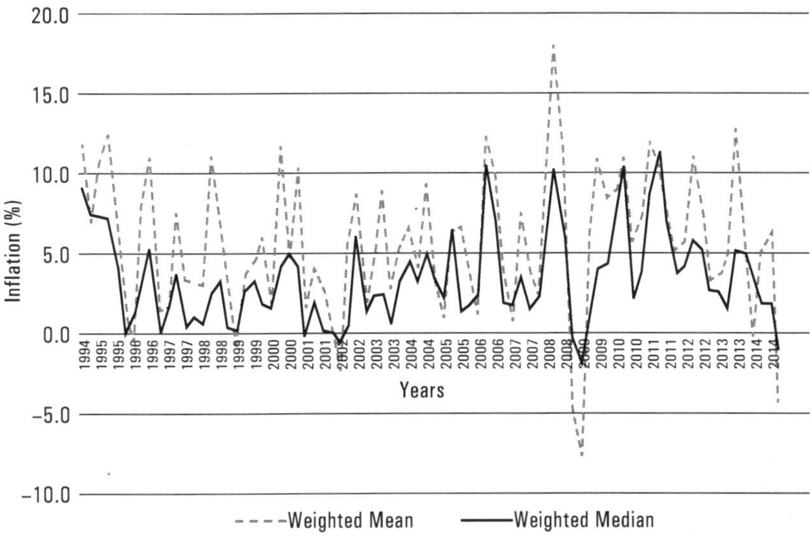

Source: Authors' computation.

FIGURE 2B. Quarterly WPI Inflation: Weighted Mean and Weighted Median (Seasonally Adjusted)

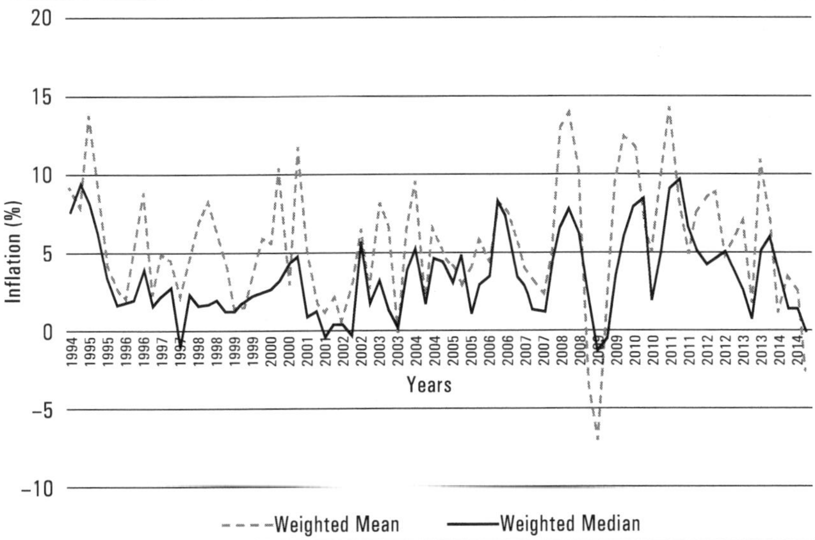

Source: Authors' computation.

FIGURE 3. Cross Sectional Distribution of Industry Price Changes

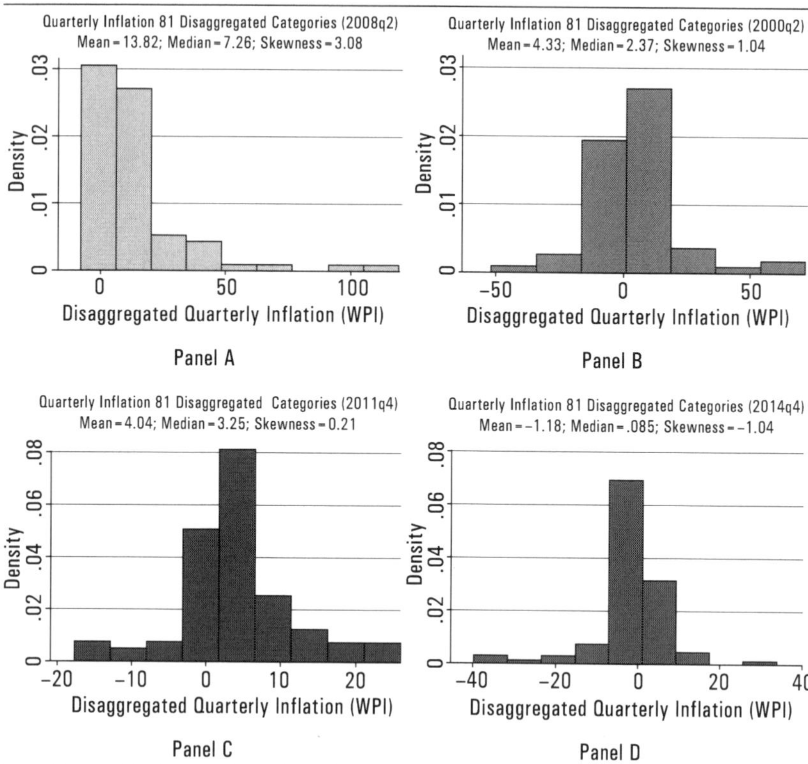

Source: Authors' computation.

metals have inflation rates greater than 35 percent, and crude petroleum, metallic minerals, coal, food (others) have rates greater than 50 percent, creating strong skewness in the distribution. In 2000Q2, milk had a rate of 40 percent and rubber and mineral oils had rates greater than 60 percent. Panel C shows a sample quarter, 2011Q4, in which the distribution of price changes is close to symmetric, implying that WPI and median inflation are approximately the same. Panel D shows 2014Q4, a quarter with negative skewness. In 2014Q4, fruits and vegetables, other food, non-food fibers and oil seeds, crude petroleum, mineral oils, manufactured food: tea and coffee, bakery products, and oil cakes were in the left tail (lowest 10 percent) of the distribution and experienced inflation rates of –7.8 percent or lower.

2.3. The Role of Food and Fuel Prices

Changes in food and fuel prices cause many of the episodes of skewed price change distributions in India, as suggested by the example of 2008Q2. The same is true in advanced economies. To demonstrate this point systematically, we examine the industries that account for the top 10 percent of the weighted distribution of inflation rates in each quarter—the right tail of the distribution, which creates skewness in many quarters and raises WPI inflation above median inflation. Many of these industries are the producers of various kinds of food and fuel such as fruits, vegetables, milk, crude petroleum, coal, and electricity. For each of our industries, we examine its contribution to the right tail; of the distribution for each quarter. This contribution is zero if the industry is not in the 10 percent tail; the industry's WPI weight times 10 if it is in the tail; and it is somewhere in between if the industry's price change puts it at the border of the top 10 percent, in which case a part of the industry's weight is included in the tail. For each industry, we compute the average contribution to the 10 percent tail over our 82 quarterly observation's on prices. These average contributions sum to 100 percent.

Recall there are 81 industries for the second part of our sample period; of these, 18 are different types of food (both primary articles and manufactured food) and four are different types of fuel or power. To see the influence of these industries more clearly, we aggregate them by one level into three broad industries: Primary Articles: food; Fuel & Power; and Manufacturing: Food. We also aggregate the other industries one level leaving us with 16 industries. For each of these industries, Table 1 shows the total of the average contributions of its components to the top 10 percent of price changes.

The results are striking. The three food and fuel industries are the three largest contributors to the 10 percent tail, with a contribution that sums to 63.5 percent. Notice if we add in non-food commodities, the fourth largest contributor, the total rises to 72 percent. Thus, if inflationary supply shocks are captured by right skewness in the price change distribution, Indian data confirm the common view that a large share of supply shocks originate in food and fuel industries—but not all. Notice that metals, chemicals, and textiles are also significant contributors to the 10 percent tail.

Figure 4 illustrates the importance of food and fuel in a different way. It shows two series: the difference between WPI inflation and median inflation, which captures the asymmetry in the distribution of price changes; and the change in the relative price of food and fuel, calculated as average inflation

TABLE 1. Contributors to Top 10% of Price Changes

Industry	*Rescaled Weighted Frequency*
Primary Articles: Food	27.83
Fuel & Power	23.50
Mfg: Food	12.22
Primary Articles: Non-Food	8.50
Mfg: BM: Basic Metals, Alloys and Metal Products	7.55
Mfg: CC: Chemicals & Chemical Products	6.02
Mfg: Textiles	4.46
Primary Articles: Minerals	2.31
Mfg: NM: Non Metallic Mineral Products	1.95
Mfg: Paper & Paper Products	1.21
Mfg: MM:Machinery & Machine Tools	0.96
Mfg: BT: Beverages, Tobacco & Tobacco Products	0.95
Mfg: TE: Transport, Equipment & Parts	0.93
Mfg: Rubber & Plastic	0.85
Mfg: Leather & Leather Products (LL)	0.52
Mfg: Wood & Wood Products	0.25

Source: Authors' computation.

Notes. Weighted frequency is rescaled to sum to 100. Industries are sorted by weighted frequency. Total number of quarters = 82 (1994q3:2014q4)

FIGURE 4. (Mean-Median) WPI Inflation & Food + Fuel Inflation – WPI Inflation

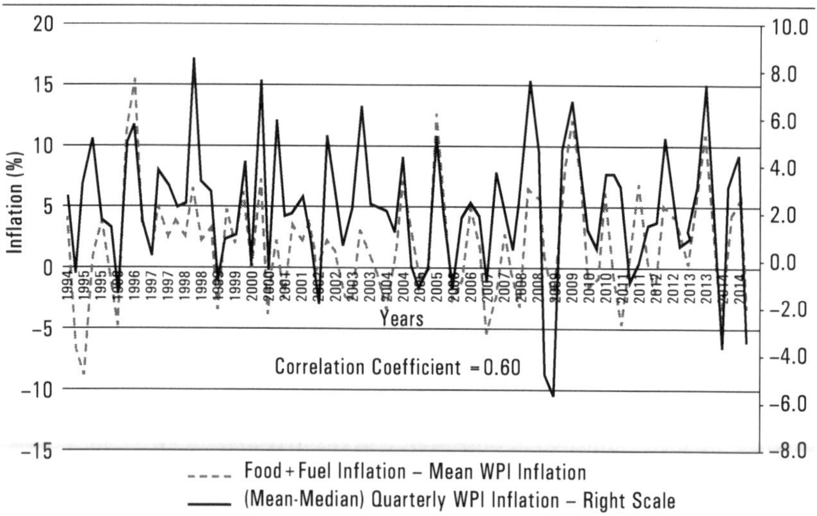

Source: Authors' computation.

for food and fuel minus WPI inflation. We can see that the two series have a strong positive relationship. For the non-seasonally adjusted series shown here, the correlation is 0.60. The correlation is somewhat lower, 0.41, when we seasonally adjust both series. Once again, we see that increases in food and fuel prices explain a large share but not all of the right tails in the distribution of inflation rates.

3. A Phillips Curve for Core Inflation

The canonical Phillips curve explains inflation with expected inflation and the level of economic activity relative to the economy's potential. In many applications, researchers assume that expected inflation can be captured by lagged values of actual inflation. Here we examine the fit of a simple Phillips curve to core inflation in India, as measured by the weighted median.

3.1. Milton Friedman's Phillips Curve

A large body of research is based on the Phillips curve introduced in Milton Friedman's Presidential Address to the American Economic Association (AEA) in 1968. This relationship can be written as:

$$\pi_t = \pi_t^e + \alpha\,(x_t - x_t^*) + \epsilon_t \qquad (1)$$

where π_t is inflation, π_t^e is expected inflation, and x_t is a measure of economic activity, typically either the log level of output or the unemployment rate. The variable x_t^* is the long-run level of x, which is called the natural rate when it is unemployment and potential output when it is output. The term $x_t - x_t^*$ captures short-run fluctuations in output or unemployment. The error term ϵ_t captures unobservable factors that influence inflation.

This Phillips curve is exposited in leading textbooks in macroeconomics. The expected inflation term captures the idea that expectations of inflation tend to be self-fulfilling: if price and wage setters expect a certain level of inflation, they raise their nominal prices to keep up, and in aggregate their price increases create the inflation they expect. The $x_t - x_t^*$ term captures the idea that an increase in activity relative to the economy's normal level raises firms' marginal costs, which causes them to raise prices by more than they otherwise would.

Here we examine the fit of equation (1) to the behavior of core inflation. In Section 4 of this paper, we examine how core inflation and supply shocks interact to determine the behavior of headline WPI inflation in India.

To estimate equation (1), we must choose the measures of x_t, x_t^*, and π_t^e.

3.2. Measuring Economic Activity

We lack quarterly data on aggregate unemployment for India. Quarterly data on output, however, are available from the CSO. In our empirical analysis, we use quarterly GDP (at market prices) since 1996Q2. We combine the 2004–05 base-year GDP series and the 1999–2000 series to create a common series from 1996Q2 to 2014Q3, using a commonly used splicing methodology. The details of the splicing methodology are provided in Appendix 1. We measure activity x_t with the logarithm of output. Before taking the logarithm, we seasonally adjust the output series using the US Census Bureau's X-13 procedure. This adjustment is important because there are large seasonal movements in India's output.

We measure potential output by smoothing the log output series with the Hodrick–Prescott (HP) filter, using a smoothing parameter of 1600. This common approach is atheoretical but yields a plausible series for x^*, and no other approach is obviously better in the absence of accurate, direct measures of the economy's productive capacity.[6]

Figure 5 shows the levels of x and x^* that we calculate, and the output gap $x - x^*$. The fluctuations in our measured output gap are consistent with common views about India's business cycle. The output gap was positive, with its magnitude being the highest during the sample, right before the 2008 global financial crisis (GFC). Output was recorded at 1.5 percent and 1 percent above its long-run potential in 2007Q4 and 2008Q1, respectively. Not surprisingly, the output gap was the most negative in our sample during the GFC. Output was 2.2 percent below its potential in 2009Q1. Our estimates also suggest a negative output gap of –0.4 percent for 2014Q3, or the last data point in our sample.

One questionable feature of the output gap series is that the size of fluctuations is small. The estimated output gap is never more than 1 or 2 percent in absolute value; even in the wake of the GFC, the gap reaches only –2 percent. By contrast, US output gaps as measured by the HP filter reach levels around 5 percent in absolute value in deep recessions and strong expansions. We are not confident that cyclical fluctuations in India

6. See Kotia (2016) and Mishra (2013) for the shortcomings of the HP filter.

FIGURE 5. Output, Trend, and Output Gap

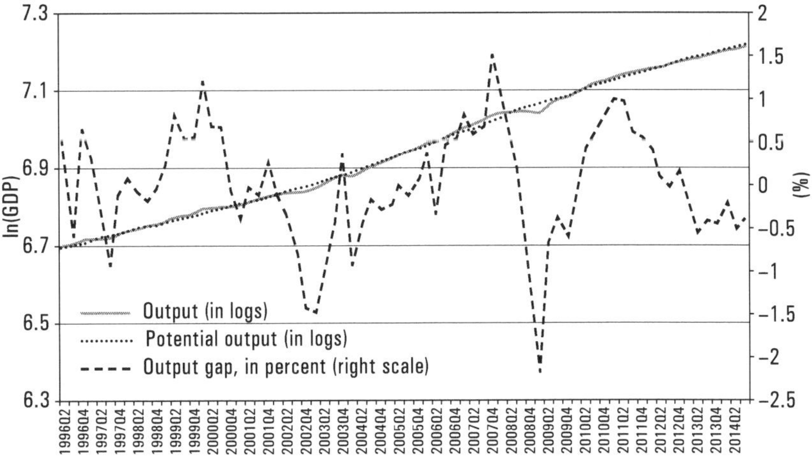

Source: Authors' computation.

are as small as our estimated gaps suggest, and suspect that the quarterly data reported for real GDP could be smoother than true GDP. We will keep this issue in mind in interpreting our estimated effects of the output gap on inflation.[7]

3.3. Measuring Expected Inflation

In presenting his Phillips curve, Friedman said that "unanticipated inflation generally means a rising rate of inflation." This is the same as saying that expected inflation is determined by past inflation. Following Friedman, much of the US Phillips curve literature (for example, Ball and Mazumder 2011; Gordon 1982; Stock and Watson 2007) has used lags of inflation to capture expected inflation. With quarterly data, researchers typically include a number of inflation lags in the Phillips curve, with the restriction that the coefficients on the lags sum to one.

In recent years, inflation expectations have appeared to be "anchored" in advanced economies, including the United States and Europe. Since around 2000, the Federal Reserve and the European Central Bank have been targeting inflation rates near 2 percent, and expected inflation has stayed close to that level: expectations have *not* varied based on lagged values of actual

7. Some suggest using a lower HP smoothing parameter for emerging economies. This would produce even smaller estimated output gaps.

inflation. We doubt, however, that inflation expectations were anchored in India over our sample period. The RBI formally announced an inflation target only in 2015.[8] Over our sample, the inflation rate was volatile without a clear tendency to return to some fixed level, much as inflation rates wandered in the United States and Europe between 1960 and 2000. In such a regime, it is natural to assume that expected inflation responds to lagged values of actual inflation.

As we saw in Figure 2, quarterly core inflation is quite volatile in India—more volatile than core inflation in advanced economies. We conjecture that expected inflation is less volatile: A few quarters of high or low inflation do not change expectations dramatically. To capture this idea, we want to allow expected inflation to depend on lagged inflation over many quarters. At the same time, we do not want to include numerous lags with unrestricted coefficients; we want a parsimonious Phillips curve with a minimum of free parameters. These goals lead us to a simple partial adjustment model of expectations.

Specifically, we assume that expected inflation is determined by:

$$\pi_t^e = \gamma\pi_{t-1}^e + (1-\gamma)\pi_{t-1} \tag{2}$$

In this specification, expected inflation depends on its own lag and the lag of actual inflation with weights γ and $1-\gamma$. This implies that a one percentage point deviation of lagged inflation from its expected level changes current expected inflation by $1-\gamma$ percentage points. Repeated substitution for lagged inflation leads to the following reduced form:

$$\pi_t^e = (1-\gamma)\pi_{t-1} + \gamma(1-\gamma)\pi_{t-2} + \gamma^2(1-\gamma)\pi_{t-3} + \gamma^3(1-\gamma)\pi_{t-4} + \cdots \tag{3}$$

Here, expected inflation depends on all lags of past inflation, with exponentially declining weights. The adjustment parameter γ determines the relative weights on recent and less recent inflation rates. We treat γ as a parameter to be estimated.

If we write our equation for expected inflation compactly and substitute it into Friedman's Phillips curve (1), we get

$$\pi_t = (1-\gamma)[\Sigma_{k=1}^{\infty}\,\gamma^{k-1}\,\pi_{t-k}] + \alpha(x_t - x_t^*) + \in_t \tag{4}$$

8. See http://finmin.nic.in/reports/MPFAgreement28022015.pdf on agreement between the Government of India and RBI on the new monetary policy framework.

To estimate this equation with the available data, we must make two approximations, which we describe in Appendix 2. First, we truncate the infinite sum in the theoretical Phillips curve: We include only 40 lags of inflation with exponentially declining weights while maintaining the restriction that the weights sum to one.[9]

Second, we must address the problem that, even with the lags truncated at 40, we do not have data on median inflation that extends far enough back to include 40 lags in the early part of our sample. In our regressions, the sample starts in 1996Q2, the first quarter for which output data are available, and our median inflation series extends back only seven quarters before that, to 1994Q3. Since we cannot measure π_t^e for our entire sample, we treat π_t^e in 1996Q2 as an unobserved parameter, which we estimate along with the parameters γ and α in the Phillips curve. We estimate the initial π_t^e, γ, and α by non-linear least squares: We find the values of these three parameters that minimize the sum of squared residuals in the equation. Notice that an estimate of the initial π_t^e and an estimate of γ allow us to calculate π_t^e for all observations in our regression using the partial adjustment equation (3).

3.4. Estimates

Table 2 presents our estimation results. The estimate of the initial level of expected inflation is about 1.9, and the estimate of γ is 0.90, with a standard error of 0.05. If we put this estimate into our reduced-form equation for expected inflation, it implies that the first four inflation lags have coefficients of approximately 0.1, 0.09, 0.08, and 0.07, which sum to 0.34 out of the total sum of coefficients of one. This confirms that relatively long lags of inflation—beyond one year—have substantial weight in determining the current levels of expected and actual inflation in India, as we conjectured based on the volatility of quarterly inflation.

The estimate of the output gap coefficient α is 1.07 with a standard error of 0.54. The *t*-statistic of 1.99 puts the coefficient at the borderline of

9. Some readers of this paper have questioned the structure of inflation lags that we assume, so we have experimented with alternatives. As we expect, based on the volatility of inflation, a large number of lags is needed to capture the behavior of expectations. We verify this point by estimating a version of equation (4) in which we replace the exponentially weighted sum of inflation lags with 16 lags with unrestricted coefficients. In this specification, we reject the hypothesis that the coefficients on lags 13–16 are zero ($p = 0.0383$), which suggests that at least 16 lags are needed to fit the data. At the same time, when we include 16 unrestricted lags, the pattern of estimated coefficients on the lags is erratic, suggesting the model is over-parameterized. These findings confirm the usefulness of restricting the coefficients with our partial adjustment model.

TABLE 2. Phillips Curve Estimates

Dependent Variable	*Weighted Median WPI Inflation*
Output gap, α	1.074**
	[0.540]
Adjustment parameter, γ	0.902***
	[0.053]
Number pf observations	74
R-squared	0.19
Adjusted R-squared	0.179

Source: Authors' computation.

Notes: ***, **, and * denote statistical significance at 1,5, and 10 percent respectively. Standard errors are denoted in parentheses.

statistical significance at the 5 percent level. Thus, we find evidence of a substantial effect of output on inflation, the central prediction of the Phillips curve, but with considerable uncertainty about the magnitude of the effect.

The top panel of Figure 6 shows our series for core inflation and the fitted values of this variable based on our estimated Phillips curve. This graph also shows the level of expected inflation implied by our estimate of the parameter γ; the deviation between this level and the fitted value of inflation is the estimated contribution of the output gap (the gap times the estimated value of α). The bottom panel of Figure 6 shows eight-quarter moving averages of the actual inflation, expected inflation, and fitted value series in the top panel. This graph smooths out much of the quarterly volatility in median inflation, allowing us to see how well our equation fits the somewhat longer-term movements in inflation.

With eight-quarter averages, the inflation movements over our sample are dominated by upward trends in actual and expected inflation from the early 2000s to 2012. Output movements help to explain some of the movements in inflation, such as the period around 2011–12 when the output gap was positive—as indicated by fitted values for inflation that exceed expected inflation—helping to push median inflation to its peak of around 7 percent. However, much of the long rise of inflation was generated by unexplained shocks to our Phillips curve, indicated by actual inflation above its fitted values. These shocks feed back into expected inflation in our partial adjustment equation, so a series of shocks pushed the level of inflation higher and higher. Negative shocks have partially reversed this process since 2012. We explore the nature of these shocks in Section 4 of this paper.

3.5. The Sacrifice Ratio

The RBI aims to reduce the inflation rate to 4 percent by 2018. The Phillips curve implies a cost to reducing inflation: absent a lucky disinflationary

FIGURE 6A. Phillips Curve Estimates with Weighted Median

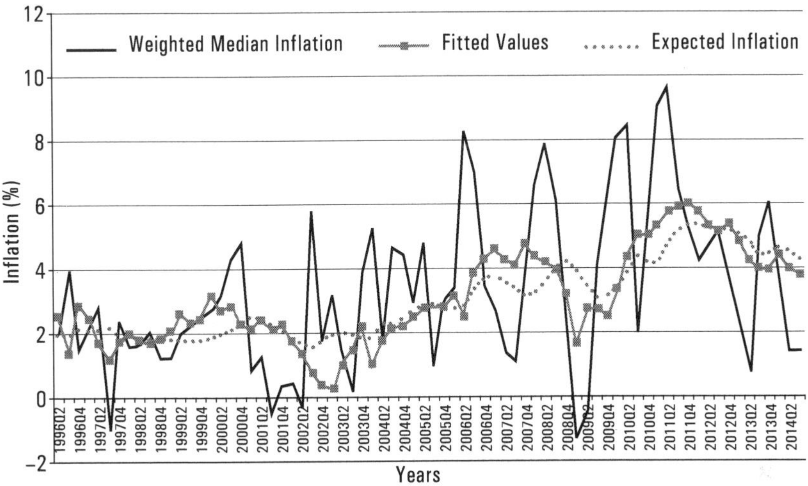

Source: Authors' computation.

FIGURE 6B. Phillips Curve Estimates with Weighted Median: 8-quarter Moving Averages

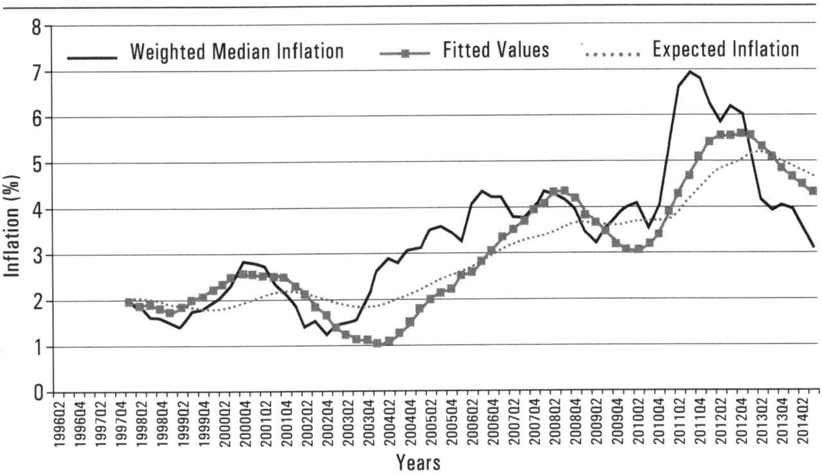

Source: Authors' computation.

shock, policymakers need to reduce output temporarily below its trend to reduce inflation.

A common measure of the cost of disinflation is the "sacrifice ratio." This concept is the number of percentage points of reduction in annual output needed to reduce the inflation rate permanently by one percentage point. Estimates of sacrifice ratios in advanced economies in the 1980s and 1990s, before the recent period of anchored expectations, are often on the order of two or three. In other words, roughly a 2–3 percentage point loss of output relative to trend is needed to reduce the inflation rate in advanced economies by one percentage point (see Mitra et al. 2015, for a literature review).

Using our Phillips curve, we can calculate the sacrifice ratio as follows. A loss of output of one percentage point for one quarter reduces current inflation by α percentage points. Given our specification of expectations, that fall in inflation reduces expected inflation by $(\alpha) \times (1 - \gamma)$ in the following period. If output returns to normal at that point and there are no shocks to the Phillips curve, then actual inflation is $(\alpha) \times (1 - \gamma)$ below its initial level and stays there.

Thus, a one-point fall in output below normal for one quarter reduces inflation by $(\alpha) \times (1 - \gamma)$ points. A one-point fall in output that lasts for four quarters—a loss of one point of annual output—reduces inflation by $4 \times (\alpha) \times (1 - \gamma)$. The sacrifice ratio is the inverse of this effect: In order to reduce the inflation rate by one percentage point, a loss of $1/[4 \times (\alpha) \times (1 - \gamma)]$ percentage points of annual output is required.

Substituting in our estimates of γ and α yields a sacrifice ratio of 2.7, which is the same order of magnitude as estimates for other countries. If the current level of inflation is 5.2 percent and the RBI wishes to reduce it to 4 percent, the cost will be $1.2 \times 2.7 = 3.2$ percentage points of annual output. Notice that our estimated sacrifice ratio for India is quite close to estimates by Mitra et al. (2015) (around 2.3 or 2.8 depending on the state of the economy), despite large differences between their methodology and ours.

Two caveats: First, the RBI is targeting CPI inflation, whereas we calculate a sacrifice ratio for core WPI inflation. Future work should examine whether the relationships of output to CPI and WPI inflation are similar.

Second, as noted earlier, we suspect that quarterly output data may understate the size of short-run fluctuations. If so, the true output gaps associated with given changes in inflation may be larger than the estimated gaps, which would imply a larger sacrifice ratio.

4. Core Inflation, Supply Shocks, and Median Inflation

The previous section found that the behavior of India's core inflation, as measured by weighted median inflation, can be explained to a significant degree by a simple Phillips curve. We saw earlier, however, that many of the fluctuations in headline inflation are deviations from core inflation caused by supply shocks, as measured by asymmetries in the cross-sectional distribution of price changes.

Here we seek a broader understanding of India's inflation by examining the interactions among core inflation, headline inflation, and supply shocks. One finding is that movements in headline inflation appear to influence expected inflation and, hence, future levels of core inflation. As a result, a one-time supply shock, such as a large spike in food prices, can have a persistent effect on inflation. Like other aspects of India's inflation, this finding is reminiscent of inflation in advanced economies in the 1970s and 1980s.

4.1. A Phillips Curve for Headline Inflation?

As a first exercise, we examine how well the simple Phillips curve fits inflation behavior if we ignore the concept of core inflation and examine the headline WPI. In Table 3, the first column repeats our Phillips curve for median inflation, for purpose of comparison, and the second column reports

TABLE 3. Phillips Curve Estimates

Dependent Variable	*Weighted Median WPI Inflation*	*Headline WPI Inflation*	*Weighted Median WPI Inflation*	*Weighted Median WPI Inflation*
	[1]	*[2]*	*[3]*	*[4]*
Output gap, α	1.074**	1.792*	1.063**	1.267
	[0.540]	[1.05]	[0.500]	[0.500]
Adjustment parameter, γ – Weighted Median	0.902***			
	[0.053]			
Adjustment parameter, γ – Headline WPI		1.022***	0.877***	
		[0.053]	[0.043]	
Adjustment parameter, γ – (constrained to be the same for Weighted Median WPI and Headline WPI)				1.086***
				[0.101]
Weight on average of past median inflation, β				0.256
				[0.277]
Number pf observations	74	74	74	74
R-squared	0.19	0.076	0.169	0.265
Adjusted R-squared	0.179	0.063	0.158	0.244

Source: Authors' computation.

Notes: ***, **, and * denote statistical significance at 1,5, and 10 percent, respectively. Standard errors are denoted in parentheses. β is the weight on an exponential average of past median inflation in the equation for determining expectations. The average of past headline WPI inflation rates has a weight of $1-\beta$. The exponential coefficient γ is constrained to be the same in the two averages.

estimates of an equation for headline inflation. This specification is the same as the first except that the dependent variable is headline WPI inflation and the lagged inflation rates with which we capture expected inflation are also WPI inflation.

It appears that this second Phillips curve is mis-specified. In particular, the estimate of the parameter γ is statistically indistinguishable from one (in fact, the point estimate is slightly above one). Our model of expected inflation, equation (3), assumes γ is less than one; as it approaches one, the adjustment of expectations diminishes to the point that expected inflation is constant. Thus, in this case, we fail to find any effect of past inflation on current inflation. Note also that the output coefficient α is less significant statistically ($p = 0.09$) than in our equation for median inflation. In sum, we fail to find strong evidence that headline WPI is explained by the variables on the right side of our Phillips curve.

This result, we believe, reflects the very great volatility of headline WPI inflation at the quarterly frequency. This noise in the series obscures any underlying Phillips curve. This negative result points to the desirability of examining median inflation when estimating the Phillips curve.

4.2. Core Inflation, Headline Inflation, and Expectations

Here we return to an equation with median inflation as the dependent variable. However, we consider the possibility that the lagged inflation terms on the right of the equation are headline WPI inflation. We interpret such a specification as saying that price setters base their expectations of inflation on past levels of headline inflation, so that movements in headline inflation are passed into future core inflation.

It is not clear *a priori* whether expected inflation should depend on the past levels of headline inflation or core inflation. Empirically, a number of studies for the United States find a sharp break in inflation behavior around the Volcker disinflation of the early 1980s. Inflation is explained by lags of headline inflation before that time and by lags of core inflation afterwards. The usual interpretation is that price setters in the 1970s based their expectations on past headline inflation, so expected inflation responded to movements in headline inflation even if those movements were the result of transitory supply shocks. After the Volcker disinflation, however, it became clear that the Federal Reserve was determined to reverse transitory inflation movements due to supply shocks, so those shocks no longer influenced expectations and actual inflation going forward. In the terminology of central bankers, in the post-Volcker era, supply shocks have first round effects—they directly affect current headline inflation—but not second round effects on expectations and future inflation.

Before using lagged headline inflation rates to explain median inflation, we account for the fact that headline inflation is systematically higher than median inflation—the difference averages 2.42 percentage points over the sample period for our regressions. We subtract this constant from the headline WPI series, resulting in an adjusted series with the same average value as the median. We can interpret this specification as explaining median inflation with lagged levels of headline inflation, both measured relative to their sample averages.

The third column of Table 3 reports this specification. The results for this case are quite close to those with median inflation on both sides of the equation, in column [1]: the estimates of α and γ are similar, and so are the *R*-squared. The estimate of γ is well below one in both economic and statistical terms, unlike the case with WPI inflation on the left. Comparing columns [1] and [3], it appears that we can explain median inflation about equally well when we measure expected inflation with the lags of median inflation and headline inflation.

For the regression with median inflation on the left and lagged headline inflation on the right, Figures 7A and 7B show actual median inflation, expected inflation, and fitted values from the regression, along with eight-quarter moving averages of these series.

FIGURE 7A. Phillips Curve Estimates with Weighted Median and Headline Inflation Expectations

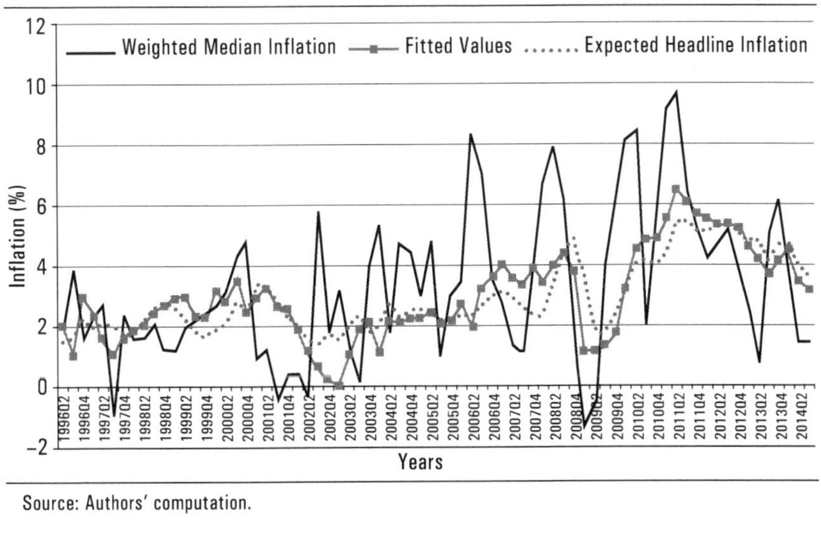

Source: Authors' computation.

FIGURE 7B. Phillips Curve Estimates with Weighted Median and Headline Inflation Expectations: 8-quarter Moving Averages

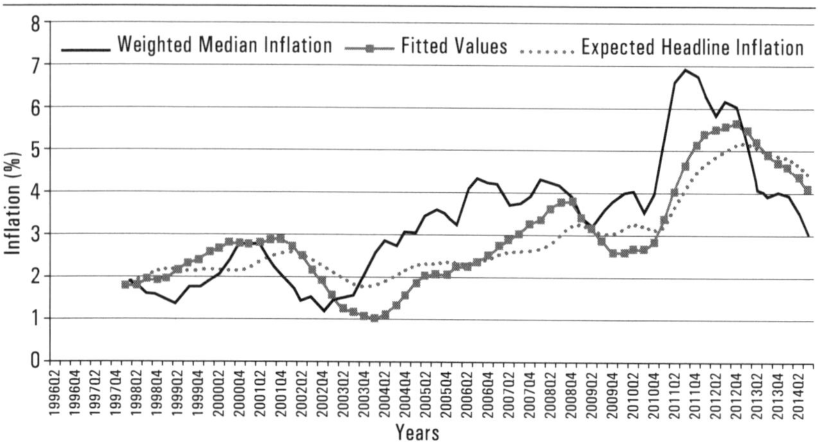

Source: Authors' computation.

In column [4] of Table 3, we investigate whether lagged headline or lagged core inflation belongs on the right side of the Phillips curve equation by including both in a horserace.

Here, we assume that an exponential average of past median inflation has a weight of β in determining expectations, and an average of past WPIs has a weight of $1 - \beta$. Notice that we constrain the exponential coefficient γ to be the same in the two averages; the qualitative results are similar if we estimate two different γs.

Our estimates for this specification are imprecise. This reflects the fact that median inflation and WPI inflation have similar medium-term movements; thus, while these two inflation rates have only a modest correlation at the quarterly frequency, the slow-moving averages of the two are strongly correlated, so there is a problem of multicollinearity.

Nonetheless, we can see where the estimates point. The key result is that the estimate of the weight β on past median inflation is 0.26 with a standard error of 0.28. A two-standard error confidence interval is [–0.30, 0.82]. While this range is wide, we can reject the hypothesis that β is one—that only past median inflation affects expectations—and cannot reject the hypothesis that is zero—that only past headline inflation matters. The estimate of γ exceeds one, but this may simply reflect sampling error, as a two-standard error band extends down to 0.88.

In sum, the data suggest that past headline inflation has a substantial effect on expected inflation, so, as in the pre-Volcker United States, a supply shock that raises inflation in one quarter can have a persistent effect on core inflation through its effect on expectations.

4.3. Food and Energy Again

Throughout our analysis, we have examined the effects of changes in the relative price of food and energy, measured by food and energy inflation minus aggregate WPI inflation. This relative price changes when there are events in the real economy affecting the supply and demand for food and energy. In our framework, large shocks of this nature influence aggregate inflation; again, the underlying theory is that of Ball and Mankiw (1995), in which large shocks have disproportionately large effects on inflation because they trigger the adjustment of nominal prices that might otherwise be sticky.

In India, economists debate the reasons for rises and falls in food prices. In particular, some cite supply-side factors such as low and stagnant production of food and others emphasize demand factors such as shifting diets. We do not take a position in this debate, and our results do not shed light on it. In our framework, a large shock to food and fuel prices has the same effect on the price change distribution and, hence, on inflation, regardless of its underlying demand or supply causes.

Much of the literature on India's inflation investigates the interactions of food inflation—the change in the nominal price of food—with non-food inflation or aggregate inflation. In our view, such empirical analyses do not have a clear interpretation. A change in food prices is an event in the real economy only to the extent it differs from aggregate inflation; otherwise, it is simply part of the inflationary process affecting all prices.

In an accounting sense, one can explain aggregate inflation with an equation that includes different components of inflation. If all the components are included, one obtains an equation with an *R*-square of one and coefficients on each component equal to its share in the aggregate price index. Even if only one or a few components are included in the equation, they can appear to have high explanatory power if movements in aggregate inflation cause correlated movements in the inflation rates for many industries.

A similar point applies to studies that regress aggregate inflation or non-food inflation on lags of food inflation or other sectoral inflation rates. In these equations, lagged food inflation may simply be a proxy for lagged aggregate inflation if there is a strong common component in the inflation rates of different sectors. Whether a measure of food inflation is contemporaneous or lagged, it can tell us something about the determinants of inflation only if it is measured relative to aggregate inflation.

In Table 4, we include the change in the relative price of food and energy, measured by food and energy inflation minus headline inflation, in the estimation of the Phillips curve. The dependent variables are weighted median and headline inflation in columns [1] and [2], respectively. Not surprisingly, as shown in column [1], the relative price of food and energy does not have a significant effect on weighted median inflation, which is stripped of volatile components. Column [2] shows that the relative price of food and energy *does* have a statistically significant effect on headline inflation. The estimated coefficient is 0.43 and the standard error is 0.14. The results support the earlier evidence that changes in the relative price of food and energy, which predominantly constitute the right tail of the distribution of price changes, strongly influence aggregate inflation.

TABLE 4. Phillips Curve Estimates with Relative Price of Food and Energy

Dependent Variable	*Weighted Median WPI Inflation*	*Headline WPI Inflation*
	[1]	*[2]*
Output gap, α	1.062**	1.918*
	[0.523]	[1.148]
Adjustment parameter, γ – Headline WPI	0.866***	1.004***
	[0.044]	[0.062]
Food and Energy Inflation – Headline WPI Inflation	0.056	0.429***
	[0.108]	[0.139]
Number pf observations	74	74
R-squared	0.1725	0.1726
Adjusted R-squared	0.1492	0.1493

Source: Authors' computation.

Notes: ***, **, and * denote statistical significance at 1,5, and 10 percent, respectively.

5. Some Policy Implications

Our findings have implications for the roles of different measures of inflation in monetary policy and for the tradeoffs facing policymakers.

We have emphasized the usefulness of the weighted median inflation rate as a measure of core inflation. Nonetheless, we believe that conventional measures of headline inflation should still have a central role in monetary policy. One reason is communication with the public. Headline inflation is a meaningful variable for non-economists, whereas the concept of median inflation and its usefulness are technical issues that would be difficult to explain. When central banks around the world discuss the inflation rate and set targets for its level, they generally refer to headline inflation, and there is no reason for India to deviate from this practice.

Even if we ignore communication issues, there is a strong case for the RBI to base policy on the headline inflation rate; for example, to tighten policy when a supply shock pushes headline inflation above median inflation. The reason is our finding that headline inflation feeds into expected inflation and, hence, future core inflation. This state of affairs contrasts with many advanced economies today, in which expectations appear not to respond to supply shocks. In those economies, policymakers can largely ignore movements in headline inflation and focus on stabilizing core inflation.

Yet, the behavior of expectations is not set in stone. In the future, a commitment by the RBI to offset the inflationary effects of supply shocks could cause inflation expectations to behave more like expectations in advanced economies. If that happens, then Indian policymakers can focus on stabilizing core inflation and pay less attention to supply shocks.

Even under current circumstances, it is vital for the RBI to examine core inflation to understand policy tradeoffs. We have used data on weighted median inflation to find a Phillips curve for India and estimate its slope, which we cannot do with headline inflation because of its quarterly volatility. Understanding the Phillips curve is essential for effective policies to control inflation.

Our finding of a Phillips curve tradeoff is both good news and bad news for policymakers. The good news is that the central bank can push inflation to a desired level by stimulating or dampening aggregate demand, regardless of supply side developments. The bad news is that lowering the level of inflation requires a sacrifice, which we estimate to be 2.7 percentage points of annual output per percentage-point reduction in inflation.

Our finding of significant costs of disinflation is consistent with the international experience. In both advanced and emerging economies, a policy of reducing inflation almost always reduces output in the short run. This is true even when disinflation is accompanied by the supply-side reforms aimed at increasing long-term growth and even when policymakers announce a clear and credible inflation target (see, for example, Bernanke et al. 1999).

6. Conclusion

Leading macroeconomics textbooks explain inflation with a Phillips curve in which the inflation rate depends on expected inflation, the level of output relative to trend, and supply shocks. Typically, the models assume that expected inflation is determined by lags of the inflation rate and that supply shocks are largely changes in the relative prices of food and energy. One-time supply shocks can have persistent effects because they feed into expectations. In this framework, a central bank can guide inflation to a desired level, but if inflation starts above this level, it is costly to reduce it, and it can also be costly to offset supply shocks and prevent them from raising inflation.

While still common in textbooks, this model of inflation is considered to be somewhat less relevant now for advanced economies including the United States and Europe. In these economies, in the 2000s, a commitment to an inflation target has led to an anchoring of inflation expectations, which makes it easier for central banks to maintain stable inflation with less cost to output stability. In contrast, we have seen that the textbook model explains much of the behavior of inflation in India in recent years. Time will tell whether inflation behavior will change under the RBI's new monetary framework.

References

Balakrishna, P. 1991. *Pricing and Inflation in India*. Delhi: Oxford University Press.

Ball, Laurence and N. Gregory Mankiw. 1995. "Relative-Price Changes as Aggregate Supply Shocks," *Quarterly Journal of Economics,* 110(1): 161–93, February.

Ball, Laurence and Sandeep Mazumder. 2011. "Inflation Dynamics and the Great Recession," *The Brookings Institution*, 42(1): 337–405.

———. 2014. "A Phillips Curve with Anchored Expectations and Short-term Unemployment," NBER Working Paper No. 20715. Cambridge, MA: National Bureau of Economic Research, Inc.

Bernanke, Ben, Thomas Laubach, Frederic Mishkin, and Adam Posen. 1999. *Inflation Targeting: Lessons from the International Experience*. Princeton, NJ: Princeton University Press.

Bhattacharya, B.B. and M. Lodh. 1990. "Inflation in India: An Analytical Survey," *Artha Vijnana*, 32(1): 25–68.

Bhalla, Surjit. 2014a. "Where Monetary Policy Is Irrelevant," *The Indian Express*, September 13.

———. 2014b. "RBI, We Have a Problem," *The Indian Express*, September 20.

Brahmananda, P. and G. Nagaraju. 2002. "Inflation and Growth in the World: Some Simple Empirics, 1970–99," in *Macroeconomics and Monetary Policy: Issues for a Reforming Economy*, pp. 43–66, New Delhi: Oxford University Press.

Bryan, M.F. and S.G. Cecchetti. (1994). "Measuring Core Inflation," in N.G. Mankiw (ed.), *Monetary Policy*, pp. 195–219, Chicago: University of Chicago Press.

Callen, Tim and Dongkoo Chang. 1999. "Modeling and Forecasting Inflation in India," IMF Working Paper, WP/99/119. Tokyo: Asia and Pacific Department, International Monetary Fund.

Chatterji, R. 1989. *The Behaviour of Industrial Prices in India*. New Delhi: Oxford University Press.

Das, S. 2003. "Modelling Money, Price and Output in India: A Vector Autoregressive and Moving Average (VARMA) Approach," *Applied Economics*, 35(10): 1219–25.

Das, Abhiman. 2014. "Role of Inflation Expectation in Estimating a Phillips Curve for India," Mimeo.

Dholakia, R.H. 1990. "Extended Phillips Curve for the Indian Economy," *Indian Economic Journal*, 38(1): 69–78.

Dua, P. and U. Gaur. 2009. "Determination of Inflation in an Open Economy Phillips Curve Framework: The Case of Developed and Developing Asian Countries," Working Paper 178. New Delhi: Centre for Development Economics.

Government of India. 2014. *Economic Survey 2013–14*, New Delhi: Ministry of Finance.

Gokarn, Subir. 1997. "Economic Reforms and Relative Price Movements in India: A 'Supply Shock' Approach," *The Journal of International Trade & Economic Development*, 6(2): 299–324.

———. 2011. "The Price of Protein," *Macroeconomics and Finance in Emerging Market Economies*, 4(2): 327–35. Doi: 10.1080/17520843.2011.593908.

Gordon, R. 1982. "Inflation, Flexible Exchange Rates, and the Natural Rate of Unemployment," in M. Baily (ed.), *Workers, Jobs, and Inflation*, pp. 89–158. Washington, DC: The Brookings Institution.

Kapur, M. 2013. "Revisiting the Phillips Curve for India and Inflation Forecasting," *Journal of Asian Economics*, 25(C): 17–27.

Kotia, Ananya. 2016. *An Unobserved Philips Curve for India*. Available at SSRN: http://ssrn.com/abstract=2315995 or http://dx.doi.org/10.2139/ssrn.2315995 (accessed on June 17, 2016).

Mazumder, S. 2011. "The Stability of the Phillips Curve in India: Does the Lucas Critique Apply?," *Journal of Asian Economics*, 22(6): 528–39.

Lahiri, Amartya. 2014. "Don't Blame MSP for Inflation," *The Indian Express*, October 7.

Mishra, Prachi. 2013. "Has India's Growth Story Withered?" *Economic and Political Weekly*. 48(15): 51–59, April 13.

Mitra, Pratik, Dipankar Biswas, and Anirban Sanyal. 2015. "Estimating Sacrifice Ratio for Indian Economy—A Time Varying Perspective," RBI Working Paper, Series 1. New Delhi: Reserve Bank of India.

Nachane, D. and R. Lakshmi. 2002. "Dynamics of Inflation in India-a P-Star Approach," *Applied Economics*, 34(1): 101–10.

NSC. 2001. Report of the National Statistical Commission, New Delhi: Ministry of Statistics and Programme Implementation, Government of India.

Patra, M.D. and M. Kapur. 2012. "A Monetary Policy Model for India," *Macroeconomics and Finance in Emerging Market Economies*, 5: 18–41.

Rajan, Raghuram. 2014. "Fighting Inflation," Inaugural speech, Governor, Reserve Bank of India at FIMMDA–PDAI Annual Conference, February 26, Mumbai.

Rangarajan, C. 1983. "Conflict between Employment and Inflation," in A. Robinson (ed.), *Employment Policy in a Developing Country—A Case Study*, pp. 114–30, London: Palgrave Macmillan.

Rangarajan, C. and R. Arif. 1990. "Money, Output and Prices: A Macro Econometric Model," *Economic and Political Weekly*, 25: 837–52.

Srinivasan, N., V. Mahambare, and M. Ramachandra. 2006. "Modeling Inflation in India: Critique of the Structuralist Approach," *Journal of Quantitative Economics*, 4(2): 45–58.

Srinivasan, T.N. 2008. "Price Indices and Inflation Rates," *Economic and Political Weekly*, 43(26): 217–23.

Stock, J. and M. Watson. 2007. "Why Has U.S. Inflation Become Harder to Forecast?" *Journal of Money, Credit and Banking*, 39(1): 3–33.

Virmani, A. 2004. "Estimating Output Gap for the Indian Economy: Comparing Results from Unobserved—Components Models and the Hodrick-Prescott Filter," Working Paper. Ahmedabad: Research and Publication Department, Indian Institute of Management.

APPENDIX

Appendix 1. Data Details

Median Inflation in 2004Q2

There is a discontinuity in the monthly series on industry price levels that we use to calculate weighted median inflation. A new series begins for each industry in April 2004, and it is not comparable to the earlier data. In addition, 20 industries are added, bringing the total number from 61 to 81. For our quarterly analysis, this break in the data makes it difficult to measure median inflation for 2004Q2.

We approximate median inflation in 2004Q2 as follows. We use the 61 industries that exist both before and after the quarter. For each industry, we assume that the gross monthly inflation rate for April 2004 is the geometric average of the gross inflation rates for February, March, May, and June 2004. With this industry inflation rate in hand, we can compute a consistent series of monthly price levels that spans April 2004. We aggregate monthly price levels to get quarterly price levels for each industry, calculate quarterly inflation rates, and then calculate weighted median inflation for the 61 industries.

Splicing Methodology for GDP Series

We compute a consistent series for real GDP (before seasonal adjustment) using two series with base years of 1999–2000 and 2004–05. Essentially, we project the 2004–05 series (which starts in 2004Q2) backwards using the growth rates from the 1999–2000 series. Specifically:

For observations starting in 2004Q2, we use the output levels from the 2004–05 base year series.

We work backward to get output in 2004Q1, 2003Q4, and so on, using the formula

$$y_t = \frac{y_{t+4}}{(1+g_{t+4})}$$

where y_t and y_{t+4} are output levels in quarters t and t + 4, and g_{t+4} is the growth rate of output from t to t + 4. For all the observations for 2004Q1 and earlier, g_{t+4} is computed from the output series for base year 1999–2000. For observations from 2004Q1 back to 2003Q2, y_{t+4} is from the output series with 2004–05 base year. For observations for 2003Q1 and earlier, y_{t+4} comes from an earlier step in our backward iteration.

Appendix 2. Details of Estimation

To estimate the Phillips curve, equation (4), we make two approximations to our equation for expected inflation, equation (3).

First, we truncate the series of inflation lags after 40 quarters, adjusting the coefficients so they still sum to one. This yields

$$\pi_t^e = \frac{(1-\gamma)}{(1-\gamma^{40})}\left[\sum_{k=1}^{40}\gamma^{k-1}\pi_{t-k}\right] + \in_i$$

Second, we must address the problem that data on 40 lags of median inflation are not available for the early part of our sample. We assume that the level of expected inflation in 1996Q3, the first observation in our regression, is some unobserved level π_0^e. This is observationally equivalent to assuming that actual inflation is constant at π_0^e in all quarters before 1996Q3. We estimate this parameter along with the parameters gamma and alpha in the Phillips curve by non-linear least squares.

Comments and Discussion*

Pami Dua
Delhi School of Economics

The paper by Ball et al. investigates the behavior of quarterly inflation in India since 1994, including headline as well as core inflation. The paper examines the distinction between headline and core inflation. Core inflation denotes the underlying trend in inflation, while headline inflation fluctuates around the core inflation due to supply shocks. Often, core inflation is measured as the inflation rate excluding the price of food and energy. Since food and energy prices are the volatile components of inflation, core inflation is considered to be less volatile than headline inflation. The authors measure core inflation by the weighted median of price changes across industries based on the approach developed by the Federal Reserve Bank of Cleveland. They find that the weighted median is less volatile at quarterly frequency than headline inflation. To implement this approach, they examine the inflation rate calculated from the wholesale price index (WPI).

First, the authors suggest that supply shocks reflect asymmetries in the distribution of price changes and that core inflation, measured by the weighted median of price changes across industries, should eliminate the effects of these asymmetries. The authors note that a measure of inflation that excludes food prices is not appropriate for the Indian economy, since food is an important component of the consumption basket. The reason mentioned by the authors for using WPI is the high level of disaggregation into industry inflation rates since 1994, which is critical for measuring median inflation. The paper uses quarterly data from Q2 April 1994 to Q4 December 2014.

Second, the paper reports the estimation of a Phillips curve for core inflation. Core inflation at quarterly frequency is modeled to depend on expected inflation, which is determined by past levels of inflation and by the level of economic activity as captured by the deviation of output from its long-run trend. The main findings of this estimation suggest the following:

* To preserve the sense of the discussions at the IPF, these discussants' comments reflect the views expressed at the IPF and do not take into account revisions to the original conference paper in response to these and other comments, even though the IPF Volume itself contains the revised paper. The original conference version of the paper is available on www.ncaer.org.

1. Current core inflation depends upon several lags of past inflation with weights that decline slowly. This finding reflects slow adjustment of expected inflation.
2. There is a positive relation between inflation and deviation of output from trend. Along with the finding regarding the slow adjustment of expectations, this implies that monetary policy can reduce inflation, but with a short-run cost in the form of a decline in output.
3. This is further shown by estimating the sacrifice ratio to be 2.7, which is of the same order of magnitude as the estimates for other countries. This implies that if the current level of inflation is 5.2 percent and the RBI wishes to reduce it to 4 percent, then the cost will be $1.2 \times 2.7 = 3.24$ percentage points of the annual output.

Third, the authors study dynamic interactions among core inflation, headline inflation, and supply shocks. One of their findings is that movements in headline inflation appear to influence expected inflation, and hence future levels of core inflation. As a result, a one-time supply shock, such as a large spike in food prices, can have a persistent effect on inflation. They also find that supply shocks in terms of food price changes feed into expectations and have an effect on aggregate inflation.

My comments on the paper are as follows:

1. The reason why the authors use the WPI index to measure core as well as headline inflation in India is quite clear. Core inflation is measured as a weighted median of prices across industries using WPI disaggregated data. The authors have added a caveat in the paper that since consumer price index- (CPI) disaggregated data is available after 2014, it can be used for future analysis. Some of the advantages of CPI are noted here for future research.

   The Government of India (2010; 2011) document provides the new CPI index from 2011 onwards while also giving the rationale for the shift in emphasis from WPI to CPI. A study by Patnaik et al. (2011) asserts that CPI should take center stage for policy purposes among all existing inflation measures in India. The CPI reflects the consumption bundle of households and is, thus, more relevant than any other measure of inflation. Second, the CPI for Industrial Workers (CPI-IW) also reflects the prices of food as accurately as the other measures. Third, CPI-IW includes the prices of services, which are not included in any other measure of inflation. Furthermore, the WPI or the Producer Price Index (PPI) largely reflects global prices of tradeables expressed in rupees. The monetary policy of the RBI has a minimal role in influencing these, other than through the exchange rate. The CPI, on the other hand, has a large share of non-tradeables. Monetary policy has a much bigger role to play in influencing the prices of domestic non-tradeables. Thus, macroeconomic analysis and policy thinking in India may steer toward CPI and away from WPI. Basu (2011), in a Finance Ministry document, cites the advantages of using CPI inflation in policy making. Gupta and Siddiqui (2014) also note the benefits of using CPI over WPI for policy purposes.

2. The authors measure core inflation as a weighted median of price changes across industries. However, other methods are available to measure core inflation. These include the exclusion method, limited influence method, trimmed mean, weighted mean, common trends method, and smoothing techniques. Studies such as Durai and Ramachandran (2007), Goyal and Pujari (2005), Dua and Gaur (2010), and Raj and Mishra (2011) provide various measures of core inflation in India. These alternative measures may also be considered.
3. For measuring expected inflation, the paper uses the partial adjustment model of expectations, which makes use of lags of inflation. The paper includes 40 lags of inflation with exponentially declining weights while maintaining the restriction that the weights sum to one. However, this lag structure is very high and a smaller lag structure may be sufficient to capture the effect of past inflation. The long lag structure may also lead to the problem of multicollinearity.
4. The authors do not give a rationale for using backward-looking expectations. The question that arises is whether this analysis will also hold for the Phillips curve with forward-looking expectations. Inflation expectations can be measured in different ways. Dua and Gaur (2010) employ four estimation specifications for forward-looking expectations, that is, naïve forecast, perfect foresight, Autoregressive Integrated Moving Average (ARIMA) model (one quarter ahead and four quarter ahead forecast), and a measure of core inflation. An IMF study by Patra and Ray (2010) also uses the ARIMA approach to measure inflationary expectations in India.
5. There is a broad comparison between the Phillips curve for core inflation and headline inflation where the results presented suggest that the Phillips curve with the WPI headline inflation as the dependent variable seems to be misspecified. When expectations are measured in terms of core inflation, the adjustment parameter is below 1, otherwise it is estimated as above 1. Similarly, the coefficient (α) for the output

gap has a value above 1. These magnitudes seem to be perverse, possibly due to the omitted variable bias in the model. Furthermore, does this imply that the authors are trying to suggest that for policy purposes in future, the central bank should target core inflation rather than headline inflation?

6. In the abstract, the authors mention that large changes in relative prices arise mainly, but not exclusively, in industries that produce food and energy. However, this point is not shown explicitly by using the econometric model.
7. The Phillips curve should be estimated in a multivariate framework. Dua and Gaur (2010) use an extensive list of variables in their paper to estimate the Phillips curve for certain countries including Japan, Hong Kong, Korea, Singapore, the Philippines, Thailand, Mainland China, and India. These factors can be further divided into demand and supply factors. The demand factors include both domestic factors (for example, output gap, real money gap) and external factors (for example, exchange rate, import inflation). The supply factors also include both domestic factors (for example, food inflation, rainfall, the differential between wage inflation and productivity) and external factors (for example, global oil prices).
8. Finally, the results of the paper may be compared with the findings for other emerging market economies that have been discussed in Dua and Gaur (2010), among others.

References

Basu, Kaushik. 2011. "Understanding Inflation and Controlling It," Ministry of Finance, Government of India, New Delhi.

Dua, Pami and Upasana Gaur. 2010. "Determination of Inflation in an Open Economy Phillips Curve Framework: The Case of Developed and Developing Asian Countries," *Macroeconomics and Finance in Emerging Market Economies*, 3(1): 33–51.

Durai, S.R.S. and M. Ramachandran. 2007. "Core Inflation for India," *Journal of Asian Economics*, 18(2): 365–83.

Government of India. 2010. "Manual on Consumer Price Index," Central Statistics Office, Ministry of Statistics and Programme Implementation, Government of India, New Delhi.

———. 2011. "Consumer Price Index Numbers—Separately for Rural and Urban Areas and also Combined (Rural plus Urban)," Central Statistics Office, Ministry of Statistics and Programme Implementation, Government of India, New Delhi.

Goyal, Ashima and Ayan Kumar Pujari. 2005, May. "Analyzing Core Inflation in India: A Structural VAR Approach," *The IUP Journal of Monetary Economics*, 3(2): 76–90.

Gupta, Kirti and Fahad Siddiqui. 2014. "Salient Features of Measuring, Interpreting and Addressing Indian Inflation," Working Paper No. 279. New Delhi: ICRIER.

Patnaik, Ila, Ajay Shah, and Giovanni Veronese. 2011, April. "How Should Inflation be Measured in India?" *Economic and Political Weekly*, 46(16): 55–64.

Patra, Michael Debabrata and Partha Ray. 2010. "Inflation Expectations and Monetary Policy in India: An Empirical Exploration," Working Paper No. WP/10/84. Washington, D.C.: IMF.

Raj, Janak and Sangita Misra. 2011. "Measures of Core Inflation in India—An Empirical Evaluation," Working Paper No. 16/2011. New Delhi: RBI.

Kenneth Kletzer

University of California

Let me begin by saying that this paper is a welcome contribution to the discussion of inflation in India and to the India Policy Forum. It provides a clear and concise presentation of the contemporary analysis of inflation dynamics for India. In particular, the authors apply a well-known and statistically straightforward method for defining core inflation and estimating the sources of short-run inflation volatility used for the USA and other advanced economies to the study of inflation in India. I appreciate the opportunity to discuss a paper by three experts, Laurence Ball, Anusha Chari, and Prachi Mishra, on inflation dynamics, based on extensive research by Ball and others on inflation in other countries.

The authors begin the paper with the measurement of core inflation. Since inflation in the short run is much more volatile than in trend, we need a measure of inflation that distinguishes transitory fluctuations from persistent movements in the price level to understand inflation dynamics. Definitions of core inflation are attempts to remove high frequency fluctuations in nominal prices from the underlying persistent components of inflation. A possibly useful way to think about core inflation is that the difference between core and headline inflation is motivated by the classical dichotomy between the monetary and real sides of the economy, that is, trend inflation ought to be due to monetary phenomenon only, as suggested by Milton Friedman in his presidential address to the American Economic Association in 1968. In the presence of nominal rigidities, short-run changes in the price level, however, can arise from either non-monetary or monetary disturbances. Short-run inflation volatility can be caused by monetary policy, and transitory shocks can lead to persistent changes to inflation through monetary policy responses. The last three words of my previous sentence are essential. Several recent commentaries on inflation in India have asserted that food price shocks cause persistent inflation. Without monetary accommodation, this is not a sensible assertion.

In this paper, core inflation is measured by a weighted median of price changes in the disaggregated WPI data. This reduces the impact of volatile and skewed price changes for individual product categories on overall inflation. Other limited influence estimators could also be used to remove the transitory effects due to price changes in the tails of skewed distributions. In their original paper, Bryan and Cecchetti (1995) proposed and compared trimmed means and dynamic factor indices in addition to weighted medians as candidates for limited influence estimators of core inflation. If nominal rigidities find their source in menu costs, then unexpected price changes are made by firms that experience the largest idiosyncratic shocks because the seller's desired price change must exceed its menu cost (as in Ball and Mankiw 1995). Such threshold effects generate differences between mean and median inflation that tend to be transitory. Limited influence estimators and alternative econometric-based estimators, for example, Quah and Vahey (1995), should be preferred to ad hoc definitions of core inflation for studying inflation dynamics, particularly the sources of inflation persistence. Ad hoc definitions such as the US version of core inflation based on all items less food and energy identify cost shocks with price volatility in particular industries rather than with shocks per se. This might be useful for transparent communication of monetary policy, but only when it provides a good approximation to a statistically based definition.

Ball, Chari, and Mishra illustrate the difference between the weighted median and weighted mean inflation in their Figure 2 and show that food and fuel contribute significantly to price changes in the upper tail of the distribution. As emphasized in the presentation, mean inflation is persistently higher than median inflation in the WPI for India, and the average weighted mean significantly exceeds the average weighted median of inflation for the sample period. This tells us that the distribution of price changes is right-skewed, and price changes in the upper tail are not symmetrically offset by lower tail changes. This is confirmed by the cross-sectional distributions of price changes illustrated in Figure 3. The distribution of price changes for advanced economies (shown for the USA in the paper) is more symmetric and does not display a pronounced difference between median and mean inflation. One concern is that the weighted mean and median measures differ on an average because price changes in the upper tail include permanent increases in the nominal prices of particular goods. This can be consistent with idiosyncratic, infrequent adjustment of nominal prices, given large menu costs. With large menu costs, the mean would always exceed the median in a steady state with constant positive inflation. However, fluctuations in the difference between the mean and median could reflect transitory inflation.

In this case, weighted median inflation may not be a very appealing measure of core inflation for guiding monetary policy. A natural, alternative approach would be to estimate permanent and transitory components of inflation, following Stock and Watson (2007). Although an econometric method does not have the transparency of a fixed, readily replicated statistic for communicating monetary policy decisions, the persistent shortfall of weighted median inflation from the trend rise in the price level for India may severely limit its usefulness in this regard. I would appreciate seeing a comparison of trend inflation from an unobserved components analysis to limited influence estimators for India included in the paper. Incidentally, the use of limited influence estimators has been suggested before for India (for example, by Mohanty, Rath, and Ramaiah 2000).

The second part of the paper uses the weighted median inflation rate to estimate the contribution of real activity to inflation using the Friedman–Phelps accelerationist Phillips curve. Expected inflation is backward-looking and represented by a moving average of lagged inflation. The implicit model of price setting behind the econometric equation suggests that producer price inflation (PPI), and not consumer price inflation (CPI), should be used. Inflation in the WPI is an imperfect substitute, but unfortunately, a proper PPI is not available for India. The estimated Phillips curves are fairly interesting; one thing I learned from the results is that these work for Indian data. Ball, Chari, and Mishra find evidence that changes in real economic activity as measured by deviations of GDP from HP-filtered trend GDP have a significant influence on current inflation.

The estimations of the Phillips curve include expected inflation and the output gap. Weighted median inflation is the dependent variable in regressions 1 and 3 of Table 3. Equation 3 uses headline inflation to estimate backward-looking inflation expectations. The model behind this specification is Ball and Mankiw (1995), in which mean inflation is regressed on lagged inflation rates and skewness of nominal price changes (the interaction between skewness and standard deviation of the cross-sectional distribution of price changes). Replacing headline inflation (weighted mean inflation) by a limited influence estimator of core inflation eliminates the need for the skewness term. Reporting regression 2, in which the dependent variable is headline inflation, reinforces the conclusion that headline inflation responds to transitory price shocks drawn from an asymmetric distribution. Regression 1 uses weighted median inflation to represent inflation expectations, thus removing fluctuations in the difference between weighted mean and median inflation from the right-hand side. Supply shocks enter the preferred regression (3) through the expectations variable. Table 4 shows the results of including food and energy inflation as a separate regressor. I think this is especially useful because it shows that food and energy prices do not influence core inflation any differently than do other sources of average inflation. Although the results do suggest that the authors' choice of a limited influence estimator is superior to headline inflation for estimating the Phillips curve, I would appreciate seeing a comparison with the alternative measure of core inflation estimated from an unobserved components model.

An alternative to the backward-looking Phillips curve is the New Keynesian Phillips curve (NKPC). Expected inflation is forward-looking in an NKPC, and the equation itself is derived from an optimizing model of price setting. In an IMF working paper, Anand, Ding, and Tulin (2014) present a new Keynesian general equilibrium model for the Indian economy that includes forward-looking expectations in the aggregate supply curve. A critique of the NKPC is that it does not perform as well empirically as the backward-looking Phillips curves, even for advanced economies. Including a discussion comparing backward-looking and forward-looking expectations would be helpful for placing the empirical model used here into the contemporary theory of aggregate supply and price dynamics. I think that this is also important for interpreting what the Phillips curve tells us about monetary policy in India. Essentially, what I glean from the estimation in Ball, Chari, and Mishra is that the output gap significantly affects inflation in India. The slope of the Phillips curve may help explain the success of the recent, post-2013, disinflation.

My first critique returns to the measurement of core inflation. The argument in favor of adopting a simple statistical measure of core inflation relies on the credibility of a transparent and easily replicated inflation statistic to communicate the objectives of monetary policy. Credibility is not likely to be gained if core inflation fails to track actual trend inflation well. Simplicity can be appealing (as seen by the US choice of definition) but not at the sacrifice of usefulness. The systematic discrepancy between weighted median inflation and headline inflation probably will not help make this a good core inflation estimator for either guiding or communicating monetary policy decisions. Both the Bank of Canada and the Federal Reserve Bank of Cleveland publish econometrically derived estimates of trend inflation.

Such estimated core inflation measures may serve better for understanding the dynamics of inflation and the efficacy of monetary policy for meeting price-level stabilization goals. At present, India probably needs better guides for monetary policy and better measures for studying the inflationary process (and inflation persistence, in particular) more than it needs an alternative to headline inflation for the central bank to communicate with the public. I suggest using the already mentioned approach of Stock and Watson to identify trend inflation for India.

The second critique is to ask whether we learn very much that is important for monetary policy in India from estimating a Phillips curve. The title of the paper, "Understanding Inflation in India," suggests that we might learn something about the persistence of inflation in India, the contribution of monetary policy to reducing or propagating inflation, and the formation of inflationary expectations in India. The paper does provide some insight into the importance of extreme price changes in particular product categories. In combination, primary food and manufactured food products comprise 40 percent of the upper tail cross-sectional price changes. The volatility of food prices drives future inflation through lagged headline inflation in the regression analysis. The predominance of food prices in outliers in individual product inflation distributions should not lead us to conclude that there is something special about food inflation, but rather about how large positive changes in individual producer prices drive inflation.

Inflation persistence has been a concern for monetary policymaking and analysis, and it has been a subject of other recent contributions to the India Policy Forum. The authors find persistence coming through the backward-looking component in the regression equations. The estimate for the geometric weight on lagged inflation, gamma, is about 0.9. The literal interpretation is that adaptive expectations adjust slowly. Another interpretation is that monetary policy accommodates aggregate supply shocks and that inflation expectations take account of this. Decomposing inflation into transitory and permanent components could help us to understand the formation of inflation expectations and how cost shocks contribute to inflation. Cogley, Primiceri, and Sargent (2010) propose that the dynamics of the gap between inflation and trend inflation measures the effectiveness of monetary policy for achieving the long-run inflation targets of monetary policymakers. I think that looking more deeply into the inflation process in India econometrically would yield greater understanding of inflation in India. The Reserve Bank of India has adopted a flexible inflation-targeting framework. We will learn if inflation expectations become better anchored in time, as we learn whether inflation in India can be tamed. A statistical analysis to elucidate our understanding and to enable monetary authorities to choose policy responses to inflationary and deflationary shocks should probably be based on econometric tools rather than on statistical simplicity.

I found this paper to be interesting and informative. It is a useful contribution to the IPF. In conclusion, I found the comparison of the recent inflation experience of India to inflation in the USA in the 1970s and 1980s very insightful and provocative. The authors point out their observation that the debates over inflation in India sound a lot like the same debates in the USA in the 1970s and 1980s. I very much look forward to more research on the inflation and monetary policy in India and further progress in taming inflation.

References

Anand, R., D. Ding, and V. Tulin. 2014. "Food Inflation in India: The Role of Monetary Policy," Working Paper No. 14/178, September. Washington, D.C.: IMF.

Ball, L. and N.G. Mankiw. 1995. "Relative-price Changes as Aggregate Supply Shocks," *The Quarterly Journal of Economics*, 110(1): 161–93.

Bryan, M.F. and S.G. Cecchetti. 1994. "Measuring Core Inflation," in N.G. Mankiw (ed.), *Monetary Policy*, pp. 195–219, Chicago: The University of Chicago Press.

Cogley, T., G.E. Primiceri, and T.J. Sargent. 2010. "Inflation-gap Persistence in the US," *American Economic Journal: Macroeconomics*, 2(1): 43–69.

Friedman, M. 1968. "The Role of Monetary Policy," *The American Economic Review*, 58(1): 1–17.

Mohanty, D., D.P. Rath, and M. Ramaiah. 2000. "Measures of Core Inflation for India," *Economic and Political Weekly*, 35(5): 273–82.

Quah, D. and S.P. Vahey. 1995. "Measuring Core Inflation," *The Economic Journal*, 105(432): 1130–44.

Stock, James H. and Mark W. Watson. 2007. "Why Has U.S. Inflation Become Harder to Forecast?" *Journal of Money, Credit and Banking*, 39(s1): 3–33.

General Discussion

Rajnish Mehra asked the authors what use their inflation data should be put to. For example, temperature data designed to assess global warming would have to be filtered very differently if we were assessing temperature changes in Delhi next week. Similarly, the paper's inflation data would have to be understood differently if it were to assess, say, short-term monetary policy vs identifying structural reforms.

Nirvikar Singh agreed with Pami Dua that the paper's 40-period-distributed lag estimation seemed like too much inertia in the adaptive equation for expected inflation. He recommended six to eight lags, which would then not need restrictions on the coefficients of the geometrically declining wages and also provide an easy robustness check. Fewer lags may mean estimating more coefficients but would mean perhaps not having to deal with missing-not-at-random data, which would make robustness checks easier and more practical.

Vijay Joshi, agreeing with Ken Kletzer, argued that to understand the trajectory of inflation in India, an important thing to consider must be the policy reaction function, which the paper seemed to lack in an explicit way. The several years of high inflation in India post the global financial crisis could possibly be attributed to the Reserve Bank of India (RBI) following an overly accommodative monetary policy. But, it would not be possible to say anything about this hypothesis using the paper, since it lacks a policy reaction function.

Joshi felt that the paper did not help understand what goes into inflationary expectations in India. The paper notes that inflationary expectations depend on supply shocks but does not go into the how or why of such a dependency. Indexation such as used for dearness allowance or Mahatma Gandhi National Rural Employment Guarantee Act (MGNREGA) wages could be a shock, but so could the announcement of the Minimum Support Price (MSP) for the government's agricultural procurement. If policy makers had a better feel for this, and research could provide the clear underlying evidence, we might then have better policies. We might, for example, do something about the MSP to deal with inflationary expectations.

Karthik Muralidharan commented on how the monetary side of inflation played into the real economy and had a question about the lowest level of aggregation at which this analysis of inflation would make sense for a continental sized economy like India's. How, for example, might the paper's most striking result about the difference between core and headline inflation vary by the level of aggregation that we adopt? This led to his second point about whether it is the lack of market integration in domestic food markets that accounts for the huge variation between the median and mean and the gap between core and headline. Should not the paper reference the considerable work done on food markets and the barriers, whether physical or policy induced, that may be preventing the emergence of an efficient national food market? Getting rid of these barriers may perhaps do more for inflation in the first instance than anything monetary policy could do.

Ila Patnaik highlighted two questions going back to the morning keynote address by Rajiv Mehrishi, India's Finance Secretary, when he mentioned the monetary policy framework agreement (MPFA) signed by the RBI and the Union Government in February 2015. First, the MPFA says that the objective of monetary policy should be price stability, with RBI targeting an inflation rate of 6 percent (±2 percent) in 2016 and 4 percent (±2 percent) beyond that, using CPI inflation as proposed by the Urjit Patel Committee. Can the findings of the paper inform the policy discussion about which measure to use, since it is likely that MPFA will get enshrined soon in an RBI Act Amendment bill? And given the analysis of volatility in the paper, what should the band be, since the ±2 percent has been put in arbitrarily? Second, Patnaik noted that if her understanding was correct, the paper showed that expectations responded more to headline than core inflation, and, if so, how should optimal monetary policy react to shocks in food and fuel prices? Overall, she felt that the paper should focus more on the policy implications of its findings.

Surjit Bhalla noted, first, that RBI should construct CPI series for both urban and rural areas and then generate a composite CPI series, going back several decades: RBI has been collecting CPI data for the last 65 years, and this should not be difficult to do since Prachi was at RBI. Second, Bhalla suggested that inflation in India can be seen in three phases: 1960 to 1996, when it averaged about 8.5 percent; 1996 to 2004–05, when it averaged about 4.3 percent; and 2006 to 2013, when it averaged above 10 percent. He felt that any policy research on inflation should answer the question of why high inflation persisted for some 35 years, then remained very low for a decade, and then rose significantly again for some six years. At a minimum, he felt that such research should be able to "reject" the following explanations for persistence, at least since the 1980s, that inflation had persisted because of: (a) globalization and the effects of global inflation on India and (b) the high, relative price of food, which he felt is not determined by droughts, but by the MSP. Once we admit that these explanations are inadequate, we can make real progress. Third, Bhalla was delighted that the paper had estimated a core inflation rate of 5 percent but wondered how this would be received at RBI, given its own expectations survey that is consistently showing inflationary expectations of 10–11 percent inflation. Finally, Bhalla noted that annual data show nothing more than two-year lags, so using 10-year lags was really a problem and could just be noise in the authors' calculations. Why not just use the annual data?

Dilip Mookherjee, professing his non-macro credentials, said that he was a little mystified why items like food and fuel should be excluded in calculating inflation. The rejection of outliers could be understood if there were significant measurement errors, but that was not the case here. While endorsing Kletzer's argument that the authors should filter out the effects of transitory supply shocks, he suggested that they could confine themselves to mean inflation and get some measure of trend inflation, even as they filter out the transitory shocks. He also suggested that there was an identification problem with respect to the lags, pointing to several other reasons for the lags, such as inventories, durables, collusion, and price fixing. He urged the authors to make stronger efforts to ascertain the cause of the lagged effects.

Anusha Chary and Prachi Mishra thanked the participants for their comments, responded to the key issues raised, and said that they would seek to incorporate them into the revised paper.

Bimal Jalan (Chair) concluded the discussion by reiterating the need for using some measure other than just CPI, even though there is a greater all-round backing for using CPI over WPI. He also suggested that the paper's discussion of the significant relationship between output and inflation would help not only in understanding inflation but also tackling inflation using policies and mechanisms that would cause the least real impact.

M. GOVINDA RAO*
NCAER and the *National Institute of Public Finance and Policy*

Tyranny of the Status Quo: The Challenges of Reforming the Indian Tax System§

ABSTRACT The paper reviews Indian tax policy and recent reforms. Against a best-practice framework, it examines changes in policy and in tax revenue trends at the Union and State levels to help identify the major shortcomings of India's tax system. A fragmented constitutional assignment of taxes on agricultural and non-agricultural income to the Union and State governments makes it difficult to levy a comprehensive income tax and opens the door to tax avoidance and evasion. Multiple objectives imposed on the tax system result in a plethora of exemptions and preferences, causing significant loss of revenue and creating unintended distortions. The government tends to tax sectors where it can raise revenue easily in an ad hoc manner, causing further distortions. The difficulty in taxing unorganized sector incomes further narrows the tax base. Tax abuse by multinational companies evading tax through base erosion and profit shifting may be equally important. A poor organizational setting and low administrative capacity have been other constraining factors. The "tyranny of the status quo" arises because those who gain from tax reforms tend to be ungrateful and those who lose tend to be vengeful, explaining why tax reforms have been slow and often ineffective in India.

Keywords: *Principles of Tax Policy, Indian Tax Reforms, Union Taxes, State Taxes, GST, Constitutional Assignment*

JEL Classification: *H21, H23, H24, H25*

* *mgrao48@gmail.com*

§ The author is grateful to Mihir Desai and Ashok Lahiri for their meticulous comments at the IPF 2015 Conference and other participants for their very useful suggestions. Thanks are also due to Richard Bird and Alan Auerbach for useful comments on an earlier draft. The usual disclaimers apply.

1. Introduction

This paper reviews tax policy and tax reforms in India. India faces the major challenge of raising resources to meet public expenditure requirements while minimizing tax distortions. Taxes matter because they affect citizens and businesses. Taxes change the behavior of people, and particularly the behavior of economic agents, in a variety of ways. They determine the incentives to work, save, and invest. No one likes paying taxes. Some use ingenious ways to avoid them, others may unhesitatingly evade them, and only a few may consider it their legitimate duty to pay them.

Writing on economic policy, Lord Keynes said,

> The ideas of economists and political philosophers, both when they are right and when they are wrong, are more powerful than is commonly understood. Indeed the world is ruled by little else. Practical men who believe themselves to be exempt from intellectual influences are usually the slaves of some defunct economist. Madmen in authority, who hear voices in the air, are distilling their frenzy from some academic scribbler of a few years back .... Soon or late, it is ideas, not vested interests, which are dangerous for good or evil. (Keynes,1936)

However, experience everywhere has shown that the impact of vested interests on tax policies is significant. Johnson and Myles (2011, p. 323) note,

> In the real world, proposals for tax reform are constrained by politics. Those who lose from tax reforms tend to be vengeful while those who gain from them tend to be ungrateful. This can lead to tax policy, perhaps, more than any other policy, to a "tyranny of the status quo."

This paper is an attempt to understand the challenges of overcoming this tyranny.

There are a number of reasons for undertaking a review of Indian tax policy. First, despite reforms attempted in India, the ratio of tax to GDP has remained remarkably stagnant and in recent years has even shown a decline. The pressure to contain fiscal deficits requires a sharp focus on identifying tax reforms. Second, the motivation for reforming the tax system has also arisen from the desire to impart greater competitiveness to the economy. Third, the federal nature of the country has posed constraints in calibrating and coordinating tax policies to evolve broad-based direct and indirect tax systems. The fragmented assignment of income tax and lack of coordination in calibrating the reform of internal and external indirect taxes have posed difficulties in evolving a harmonized and competitive income and consumption tax system in the country. Fourth, recent years have seen widespread dissatisfaction among multinational companies and frustration among tax collectors, highlighting the difficulties of taxing international capital on the one hand, and legal and administrative ambiguities in the tax system on the other.

On tax reforms, it is important to distinguish between minor changes in the tax system undertaken on an annual basis and reforms that are undertaken to change the nature of the tax system (Auerbach 2009). Given the significant impact of the tax system on economic activity, it is important for the tax system to be simple, stable and predictable, and therefore, changes in the tax system should not be disruptive. At the same time, minor changes are often necessary to take into account the conditions and conveniences of tax authorities and taxpayers. Tax reforms, in contrast, involve major shifts in the direction of policy, which is what this review focuses on: an analysis of the tax system in India, trends in tax revenues, various reform proposals, and progress in their implementation. At the same time, it must be noted that any reform is not an event, but a process, particularly in democratic societies.

The review in a way revisits and updates a similar review undertaken 10 years ago for the *India Policy Forum* (Rao and Rao 2005–06; 2010). Revisiting the Indian tax system is useful because the economy has changed, as has the political landscape, and as have the structure of taxes and the application of technology to tax administration. There has also been considerable public discussion on reforming both direct and indirect taxes recently. Besides considerable discussion on replacing multiple commodity taxes with a destination-based value-added tax on goods and services, the government has placed two discussion papers on the Direct Taxes Code (DTC) in the public domain. Therefore, a detailed review of the tax system in India is timely. Section 2 provides a framework to identify the characteristics of a good tax system in light of new developments in theory and global practice. Section 3 analyses recent changes and proposals on tax policy reforms and recent trends in Union and State revenues. In Section 4, some important tax policy reform successes are discussed. The major shortcomings of the Indian tax system and the need for further reforms are discussed in Section 5. Section 6 brings together proposals for reforming the tax system and the final section provides concluding remarks.

2. What Makes for a Sound Tax System?

Tax policy stands on the tripod of three equally important components, namely its architecture, engineering, and management (Bird 2008).

Architecture provides the design of tax policy guided by its objectives. Engineering relates to the mechanics of applying the design, dependent on the nature and quality of the systems and institutions involved in tax collection. Management determines the implementation strategy and action, depending on political support and the competence of the tax administration and its application of technology and information systems. Architecture, engineering, and management are inter-dependent. A tax policy, even if optimally designed, is only as good as its administration. At the same time, even the most competent administration cannot enhance revenue or minimize distortions if the design of the tax system is overburdened with multiple objectives. The objective of tax policy should be to raise revenues in the least distortionary manner. Tax implementation and administration become easier when the design is simple and the system is transparent, particularly in developing countries such as India, where administrative constraints can be severe.

With multiple objectives, administrative constraints, and many vested interests, it is important to have a framework for what constitutes an ideal tax system to see the departures from the ideal, to try to move towards it, and to have clarity in objectives. Of course, a single model cannot suit every country. Nor is it appropriate to assume that in the absence of taxes we would have a perfectly competitive economy with Pareto-efficient resource allocation and, therefore, that lump-sum taxes are the best, and in the absence of such taxes, we need to seek second-best solutions. When economic, political, and administrative conditions vary, as do the responses of economic agents to any change in tax policy, every country has to choose its own tax system. Nonetheless, general principles can be helpful both for tax design and reforms.

The thinking on tax policy has undergone significant changes over the years. The traditional view has been that income tax is good for reducing inequalities in incomes and should, therefore, be a preferred instrument for raising resources. An increase in the share of direct taxes in the total revenue was, therefore, considered desirable. Theory posits that the optimal tax rate schedule should depend on the distribution of abilities. In the absence of lump-sum taxes, the search for a second best optimum shows that increasing marginal tax rates to tax people with high abilities could result in disincentives for them to earn more income. Thus, as shown by Mirrlees (1971), high marginal tax rates would lead to high economic distortions relative to the revenues raised. Further, research has shown that the distortions can be significant when labor supply is relatively inelastic, which implies that the distortions from high marginal tax rates could adversely impact wage rates, thereby defeating the very purpose of reducing inequality (Feldstein 1995). Given the difficulties in getting information on abilities and efforts, it is suggested that a flat tax could be close to being optimal.

In the case of commodity taxes, Ramsey (1927) showed that distortions can be minimized by levying higher tax rates on commodities with low compensated price elasticities of demand. Tax rates for different commodities and services would then have to be designed varying inversely with their compensated price elasticity of demand to achieve an equi-proportionate reduction in their demand in response to a tax. The information required for designing such a tax system is well beyond the realm of availability, and administering a tax with multiple rates is well beyond the capacity of any tax administration. Rate differentiation could also provide scope for special interest groups. Further, since commodities with inelastic demand are the ones that constitute a larger proportion of the consumption basket of the poor, there is a clear conflict between efficiency and equity.

While the optimal theory of direct and indirect taxes provides useful insights, their practical application in tax design has been more limited. Indeed, the perfect and costless information assumed in these models simply does not exist. They also do not take into account administrative capacity, compliance costs, and enforcement tools. The focus of these models is on determining optimal tax bases and rates. Furthermore, these models essentially analyze behavioral responses in consumption and production decisions and not responses in terms of tax avoidance and evasion. There is also an implicit assumption that taxpayers understand and react rationally to the tax system, and therefore, governments have no reason to influence the perceptions of taxpayers (Slemrod and Gillitzer 2014).

Optimal tax theories emphasize efficiency. The presumption is that in the absence of taxes, the economy operates at a perfectly efficient frontier. However, another branch of literature, which analyzes market imperfections, argues that it is possible to design tax systems to correct market distortions. Stiglitz (2010, p. 14), for example, states,

> [A]nother important strand of research in the past quarter century has analyzed a large number of market imperfections, including those from imperfect and asymmetric information. Tax distortions may interact with market distortions in various ways. In particular, taxes may be used to *correct* market distortions. One distortion may, at least partly, undo the effects of the other.

Unfortunately, this would also require perfect knowledge and information about the nature of market imperfections and about the responses of economic agents to tax changes.

Optimal theories of direct and commodity taxes can only provide broad guidance in calibrating real-world tax systems. As stated by Frank Hahn (1973, p. 106), "Optimum formulas are either guides to action or nothing at all." Despite this pessimism, theoretical advances have helped us understand what constitutes a desirable tax system and develop best practice approaches to calibrating tax policies.[1] One of the most important lessons from optimal taxes is the focus on distortions. This has led to recommending uniformity and simplicity in designing and reforming taxes. While the Haig–Simons income tax was traditionally considered the bedrock of a tax system, there is much less consensus on this today in view of the undesirable economic effects of capital taxation. In fact, there has been a movement towards dual income taxation, with capital income taxed at lower and less progressive rates (Auerbach 2008). In many countries, the balance has shifted in favor of a broad-based value-added tax on goods and services (GST). Even as income taxes continue, the step progressivity that existed in most countries in the world in the 1950s and 1960s, including in the US and UK, is no longer in fashion. There is much less emphasis on high and steeply increasing marginal rates, an influence of the principles arising from optimal tax theories.

The most important objective of tax policy is to raise revenue. But revenues must be raised by minimizing the three costs associated with taxation, namely the cost of collection, compliance costs, and distortion costs. Minimizing administrative and compliance costs requires the tax system to be simple and transparent, and tax policy not to be loaded with multiple objectives but designed mainly to raise revenues in an equitable manner. Raising the same amount of revenue with lower tax rates requires a broadening of the tax base with minimum exemptions and preferences, and an effective administration and intelligence system to ensure compliance. While raising revenue is important and taxes exist primarily to meet this objective, the focus of tax policy and reforms should be on enhancing long-run revenue productivity and not meeting short-term exigencies through ad hoc changes.

Thus, as Bird and Zolt (2008) argue, a best practice approach to tax policy and reforms requires governments to move towards a broad-base-low-rate (BBLR) approach, a simple and transparent tax system that avoids arbitrary tax differentiation across people and economic activities. Distortions increase exponentially with tax rates and most countries desist from levying taxes at high rates. Therefore, in order to raise the given amount of revenue, the base should be broadened by minimizing exemptions and preferences.

1. The most recent attempt to distil balanced and well-grounded tax reform proposals in the UK was the Mirrlees Review. See Gordon (2011).

An important part of the tax advice given to most developing countries is to transform their consumption taxes into a broad-based value-added tax on goods and services (GST) with uniform rates. Even as the optimal tax theorists show that neutrality requires levying of commodity taxes with multiple rates varying inversely with the price elasticity of demand, the move has been towards evolving uniform tax rates for reasons of lack of information, administrative convenience, and more importantly, as Harberger (1990) argues, to avoid political pressures.

In most developing countries, including India, taxes are deployed to fulfil a variety of objectives besides raising revenues in an equitable manner. These include raising the levels of saving and investment, promoting investments in particular activities, regional development, enclave development to overcome institutional and infrastructure bottlenecks, exports, and use of particular technology. Even when the objectives are clear, for example, promoting investment or exports, it is difficult to ascertain the effectiveness of specific tax incentives. Very often these can be redundant and ineffective, and may merely contribute to complicating the tax system and opening up avenues for the avoidance and evasion of taxes. Often, they result in an uneven tax burden, with domestic companies bearing a higher burden than foreign companies. Although experience suggests that sound macroeconomic factors, competitive infrastructure, effective governance, and stable and predictable policies are the most important determinants of investment, most countries continue to extend a variety of incentives to attract investments, which not only causes significant revenue losses from tax expenditures but also results in distorting resource allocation.

The major challenge is to design the tax system to incorporate fairness in its impact. The most important lesson from optimal taxation is that distortions increase exponentially with tax rates and, therefore, even when the tax is seen to be progressive, its adverse effects on economic activity and employment may negate the progressivity. Furthermore, too much attention to the fairness of individual taxes is misplaced. When the tax system is designed to reduce distortions, it may contain some individual taxes that may be considered regressive. What matters is the effect of the tax system as a whole and not the impact of individual taxes on the distribution of incomes (Bird and Zolt 2005; 2008; Johnson and Myles 2011).

While it is important to assess the impact on redistribution of the totality of taxes, the notion that in the presence of a good income tax there is no need to impart progressivity to commodity taxes may be misleading. In most developing countries, the coverage of income tax is low, capital is mobile, and there are difficulties in enforcing an effective income tax (Stiglitz 2010).

Therefore, to the extent redistribution is considered as an objective, it may be necessary to design consumption taxes to ensure that they are not regressive by exempting unprocessed food and by taxing essential items at a lower rate. At the same time, it is important to ensure that the list is kept narrow because when a commodity or a service is taxed at lower rates, high income groups also benefit from the lower rate.

The general presumption is that since indirect taxes are regressive, direct taxes should be designed to reduce inequalities and, therefore, the traditional approach is to design highly progressive personal income tax systems and levy high rates on corporate incomes. This has, however, come into serious questioning. First, it is possible to design non-regressive consumption taxes by exempting essential unprocessed food items. Second, the effectiveness of personal income tax in reducing inequality itself is doubtful because only a small proportion of the people pay income tax in developing countries. This is due to the fact that in most of these countries, income tax is neither comprehensive nor progressive, and much of the revenue comes from withholding taxes and very little from the self-employed businesses due to poor information systems and the existence of a large unorganized sector. High rates of taxes on corporate incomes, given the high mobility of capital, could drive out businesses and a tax on capital might turn out to be a tax on labor. Furthermore, progressive tax systems are not costless. They increase administrative and compliance costs and, even more, economic efficiency costs. When the distortions are taken into account, the adverse impact of economic activity on the incomes of the poor may outweigh the gains from progressivity. The experience in most countries has shown that personal income tax has not been an effective instrument for reducing inequalities and, therefore, inferences about progressivity in the distribution of the tax burden being merely based on the ratio of direct and indirect taxes are misplaced (Bird and Zolt 2005).

Empirical studies in both developed and developing countries have shown that the tax system has not been effective in redistributing incomes. A study by Pechman (1985) using alternative assumptions about the distribution of the burden of individual taxes for the period 1966–85 has shown that the US tax system is not significantly progressive. Similarly, a careful study of the Chilean tax system by Engel et al. (1999) showed that the tax system was, in fact, moderately regressive, with the Gini coefficient increasing to 0.4861 after the tax, from 0.4883 earlier. Therefore, the focus of redistribution in fiscal policy needs to shift from reducing the incomes of the rich to increasing the incomes of the poor, and this implies that the focus of the redistributive instrument should shift from the tax to the expenditure side of the budget.[2]

Recent discussions on optimal tax systems have brought back the issue of an appropriate tax base and taxing income versus consumption. Most versions of a consumption tax avoid taxing normal returns on savings/capital. Of course, evolving an expenditure tax may not be an option; also, it will not be possible to impose a zero effective tax rate on normal returns to capital. Nevertheless, a consensus among tax theorists is that labor and capital incomes should be taxed differently due to their differential responses to taxation. In fact, Auerbach et al. (2010) recommend the replacement of the present system of corporate taxation with a destination-based VAT on goods and services, with labor costs deductible in addition to other input costs.

While doing away with the corporate tax would be socially unacceptable in any country, a comprehensive value-added tax on goods and services is an important instrument in any modern tax system. The tax is found to be particularly important to overcome a decline in revenues when developing countries embark on their rationalization of import duties. This is demonstrated in the study by Keen and Ligthart (2005), which shows that revenue-neutral tariff reductions, accompanied by a price-neutral GST, will enhance both revenue and efficiency. A revenue increase arises from the self-enforcing nature of the tax. An efficiency increase arises as it avoids distorting input prices and, to that extent, reduces production inefficiency (Keen 2007). Emran and Stiglitz (2005), however, contest the claim that GST, being a tax on recorded transactions, when combined with weak administrations in developing countries can work as a tax on the formal sector. In contrast, Keen (2007) considers the GST as one of the least costly ways of taxing the informal sector due to its self-enforcing nature. Although B2B sales provide information on input purchases to enable the tax administrations to do their job better, both sides can easily evade tax through collusion, especially if one of them is a fraudulent enterprise with a VAT number and there is no check on B2C transactions, and they are wide open to fraud. The impact of the GST is best seen empirically; as long as the gains from participating in the formal market are greater than the tax loss, the taxpayer would prefer to pay the tax and it is here that the simplicity of

2. As Harberger (1990, p. 13) argues, "Society is not going to bring about major changes in the income distribution by operating either on the tax side or on the expenditure side of the budget of the public sector…. it is more realistic to think of the struggle against poverty to be a major goal." He recommends that this should be done by helping the poor in meeting their basic needs and providing opportunities for advancement by ensuring access to education and healthcare to those who cannot afford it. For similar arguments also see Bird and Zolt (2008).

the tax becomes important. Thus, as Bird and Gendron (2007) argue, "On the whole, while further theoretical and particularly empirical research on the effects of VAT in developing and transitional countries is needed, the case for VAT in most such countries remains solid."

Thus, GST is an important component of modern tax design in most developing countries. A destination-based GST is considered neutral as it removes the taxation of inputs and capital goods. In terms of total impact, a retail sales tax levied at the last point is equivalent to VAT. However, under sales tax, if the last seller evades the tax, the revenue is completely lost, whereas under VAT only the last transaction escapes the net. Given that the tax paid at each stage is only on value added at that particular stage, the incentive for evasion is less under a VAT. More importantly, as crediting the tax paid at the previous stage of transaction requires invoices, the tax is self-enforcing. In addition, harmonization of VAT registration numbers with income tax permanent account numbers can throw up valuable information for the income tax administration, which can significantly improve the compliance of the latter.

As mentioned above, management of the tax system is an important leg in the tripod of tax policy, and this is provided by tax administration, including its information systems. A tax policy is only as good as it is administered and, therefore, it is important to keep in mind the capacity of the tax administration in designing a tax system, while at the same time constantly upgrading administration capacity and the application of technology in tax administration. Confidence and trust between the tax administration and taxpayers is important in tax compliance and, therefore, tax administration should be transparent and should consider taxpayers as agents rather than adversaries. A complementary part of administration is the building of a proper information system, its exchange among tax departments, and application of technology for tax administration and enforcement. Tax administration should be an independent department that is insulated from political pressures. Another important part of a good tax system is an efficient taxpayer service. This would help in building the trust of the taxpayers and in improving tax compliance.

Thus, a good tax system is one that minimizes administrative cost, compliance cost, and distortion cost to the economy. It should have a broad base, low marginal rates, and less differentiated rates with a simple structure. Fairness in tax policy should be judged in totality and not by individual taxes. Furthermore, tax policy has not been found to be effective in bringing about a redistribution of incomes and, therefore, the focus should shift from reducing inequality to alleviating poverty, which is better done through the expenditure side of the budget. An important component of a good tax system is a comprehensive GST. In a multilevel fiscal system, it is important to coordinate tax reforms between different levels of government so that they do not work at cross purposes (Rao and Sen 2013). It is not enough to focus on the design of the tax structure; building capacity as well as orientation in tax administration is equally important. A good tax system is supported by a good information system, not only to enforce tax but also to calibrate changes with full information. A hallmark of a good tax administration is a taxpayer service, which not only builds confidence among taxpayers, but also improves compliance. The use of information technology promotes transparency and provides information for the enforcement of taxes.

3. Trends in Indian Tax Policy and Revenues

The basic framework for the levy of taxes by the Union of India and States is provided in the Indian Constitution's Seventh Schedule, which, following the principle of separation, assign taxes to either the Union or State governments. The Union Government can levy taxes on non-agricultural income, wealth, and corporate income, on services, and customs and excise duties. The tax powers assigned to the States include taxes on agricultural income and wealth, the tax on the sale and purchase of goods, excise duties on alcoholic products, taxes on motor vehicles and goods and passengers, stamp duties and registration fees on property transactions, entertainment tax, and taxes and duties on electricity. The Union Government can levy a tax on the inter-state sale of goods, which can be collected and appropriated by the States.[3] States have the powers to levy taxes on professions, trades, and employment, and while some States levy the tax themselves, some others have passed the power on to local governments. The State List also includes taxes on immovable properties, and the tax on the entry of goods for consumption, use, or sale, which are generally assigned to local bodies.

The legal separation of tax powers in the Constitution was done to minimize overlap and avoid disharmony. However, the separation is entirely legal and cannot avoid the economic inter-dependence of the tax bases. The separation

3. Article 301 of the Constitution mandates that "Subject to other provisions ..., trade, commerce and intercourse throughout the territory of India shall be free." Article 286 prohibits any State from imposing a tax on the inter-state sale or purchase of goods. However, it authorizes the Union Government to formulate principles for such a levy. Thus, after the 6th amendment to the Constitution, Entry 92A was added to the Union List, which authorized the Union Government to levy the tax to be collected and appropriated by the States.

of income tax from agricultural and non-agricultural sources has provided a route to evade and avoid tax on non-agricultural income by misclassifying it as agricultural income. Similarly, the excise duty on manufactured products levied by the Union is nothing but a sales tax at the point of first sale, which has created a significant overlap in the consumption tax system. In assigning the sales tax on the sale or purchase of goods to the States, the Constitution has favored revenue autonomy for the States over fiscal disharmony. However, States do not have the power to levy the tax on services, and it is not possible, therefore, to evolve a comprehensive GST unless the Constitution is amended. As a result, coordination and harmonization of consumption tax reform between the Union and States and among the States themselves is a major challenge, as is seen in the ongoing impasse on introducing GST.

The division of tax powers requires coordination in calibrating tax reforms between the Union and State governments, which in the Indian context has been a problem. For example, opening up the economy in 1991 required a substantial reduction in customs duties. The solution to overcome revenue loss would have been to coordinate the reform of domestic trade taxes with a reduction in import duties to evolve a broad-based GST. However, as the power to levy sales tax lay with the States, the reduction in customs duty was not accompanied by the replacement of a cascading type sales tax with a comprehensive value-added tax, and this resulted in a net loss of revenue of over two percentage points of GDP between 1991 and 2001. Furthermore, even as the discussion on the introduction of destination-based GST at the Union and State levels in a coordinated manner has continued for over a decade, its implementation has faced several problems. Thus, Constitutional tax assignments have posed constraints on evolving a national harmonized tax system since it has not been possible to amend the Constitution to meet the requirement of changing times.[4]

During the initial years after India's independence, tax policy was designed to meet the objectives of planning in a mixed economy framework. The details of how tax policy evolved then is not discussed here as it has been detailed in an earlier paper (Rao and Rao 2005-06). Essentially, tax policy was considered a major instrument to finance a public-sector-led import-substitution industrialization strategy and to reduce inequalities in income and wealth arising from the industrial license regime. Tax policy was also one of the instruments for prioritizing the allocation of resources among

4. There is a clear trade-off between sub-national fiscal autonomy and tax disharmony. In regard to tax assignments, the founding fathers of the Constitution seem to have preferred the former.

different sectors of the economy. The multiplicity of objectives assigned to tax policy is a legacy in part of this planned era.

3.1. Reform of Union Taxes

Since 1991, a number of attempts have been made at reforming both direct and indirect taxes at the Union level to simplify and rationalize the tax system. The Tax Reform Committee (TRC) with Raja Chelliah as the Chairman, appointed immediately after the 1991 economic reforms were initiated, made far-reaching recommendations for the simplification and rationalization of both direct and indirect taxes (Government of India 1991; 1993). These recommendations were implemented during 1991–95, and the direction of reforms set in these recommendations continued thereafter. A comprehensive review of the tax system was made in 2003–04 in the two reports chaired by Vijay Kelkar on direct and indirect taxes (Government of India 2003a; 2003b). In addition, reviews have been done on specified taxes, such as the *Report of the Expert Group on Taxation of Services* (Government of India 2001a) and *Report of the Advisory Group on Tax Policy and Tax Administration for the Tenth Plan* (Government of India 2001b). More recently, the Tax Administrative Reform Committee chaired by Parthasarathi Shome has comprehensively dealt with the reform of tax administration, including revenue forecasting and research, in a series of four reports (Government of India 2014; 2015).

Successive governments have attempted to reform both the direct and indirect tax systems to improve their revenue productivity by expanding the tax base and simplifying and rationalizing tax structures. In the case of non-corporate income tax, as per the recommendations of the Chelliah Committee, the number of tax brackets was reduced to 3, with the highest bracket taxed at 40 percent (as against 50 percent earlier). This was further rationalized to reduce the highest marginal rate to 30 percent in 1997. However, a surcharge and a cess were levied later to earmark revenues for elementary and higher education. At present, tax is levied at 10 percent for incomes above ₹2.5 lakhs up to ₹5 lakhs,[5] 20 percent on incomes between ₹5 lakhs and ₹10 lakhs, and 30 percent above that. In addition, there is an education cess of 3 percent. On incomes above ₹1 crore, there is also a surcharge of 12 percent, which implies that the marginal tax rate for those earning above ₹1 crore works out to 36.66 percent.

5. The exemption limit for those above 60 years of age is ₹3 lakh.

The important administrative measures taken to expand the tax base include: (a) every individual living in a large city and covered by any one of six conditions (ownership of a house, ownership of a car, membership in a club, ownership of credit cards, foreign travel, and a telephone subscriber) is required to file a tax return, and (b) expanding tax deduction at source beyond salaries to most transactions, including interest and dividend receipts and payments to contractors.

In the case of corporate tax, based on the recommendations of the TRC, the distinction between closely held and widely held companies was done away with and tax rates were unified at 40 percent in 1993–94. In 1997–98, the corporate rate was further reduced to 35 percent, and the 10 percent tax on dividends was shifted from individuals to companies. Since then, the measures adopted have lacked direction. The dividend tax rate was increased to 20 percent in 2000–01, then reduced again to 10 percent in 2001–02, and levied on shareholders rather than the company. The policy was reversed once again in 2003–04, with the dividend tax imposed on the company. In the 2015–16 budget, the Finance Minister has promised to reduce tax preferences progressively and reduce the corporate tax to 25 percent in the next three years.

The legal framework for the levy of income tax in India goes back to the Income Tax Act, 1961. The various amendments to the Act carried out over the last 55 years have made it unwieldy and complex. With a plethora of exemptions, concessions, and deductions introduced over the years, the income tax system has become complicated, leading to ambiguity and discretions in interpretation. This has increased both administrative and compliance costs and has piled up arrears on account of disputes, besides causing serious distortions in resource allocation. Further, the Act has not kept pace with the changes in international business models and mechanics of the multinationals. This provides scope for evasion and avoidance, invites adverse international publicity, and blocks a huge amount of revenue in litigations. Keeping these in view, the first discussion paper on the DTC was put out in the public domain with the principal objective of simplifying and rationalizing the tax and phasing out various tax preferences to make it broad-based. As expected, everyone wanted tax rates to be low and tax concessions to be abolished on all sectors except their own. After taking the feedback into account, the Finance Ministry put out a second discussion paper in which the objective of expanding the base was substantially diluted. The Union Finance Minister in his 2015–16 budget speech has given a sound burial to the proposal stating that he does not intend proceeding in producing a new DTC.

The thrust of reforms on indirect taxes since 1991 has been to reduce and rationalize customs duties, simply and unify excise duties, and expand the base of service tax. In the case of customs duties, tariff rates have been lowered, quantitative restrictions replaced by tariffs, and the dispersion in the rates reduced. In 1990–91, duty rates ranged from 0 to 400 percent and the peak rate was over 150 percent. The peak rate had been lowered progressively to 15 percent by 2005–06. The number of duty rates covering 90 percent of duty collected was reduced from 22 in 1990–91 to 4 in 2003–04. At the same time, a special additional duty was imposed on goods imported into the country on the rationale that if the commodity was domestically produced and sold inter-state, it would have attracted a tax rate of 4 percent. This duty was abolished in January 2004, only to be reintroduced in 2005–06. The weighted average of import duties has steadily declined from 77.2 percent in 1991–92 to 9 percent in 2007–08. Despite these attempts to rationalize, there are still a large number of rates including specific rates. Higher rates are specified for agricultural products. Furthermore, lower tariffs rates are applied on inputs, resulting in very high effective rates of protection on the outputs.

Ill-prepared tax reforms can be more harmful than any reform. This was clearly demonstrated in the reform of Union excise duty undertaken in 1986–87. The Jha Committee (Government of India 1976) had recommended in 1976 that Union excise duties should be transformed into a manufacturing stage value-added tax. It had, however, recommended that this should be preceded by adequate preparation in terms of converting the specific duties into ad valorem ones, unifying the rates, and building capacity in tax administration to administer the new tax. However, the measure was introduced without any prior preparation, resulting in the emergence of a highly complicated tax with several tax rates, both specific and ad valorem, with presumptive ways to provide input tax credit and refund of the duty on exports, and called a modified vat (MODVAT). This "learning by doing" approach resulted in huge complications in MODVAT, excessive tax credits and a huge loss of revenue. After 1991, based on the recommendations of the TRC, the process of converting specific duties into ad valorem was initiated. Even so, the number of tax rates continued to be large, and this perpetuated the problem of misclassification and disputes. Subsequent years have seen substantial convergence of tax rates until 2008–09, when there were again attempts to reduce the rates on some items including processed food items. At present, most of the commodities are subject to two rates, one levied at a lower rate (6 percent) and the second at the general rate (12.5 percent), though some items are taxed at different rates including specific rates (cement, cigarettes). Clearly, there is considerable scope for further rationalization by lowering the threshold from the prevailing ₹1.5 crore, pruning the exemption list from about 300 items prevailing at present, and moving items like processed food into the higher rate category.

The Constitution did not originally assign the power to levy tax on services either to the Union or to State governments. However, taking advantage of the residual powers assigned to it under Article 246, the Union Government introduced the levy on three services: non-life insurance, stock brokerage, and telecommunications in 1994. Later, the 88th Amendment of the Constitution specifically empowered the Union Government to levy the tax by inserting Entry 92-C in the Union List. The list of taxable services was steadily expanded and finally in the budget of 2012–13, the tax was applied to all services except those specified in the negative list. Initially, the tax was levied at 5 percent, and thereafter increased to 8 percent in 2003–04 and to 10 percent in 2004–05. This was brought down to 8 percent in the aftermath of the global financial crisis, but was increased to 10 percent, and the education cess (0.3 percent) was levied in 2010. The 2012 Budget increased the tax to 12 percent (excluding the education cess) and in the 2015–16 Budget, it was raised to 14 percent by adding additional cess for *Swachh Bharat*.

The Expert Group on Taxation of Services in 2011 had recommended switching over to the negative list, unifying the threshold and rates between excise duty and service tax, and enabling input tax credit between goods and services to evolve a manufacturing stage GST (Government of India 2011). It took over 11 years for the government to move over to the negative list. Perhaps, had the recommendation to introduce the manufacturing state GST been implemented, the transition to a full-fledged GST would have been easier, as it would have provided valuable experience to make a smoother transition at the State level without much acrimony. In fact, the expert group had also recommended that the power to levy service tax be shared with the States and in return, inter-state sales tax be abolished to reform the sales taxes levied in the States into a destination-based GST. Instead, the reform in 2005 resulted in the partial roll over of the value-added tax only on goods at the State level. The issue of evolving a broad-based dual GST continues to remain elusive. This issue is discussed in greater detail below.

3.2. Reform of State Taxes

Although the Constitution assigns the power to levy a number of taxes to the States, only the tax on sale and purchase of goods is a broad-based tax generating about 60 percent of the States' own tax revenues. In general, the States raise 38 percent of the total tax revenues raised in the country. Other important State taxes include stamp duties and registration fees on property transactions, excise duties on alcoholic products, and taxes on transport by way of motor vehicles tax and passengers and goods tax. Land revenue and agricultural income tax have ceased to be important from the point of view of revenue. There are also less important taxes such as entertainment tax and electricity duty. Many States have assigned profession tax, property tax, and entry taxes to local bodies. An important development over the years has been the gradual phasing out of the tax on the entry of goods into a local area for consumption, use, or sale. All the States except Maharashtra have abolished the levy. Another important development over the years has been the gradual reduction in the rates of stamp duties and registration fees on immovable properties. The rates which were above 10–12 percent in most States in the early part of the millennium have been reduced to an average of 6 percent over the years.

The major reform at the State level was the introduction of value-added tax on goods from 2005–06. Discussion has been going on for the introduction of dual GST by the Union and State governments. As mentioned above, the expert group on the taxation of services recommended in 2001 that the Union Government could introduce the GST in the manufacturing state and the States could transform their cascading type sales taxes into a destination-based GST by enabling them to levy tax on services by amending the Constitution. The Empowered Committee of State Finance Ministers has put out two papers for public discussion. However, consensus on a number of issues relating to the structure and operation of the tax is yet to be reached between the Union and States and among the States. The reform is supposed to transform the prevailing value-added tax, which is partly origin-based due to the continuation of Central sales tax into a destination-based GST.[6]

Even though both the Union and States see the GST reform as important, a number of issues need to be finalized before the tax can be implemented (Rao 2013). The target date for implementation of GST has been repeatedly changed as the Union and States, as well as the States among themselves,

6. Central sales tax is levied by the exporting state. The tax, which was 4 percent, was brought down to 2 percent in 2008, and this was supposed to be done away with and after imposition of the GST, to make the GST completely destination-based. The Union Government agreed to pay compensation for the loss of revenue in 2010 when the GST was to be implemented. However, with no consensus emerging, the implementation date was shifted. The Union Government's refusal to pay compensation after 2010 also resulted in a trust deficit between the Union and States, and in the process, the reform itself took a back seat. The discussion has resumed after the Union Government agreed to pay the compensation.

have not been able to agree on many issues. In his 2008–09 Budget, Mr Chidambaram declared that the reform would be implemented in April 2010. The rate of inter-state sales tax was reduced from 4 percent to 2 percent in preparation for moving over to a destination-based GST and the Union Government agreed to compensate for the revenue loss until 2010 when the GST was supposed to have been implemented. However, consensus on many of the issues relating to the structure and operation of the new levy could not be reached and successive finance ministers had to postpone its implementation. The Thirteenth Finance Commission recommended that compensation for any loss of revenue to the States should be paid only if the States implemented a "flawless GST," and this put the clock back as the States wanted to negotiate and settle for a compromise structure. The reluctance of the Union Government to give compensation for reducing the rate of central sales tax from 4 percent to 2 percent beyond 2010 created a serious trust deficit, and progress in evolving a consensus stalled as a result. The present Finance Minister, in his keenness to embrace the reform, has now set April 2016 as the date of implementing the tax. The 122nd Constitution Amendment Bill has been passed in the Lok Sabha, but not in the Rajya Sabha, where it has been referred to the Select Committee of the Rajya Sabha. The Select Committee has made recommendations, with a dissenting note by members of the Indian National Congress. The Government has received the report of the committee under the chairmanship of the Chief Economic Adviser on the rate structure for the GST. However, lack of political consensus continues to plague the passage of the Bill in the Rajya Sabha. Even if the Bill had been passed in the Budget Session in February 2016, it is unlikely that the reform can be implemented before April 2017. Issues relating to the GST reform are discussed in greater detail below.

3.3. Tax Revenue Trends in India

There have been several studies on the trends in tax revenues across different countries and these bring out four important generalizations (Bird and Zolt 2005; IMF 2011; Tanzi and Zee 2000). First, the tax–GDP ratio varies positively with the level of development of the country. Second, the tax–GDP ratio in developing countries has shown an increase, though in developed countries, it has tended to plateau. Third, in terms of composition, the general tendency has been to replace tariffs with domestic trade taxes, particularly the value-added tax on goods and services. Finally, the share of consumption taxes has shown an increase over the years in both developed and developing countries, with the value-added tax becoming important due to its high revenue productivity.

FIGURE 1. Percentage of Tax to GDP in India 2000–15

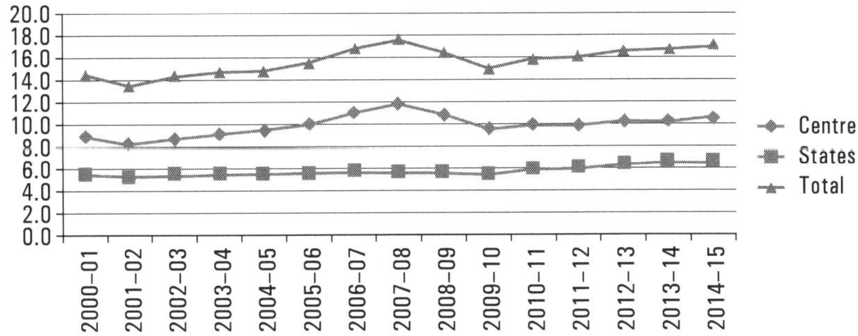

Source: Indian Public Finance Statistics, Ministry of Finance, Government of India.

International comparisons can provide broad trends and directions for policy calibration . Analysis shows that India's tax revenue is substantially lower than the average for countries with comparable level of development. The analysis of Bird and Zolt shows that the average for the middle-income countries (with per capita incomes ranging from USD 1000 to USD 17,000) had a tax–GDP ratio of 22 percent. Similarly, the more recent study by the IMF covering 174 countries shows that the average tax ratio for middle-income countries (with per capita GNP ranging from USD 995 to USD 3,945) for the time period 1980–2009 was close to 18 percent. India's tax ratio at 16.4 percent of GDP compares unfavorably with this international experience (Table 1 and Figure 1).

In India, the tax–GDP ratio is not only low by international standards, but it has also been stagnant or declining over the years. The average tax–GDP ratio in India during the decade of the 1980s was 14.7 percent but declined to 13.9 percent during the 1990s. In fact, after economic reforms were initiated in 1991, the tax ratio declined from 15.3 percent in 1991–92 to 13.3 percent in 2001–02. More recently, there has been a steady increase in the ratio after 2003–04 to reach the highest level at 17.5 percent in 2007–08. However, following the deceleration in economic growth and, more importantly, reduction in the tax rates of Union excise duty and service tax in 2009–10 as a part of the stimulus following the global financial crisis, it has remained stagnant at about 16.5 percent in subsequent years. This low and stagnant tax ratio has limited the fiscal space of the government to spend on much needed expenditures on physical infrastructure and human development.

The decline in the tax–GDP ratio during the 1990s, its sharp increase from 2003–04 to 2007–08, and the subsequent decline were mainly due to movements in Union tax revenues. The Central Government's tax ratio

TABLE 1. Trends in Tax–GDP Ratio at Union and State Levels (percent)

	Union			*States*			*Total*		
Year	*Direct*	*Indirect*	*Total*	*Direct*	*Indirect*	*Total*	*Direct*	*Indirect*	*Total*
1950–60	1.57	2.77	4.33	0.65	1.69	2.34	2.22	4.46	6.68
1961–70	1.93	4.49	6.42	0.44	2.48	2.92	2.37	6.97	9.34
1971–80	2.21	6.21	8.42	0.26	3.71	3.97	2.47	9.91	12.39
1981–90	1.96	7.77	9.74	0.20	4.79	4.99	2.17	12.56	14.73
1991–2000	2.64	6.21	8.85	0.16	4.97	5.13	2.80	11.18	13.98
2001–08	4.43	5.46	9.89	0.15	5.57	5.72	4.58	11.03	15.61
2007–08	6.26	5.63	11.89	0.13	5.43	5.56	6.39	11.06	17.45
2008–09	5.68	5.07	10.75	0.14	5.37	5.51	5.83	10.43	16.26
2009–10	5.67	3.97	9.64	0.15	5.66	5.81	5.82	9.63	15.45
2000–11	5.63	4.55	10.19	0.16	5.99	6.15	5.79	10.55	16.34
2011–12	5.42	4.45	9.87	0.15	6.28	6.43	5.57	10.73	16.29
2012–13	5.48	4.77	10.25	0.14	6.33	6.47	5.62	11.10	16.72
2013–14	5.54	4.42	9.96	0.14	6.44	6.59	5.69	10.87	16.55
2014–15	5.53	4.36	9.89	0.14	6.49	6.64	5.67	10.85	16.53
2008–2015	5.55	4.50	10.05	0.15	6.18	6.33	5.69	10.68	16.37

Source: Public Finance Statistics, Ministry of Finance, Government of India (various years). For 2013–14 and 2014–15, the Budget documents of the Union government and article on State Finances: A Study of Budgets 2014–15, Reserve Bank of India.

Note: The data for 2014–15 refer to revised estimates for the Union government and budget estimate for the States.

declined from 10 percent in 1991–92 to 7.9 percent in 2001–02, or looking at its average tax ratio over a decade, from 9.7 percent in the 1980s to 8.8 percent in the 1990s. The decline was mainly on account of indirect taxes, which fell from 6.2 percent during the 1980s to 5.5 percent during the 1990s. More recently, the sharp increase in the tax ratio from 2003–04 to 2007–08 and the decline thereafter was also due to revenue trends in Union taxes. The ratio of State taxes relative to their GDP, in contrast, was broadly constant until 2008–09, and showed a steady but slow increase thereafter.

The trends in the level and composition of Union taxes after 1991–92 presented in Table 2 show three distinct phases. The first phase from 1991–92 to 2001–02 was marked by a sharp decline in revenues relative to the GDP, mainly due to a decline in customs and excise duties. During this period, the Union Government's tax revenues relative to GDP declined by over two percentage points. This was due to the decline in indirect taxes from 7.6 percent in 1991–92 to 5 percent in 2001–02. The average growth rate of tax revenues during this period was just about 12.7 percent, indicating a buoyancy of 0.87. This was mainly due to a decline in revenues from both customs and excise duties; the former declined from 3.3 percent to 1.7 percent of GDP, while the latter declined from 4.1 percent to 3.1 percent. The decline in Union excise duties at a time when customs duties were falling as a result of the opening up of the economy shows a lack of coordination in calibrating domestic and foreign trade taxes. The decline in revenue from excise duties during the 1990s also shows that the reform of Union excise duty in 1987 leading to the introduction of MODVAT caused a decline rather than an increase in tax revenues. In contrast, the average buoyancy of direct taxes was 1.5 as this revenue grew at 19.3 percent during the 1990s. As mentioned earlier, the reduction in the number of tax brackets after the recommendations of the tax reforms committee and reduction in tax rates, particularly in 1996–97, led to a significant increase in compliance and in revenue productivity (Das-Gupta 2002). In contrast, the growth rate of indirect taxes remained low at 10.6 percent, indicating a buoyancy of 0.7.

The trend in Union tax revenue from 2001–02 to 2007–08 is marked by an acceleration in the growth of revenue from income and service taxes. The revenue from corporate and personal income tax increased at an average annual rate of 27.8 percent, showing an average buoyancy of over 2 during this period. Similarly, service tax revenues grew at an average annual rate of 63 percent due to the steady expansion in the base with the inclusion of more and more services in the tax net. Although total indirect taxes registered an average annual growth of 17 percent, the share of excise duty in the total revenue as well as the ratio to GDP continued to decline during

TABLE 2. Trends in Tax–GDP Ratio: Union Government (percent)

Year	*Corporate Tax*	*Personal Income Tax*	*Total Direct Taxes*	*Customs Duty*	*Excise Duty*	*Service Tax*	*Total Indirect Taxes*	*Total tax-Union*
1991–92	1.17	1.00	2.26	3.30	4.17	0.00	7.55	10.00
1995–96	1.34	1.27	2.74	2.91	3.28	0.07	6.31	9.07
2001–02	1.55	1.36	2.94	1.71	3.08	0.14	4.98	7.94
2005–06	2.74	1.55	4.30	1.76	3.01	0.62	5.62	9.95
2006–07	3.36	1.97	5.34	2.01	2.74	0.88	5.88	11.03
2007–08	3.87	2.17	6.05	2.09	2.48	1.03	5.93	11.89
2008–09	3.79	1.88	5.68	1.77	1.93	0.55	4.51	10.75
2009–10	3.78	1.89	5.68	1.29	1.59	0.90	3.94	9.64
2010–11	3.84	1.79	5.63	1.74	1.77	0.91	4.53	10.19
2011–12	3.58	1.83	5.42	1.66	1.61	1.09	4.43	9.87
2012–13	3.52	1.94	5.48	1.63	1.74	1.31	4.74	10.25
2013–14	3.45	2.08	5.54	1.51	1.48	1.35	4.39	9.96
2014–15	3.37	2.15	5.53	1.49	1.46	1.33	4.33	9.89
2015–16	3.34	2.27	5.61	1.48	1.62	1.49	4.64	10.27
Growth rate: 1990–91 to 2001–02	19.58	18.57	19.29	10.06	10.47	33.07	10.62	12.74
Growth rate: 2002–03 to 2007–08	31.80	21.29	27.76	17.23	9.40	63.25	17.00	21.26
Growth rate: 2007–08 to 2014–15	12.13	17.46	14.00	13.54	10.65	31.42	15.23	13.91

Source: Budget Documents, Ministry of Finance, Government of India.

Note: 1. Total direct taxes include revenue from other minor taxes such as estate duty and wealth tax.

2. Total taxes also include Union Territory taxes.

this phase, registering a growth rate of 9.4 percent per year, which works out to a buoyancy of 0.7.

The spectacular increase in revenue from income taxes is attributed in the main to the application of technology in tax administration. In particular, following the Comptroller and Auditor General's comment that a large proportion of those who were required to deduct tax at source were not submitting their returns to the tax department, the tax identification number (TIN) was introduced for tracking tax deduction at source and matching it with actual payments to banks in cities that were increasingly covered from 2003–04 to 2007–08. This progressively resulted in improving tax revenue as efficient networks, and information systems helped improve compliance in tax payments. Thus, until 2007–08, there was a spectacular increase in both personal and corporate income tax revenues. The steady expansion in the service tax base by including more and more services increased service tax revenue. However, revenue from Union excise duties in spite of buoyant economic conditions and high growth of the manufacturing sector continued to be low. The revenue from Union excise duties grew only at 9.4 percent even when the nominal growth of GDP during this period was 14.5 percent.

Revenue trends in the third phase are marked by a decline in the revenue–GDP ratio, partly due to the reduction in excise and service tax rates by two percentage points in the 2009–10 budget as a part of the stimulus given in the wake of the global financial crisis. The CENVAT rate was reduced from 10 percent to 8 percent and the service tax rate was reduced from 12 percent to 10 percent. The lowering of these tax rates, along with a decelerating manufacturing sector, caused a decline in the Union Government's tax revenues relative to GDP from 11.9 percent in 2007–08 to 9.6 percent in 2009–10. The largest decline in the ratio was in the case of excise duties by 0.9 percentage points, followed by customs duty (0.8 percentage points). The revenue from income tax remained static following the completion of TIN coverage. In subsequent years, even as the stimulus provided by reduced tax rates was withdrawn, the revenue–GDP ratio remained stagnant.

3.4. Trends in State Tax Revenue

In contrast to the Union tax revenues, revenues from State taxes relative to GDP showed an increase from 6.3 percent in 2000–01 to 7 percent in 2005–06, mainly on the strength of an increase in revenue from sales tax and stamps and registration. However, subsequently, the ratio declined to 6.5 percent in 2009–10 before recovering to 7.6 percent in 2012–13. The trend is broadly the same in the case of non-special category States.

The tax–GDP ratio increased from 6.3 percent in 2000–01 to 7.2 percent in 2006–07, then declined to 6.6 percent in 2009–10, before recovering to 7.7 percent in 2012–13. Interestingly, the growth of revenues in the special category States was faster—increasing by one percentage point from 4.1 percent in 2000–01 to 5.1 percent in 2005–06 and eventually increasing to 6 percent in 2012–13 (Table 3).

An important feature of state-level taxation is the wide variations in revenue among the States, which cannot be explained by taxable capacity alone even when general and special category States are considered separately. Analysis by the Fourteenth Finance Commission (Government of India 2015) showed that among general category States, the tax ratio in 2013–14 (RE) varied from 11.2 percent in Tamil Nadu to 10.2 percent in Karnataka and 5.5 percent in West Bengal.[7] The per capita GSDPs of Gujarat, Haryana, Maharashtra, and Punjab were higher than those of Karnataka and Tamil Nadu, but their tax–GSDP ratios were at least two percentage points lower at 7.8, 6.8, 7.2, and 8.3, respectively. Similarly, Chhattisgarh, Madhya Pradesh, Uttar Pradesh, and Bihar had tax–GSDP ratios at 8.9 percent, 7.5 percent, 8.1 percent, and 6.7 percent, respectively, which were much higher than that of West Bengal at 5.5 percent. The tax–GSDP ratios of Bihar and Haryana were similar. These comparisons showed that there were significant differences in tax effort among the States.

Table 4 presents the analysis of the growth of the individual state's own tax revenues and sales tax revenue for the period 1991–92 to 2012–13. The growth rates were estimated for the periods 1991–92 to 2004–05 and 2005–06 to 2012–13 to assess whether the replacement of cascading sales taxes based on multiple rates with a value-added tax on goods with two rates accelerated the growth of tax revenue in States. As Table 4 shows, growth rates during the second period were generally higher at 16.5 percent as compared to 13.7 percent. Similarly, sales tax revenue growth for all States was higher at 16.7 percent as compared to 14.3 percent in the earlier period. Broadly, a similar trend was seen in the case of the general category States. In the case of special category States, the acceleration was even higher.

The analysis presented for individual States suggests that acceleration in the average annual growth of tax revenue as well as in sales tax revenue was substantially higher in the case of some of the poorest States. In Bihar, for example, the growth of tax revenues accelerated from 11.9 percent

7. In Annex 4.34 in Volume 2 of the Report, the data on the tax–GSDP ratio are presented for the period 2004–05 to 2014–15 (BE). Since generally, the budget estimates are more in the nature of targets than actual realizations, the revised estimates of 2013–14 are analyzed here.

TABLE 3. Trends in Tax–GDP Ratio in States (percent)

Year	Tax on Land and Agri. Incomes	Stamp and Registration	State Excise Duties	Sales Tax/ VAT	Taxes on Transport	Other Taxes	Total- States' Own Tax
I. Non-Special Category States							
1991–92	0.13	0.48	0.96	3.72	0.53	0.34	6.31
1995–96	0.14	0.55	0.76	3.19	0.48	0.52	5.79
2001–02	0.09	0.57	0.84	3.80	0.57	0.18	6.31
2005–06	0.09	0.84	0.83	4.26	0.61	0.19	7.04
2006–07	0.10	0.94	0.83	4.33	0.57	0.18	7.15
2007–08	0.11	0.93	0.83	4.20	0.53	0.16	6.97
2008–09	0.11	0.78	0.87	4.16	0.52	0.15	6.78
2009–10	0.10	0.75	0.89	4.03	0.52	0.16	6.66
2010–11	0.13	0.83	0.91	4.26	0.54	0.19	7.07
2011–12	0.12	0.89	0.97	4.60	0.54	0.16	7.47
2012–13	0.12	0.92	0.98	4.76	0.58	0.19	7.75
II. Special Category States							
1991–92	0.47	0.09	0.59	1.49	0.24	0.12	3.47
1995–96	0.18	0.09	0.63	1.49	0.28	0.13	3.10
2001–02	0.13	0.18	0.76	2.23	0.46	0.24	4.12
2005–06	0.06	0.32	0.65	3.28	0.47	0.18	5.13
2006–07	0.06	0.40	0.64	3.42	0.45	0.14	5.31
2007–08	0.06	0.31	0.64	3.49	0.40	0.18	5.29
2008–09	0.09	0.24	0.61	3.37	0.47	0.19	5.16
2009–10	0.08	0.23	0.64	3.29	0.52	0.14	5.06
2010–11	0.10	0.22	0.63	3.49	0.48	0.15	5.21
2011–12	0.07	0.25	0.68	3.93	0.52	0.24	5.90
2012–13	0.09	0.28	0.73	4.01	0.47	0.23	5.99

(Table 3 Contd)

(Table 3 Contd)

Year	*Tax on Land and Agri. Incomes*	*Stamp and Registration*	*State Excise Duties*	*Sales Tax/ VAT*	*Taxes on Transport*	*Other Taxes*	*Total- States' Own Tax*
				III. All States			
1991–92	0.33	0.15	0.46	0.94	3.60	0.52	6.15
1995–96	0.50	0.14	0.53	0.75	3.10	0.47	5.66
2001–02	0.18	0.09	0.55	0.83	3.70	0.56	6.18
2005–06	0.19	0.09	0.81	0.82	4.20	0.60	6.93
2006–07	0.18	0.10	0.91	0.82	4.28	0.56	7.05
2007–08	0.16	0.10	0.89	0.82	4.16	0.52	6.88
2008–09	0.15	0.11	0.75	0.85	4.12	0.52	6.69
2009–10	0.16	0.10	0.72	0.88	3.99	0.52	6.57
2010–11	0.19	0.13	0.80	0.89	4.22	0.54	6.96
2011–12	0.17	0.12	0.85	0.95	4.56	0.54	7.38
2012–13	0.19	0.12	0.88	0.97	4.71	0.58	7.65

Source: Finance Accounts of different States.

TABLE 4. Growth Rates of States' Own Tax Revenues (percent)

	Sales Tax/ VAT			*Total States' Own Tax Revenues*		
	1991–2012	*1991–2004*	*2005–2012*	*1991–2012*	*1991–2004*	*2005–12*
Andhra Pradesh	15.99	18.13	17.01	15.56	15.23	17.06
Bihar	9.20	11.90	17.51	11.11	11.07	19.10
Chhattisgarh		23.29	19.99		21.70	18.54
Goa	14.74	17.95	14.55	15.74	17.43	16.52
Gujarat	9.70	0.00	17.37	13.50	13.36	17.65
Haryana	18.21	18.70	27.05	14.97	13.61	14.74
Jharkhand		18.05	15.87		18.24	15.86
Karnataka	13.90	14.26	16.77	14.69	13.53	16.85
Kerala	14.18	16.64	15.33	13.71	15.22	15.46
Madhya Pradesh	13.04	13.25	17.50	12.47	12.86	17.99
Maharashtra	13.40	13.32	15.35	13.89	14.13	15.79
Odisha	16.27	14.34	19.27	16.36	13.18	18.14
Punjab	14.43	13.10	15.59	12.76	11.96	14.32
Rajasthan	15.71	14.66	17.81	14.66	14.81	16.30
Tamil Nadu	13.68	14.20	15.24	14.13	14.44	16.44
Uttar Pradesh	14.98	14.30	17.78	14.09	13.54	16.90
West Bengal	12.00	11.22	15.34	12.01	10.01	14.63
All General Category States	14.36	14.26	16.60	14.21	13.74	16.46
Arunachal Pradesh	45.00	11.80	28.65	25.13	19.93	25.44
Assam	16.40	12.12	15.83	14.80	11.92	15.75
Himachal Pradesh	19.70	17.61	22.08	15.96	16.19	17.12
Jammu and Kashmir	23.36	19.57	22.64	18.69	17.35	18.44
Manipur	18.87	16.12	23.40	16.24	14.01	19.77
Meghalaya	18.98	15.39	20.76	15.24	12.32	18.03
Mizoram	32.89	25.73	26.98	23.03	16.00	23.30
Nagaland	18.23	12.72	20.19	16.19	13.79	18.37
Sikkim	22.02	23.08	16.79	19.10	16.42	19.09
Tripura	20.72	20.10	19.09	18.41	17.63	17.73
Uttarakhand			22.79			19.65
All Special Category States	20.63	15.21	19.77	17.54	14.09	17.82
All States	14.56	14.29	16.73	14.33	13.75	16.52

Source: Author's estimates from States' Finance Accounts data.

during 1991–2004 to 19.1 percent during 2005–13. There was an increase of at least 3.5 percentage points in growth rates in the other low-income States of Odisha, Madhya Pradesh, Rajasthan, and Uttar Pradesh. In contrast, the acceleration was not very high in the case of the more affluent States of Kerala (from 15.2 percent to 15.5 percent), Haryana (13.6 percent to 14.7 percent), and Punjab (12 percent to 14.3 percent). During 2005–13, despite the acceleration, the growth of tax revenues in the States of Haryana

(14.7 percent), Punjab (14.3 percent), and West Bengal (14.6 percent) were only marginally higher than the growth of GSDP in these States. While tax revenues in the three States during 2005–13 grew at 14.7 percent, 14.3 percent, and 14.6 percent, respectively, their growth rates in GSDP were 16.9 percent, 13.3 percent, and 13.4 percent, respectively, indicating a buoyancy of less than 1 in the case of Haryana and marginally more than 1 in the case of the other two States.

Although the periods above for analyzing revenue growth were chosen with a view to examining the structural break due to the introduction of VAT in 2005–06, it would be misleading to attribute the acceleration entirely to policy reform since during the second period, the economy was also buoyant and commodity prices were high. The economy registered a 14.9 percent nominal growth rate as compared to 12.6 percent during the previous period. With revenue from petroleum products constituting 30–35 percent of the ad valorem sales tax revenue in the States, an important reason for the acceleration in the growth of tax revenues during the second period was the sharp increase in the price of petroleum products after 2008–09.

To examine whether the introduction of VAT by itself led to an acceleration in revenues, sales tax revenues in each of the States for the period 1991–92 to 2013–14 were regressed on the per capita GSDP, the proportion of GSDP from the non-agricultural sector, the wholesale price index of petroleum products, and the VAT dummy after 2005–06 in a log-linear model.[8] The regression estimates are summarized in Table 5. The analysis shows that in all the States, per capita GSDP was a significant determinant of sales tax revenues. In 10 out of the 25 States, the proportion of non-agricultural income was significant with the correct sign. Similarly, in 10 States, the wholesale price index of petroleum products was significant. The VAT dummy was significant only in Gujarat and Manipur. Thus, while the introduction of VAT could have substantially rationalized the tax system, it would be unrealistic to claim that it led to a significant increase in revenues. The major reasons for the increase in revenues must be attributed to acceleration in the growth rate of GSDP and sharp increase in the prices of petroleum products, particularly after 2008–09.

8. Thanks are due to Ms Suranjali Tandon of NIPFP for estimating these equations.

TABLE 5. Impact of VAT Reform in Indian States

State	*Log GSDP per capita*	*Petrol Price Index*	*Non-Agricultural GDP share*	*VAT dummy*	*Constant*	*Adjusted R-Square*
Andhra Pradesh	1.082***	-2.9E-05	0.0105**	-0.067**	-2.42***	0.9921
Arunachal Pradesh	3.611*	-0.0026	0.054*	0.512	-17.201**	0.7998
Assam	0.75**	0.0012	0.0219***	-0.0208	-2.032**	0.9860
Bihar	1.07**	0.0012	-0.018**	-0.098	-0.715	0.8557
Goa	0.91***	-0.0005	-0.01	0.0469	0.109	0.9851
Gujarat	0.485***	0.003***	0.0014	0.049*	0.547	0.9927
Haryana	0.605***	0.0079	0.0187***	0.0025	-0.957**	0.9925
Himachal Pradesh	1.214***	0.0005	0.0003	0.05	-2.667***	0.9948
J&K	1.89***	-0.0021	0.01	-0.034	-5.91***	0.9772
Karnataka	0.807***	0.001***	-0.0005	0.007	-0.544*	0.9963
Kerala	0.951***	0.0013*	-0.00007	-0.089***	-1.093***	0.9927
Madhya Pradesh	0.705***	0.0024***	0.0036	-0.0039	-0.696	0.9909
Maharashtra	0.898***	0.001	0.003	-0.059*	-1.28**	0.9896
Manipur	1.216***	0.0026	-0.017	0.138*	-1.92*	0.9638
Meghalaya	1.17***	0.0015	-0.004	0.0038	-2.55***	0.9903
Mizoram	2.26***	-0.003	0.038**	0.153	-10.37***	0.9654
Nagaland	1.067***	0.002**	-0.0019	0.052	-2.4***	0.9928
Odisha	0.73***	0.0017**	0.008**	-0.019	-1.088**	0.9904
Punjab	1.106***	0.0001	0.008	-0.063	-2.43**	0.9696
Rajasthan	0.82***	0.002***	0.0095***	-0.0039	-1.56***	0.9975
Sikkim	-0.0116	0.0042	0.036***	-0.0019	-0.433	0.9088
Tamil Nadu	0.6***	0.0022***	0.0097***	-0.011	-0.495*	0.9967
Tripura	1.015***	0.0018**	0.016**	-0.02	-3.17***	0.9942
Uttar Pradesh	1.4***	0.00005	-0.002	-0.047	-2.98***	0.99
West Bengal	0.636***	0.0023***	-0.0027	0.027	-0.009	0.9864

Sources: 1. Finance Accounts of the States, Comptroller and Auditor General, Government of India (for data on VAT revenues); 2. Ministry of Petroleum and Natural Gas, Government of India. (Price index of petroleum products); 3. Central Statistical Organization, Ministry of Statistics and Programme Implementation, Government of India (for data on non-agricultural GSDFP share).

Note: Estimated Equation: log(*sales tax per capita*) = $\alpha + \beta_1$ log(*GSDP per capita*) + β_2 *Petrol price index* + β_3 *Share of non-agricultutral GDP* + β_4 *VAT dummy*

*Significant at 10 percent; **significant at 5 percent; *** significant at 1 percent.

4. Successful Reform Initiatives in India's Tax System

The analysis of Indian tax policy suggests remarkable successes as well as important failures. Understanding successes is important in order to replicate them wherever possible, and the analysis of failures provides lessons for the future to devise strategies to avoid them.

The most important success story in Indian tax policy is the simplification of the personal income tax in terms of reducing the number of brackets and marginal tax rates. The number of brackets was reduced from 12 in the early 1970s to 3 in 1997 and the marginal tax rate was reduced from 97.75 percent to 30 percent during the same period. There is considerable anecdotal evidence to show that the reduction in marginal rates led to a significant improvement in tax compliance. The impact on revenues could have been even higher had the reduction in the marginal rate of tax been accompanied by administrative reforms.

The second important success story of the Indian tax system is the application of technology to improve revenue productivity. The introduction of the TIN in 2003–04 led to an increase in income tax revenues relative to GDP by almost 2.7 percentage points in just four years from 3.3 percent in 2002–03 to 6 percent in 2007–08, registering a growth rate of close to 30 percent per year during the period. The use of technology was simply to ensure that those who were required to deduct tax at source paid tax and filed the returns. The TIN has also generated a vast amount of data on the sources of income of individuals and could be usefully mined to get much more information to improve compliance. It is also hoped that when GST is introduced, the seeding of PAN numbers in GST numbers can lead to enormous information on small businesses and self-employed traders and service providers, and this could substantially improve tax compliance.

The third most successful tax reform in the Indian context is the introduction of the value-added tax at the State level in 2005. This was truly a major reform involving all the States and Union Territories in which cascading sales taxes with 14–16 rates were replaced with a value-added tax with broadly two rates (excluding a low rate on bullion and specie and precious metals, and a high rate on motor spirit and high-speed diesel). Besides, being revenue-neutral, this reform seems to have substantially improved the competitiveness of Indian manufacturing and has led the way for a further reform of implementing the GST.

The fourth important reform initiative that has helped to broaden the base and balance tax burden is the introduction of service tax. The tax, first introduced in 2004 on three services, was progressively expanded into other services and finally, in 2012, coverage was extended to all services excluding those specified in the negative list. There is still scope for pruning the negative list and doing away with exemptions, but expansion in the coverage of the tax is no mean achievement. In fact, in the Indian context, this has helped to offset the revenue loss from customs duty undertaken to open up the economy and to ensure a measure of balance in the tax burden between commodities and services.

Another important initiative that has helped to improve the ease of doing businesses is the creation of large taxpayers units (LTUs). Beginning with

Bangalore in 2009, the LTUs have been set up in Chennai and Mumbai. Taxpayers with a turnover of more than ₹5 crores in service tax or excise duty, or those paying an advance tax of more than ₹10 crore, are eligible to be served by the LTUs. They function as a one-stop shop for all central taxes and, hence, enable a coordinated approach to taxpayer services. However, joining an LTU is optional for eligible taxpayers. Reducing eligibility thresholds, making participation mandatory, providing fast services, and facilitating payments could go a long way in improving taxpayer services.

5. What Ails the Indian Tax System?

In contrast to the few successful initiatives, the failures of the Indian tax system are many and there is much to be done to evolve a broad-based, simple, productive and less distorting tax system. As discussed in Section 2, the tax system is supposed to raise required revenues by minimizing collection, compliance, and distortion costs, that is, have high revenue productivity, low cost of paying tax, and few adverse impacts on resource allocation.

The low revenue productivity of the Indian tax system has been a matter of concern, and despite several rounds of reform, the tax–GDP ratio has remained stubbornly low. The highest tax–GDP ratio of 17.5 percent was reached in 2007–08, and after declining to 15.5 percent due to reductions in the rates of excise and service taxation, revenues recovered only marginally and hovered around 16.5 percent of GDP, mainly due to a marginal increase in the tax–GDP ratio of the States. The ratio of Union tax revenue to GDP in 2014–15 is estimated to be less than 10 percent, a clear two percentage points lower than in 2007–08.

5.1. Constitutional Assignment and Narrow Base

The most important reason for the low productivity of the Indian tax system is its narrow tax base. The base is narrow for a number of reasons: the fragmented Constitutional assignment of revenues, wide-ranging exemptions, concessions and deductions, complications and ambiguities in tax laws due to a multiplicity of objectives assigned to tax policy, large and increasing tax arrears held in disputes, base erosion and profit shifting (BEPS) by multinationals, organizational shortcomings and the poor capacity of tax administrations, and less than full use of information systems to administer and enforce tax compliance.

The difficulty of levying a comprehensive income tax in India lies in part in the Constitutional assignment itself. The assignment of income tax on agriculture to the States means that the Union Government can levy tax only on non-agricultural incomes. The States do not levy agricultural income tax except on income from plantation crops. Even corporates earning income from agriculture do not pay tax. A recent study by Rao and Sengupta (2012) for 2008–09 estimates the potential loss from not taxing agriculture at 0.6 percent of GDP. Exempting agricultural income provides an easy avenue for the evasion and avoidance of tax.

5.2. Tax Exemptions and Preferences

The second important reason for India's narrow tax base is the plethora of exemptions, concessions, and deductions in direct and indirect taxes, all justified in one way or the other by the multiple objectives of the tax system. Besides raising revenue, the tax system is expected to incentivize savings, promote exports, achieve balanced regional development, promote investments in infrastructure, expand employment, promote scientific research and development, and encourage cooperatives and charitable activities. Similarly, excise duty is used to provide preferential treatment to small-scale industries by keeping the threshold high and to promote backward area development. The resulting exemptions, concessions, and deductions create enormous opportunities for tax evasion and avoidance. No one can be sure how far these objectives are being achieved, if at all. What is worse, having given these concessions, when companies take advantage of them to reduce tax liability, the government comes up with a minimum alternative tax.

Since 2006, the Government of India has been publishing estimates of revenue foregone from tax concessions in its annual budget. For 2014–15, the government estimates revenue foregone at a staggering ₹5,89,285 crore, ₹3,01,688 crore from customs, and ₹1,84,764 crore from excise. These may appear to be over-estimates to some due to the methodology employed. The difference between rates specified in the tariff schedule and the actual rate applied on imports is taken as the basis for revenue foregone in the case of customs duty. However, when an "essential" commodity is imported due to domestic shortages, the government applies lower tariff rates in the public interest. There is the basic question of the right level of customs duty used for such calculations because the duty is simply protection given to domestic producers: all import duties are taxes imposed on citizens to provide subsidies to domestic producers. Similarly, customs revenue lost due to exemptions given to imports used in re-exports could be left out since the exemptions are provided to help the competitiveness of domestic exporters. The same logic might hold when excise rates are lowered for commodities to control prices during periods of shortages of essential goods. These arguments have led to the concept of tax expenditures.

Whatever be the logic, the tax-expenditure estimates bring out glaring shortcomings in the tax system that constrain revenue productivity. The revenue lost on account of concessions for special economic zones (SEZs) for 2014–15 is estimated at ₹20,376 crore from corporate tax alone. The rationale for tax concessions for companies in SEZs is that they need to be compensated for the overall infrastructure deficit to help their competitiveness. But exporters located in non-SEZ areas do not get the benefit and yet face perhaps even worse disadvantages due to poor infrastructure and governance. Not surprisingly, companies prefer to locate in these enclaves. The Union Commerce Ministry showcases this as additional investment and argues for the continuation of tax benefits. The revenue cost of area-based incentives for 2014–15 is estimated at ₹17,284 crore from excise duty and almost ₹8,000 crore in the case of corporate tax. The revenue foregone on account of tax concessions to infrastructure industries works out to ₹22,230 crore. There are also customs duty reductions in the case of items like fertilizers. A closer scrutiny and weeding out of these tax preferences could easily result in enhancing the ratio of tax to GDP by at least 1 percent, helping to contain the revenue and fiscal deficits and augment much-needed education, health, and capital expenditures.

5.3. Lopsided Revenue Concentration

Revenue from Union excise duties has declined steadily from 4.2 percent of GDP in 1990–91 to 1.5 percent in 2014–15 (Revised Estimate, RE). Even during 2001–02 to 2007–08, when the economy was in its high growth phase, excise revenue grew at an average rate of 9.4 percent, actually lower than the average growth rate of about 10 percent in the following years. The low growth of excise duty has been a major constraint in improving the revenue–GDP ratio. The detailed commodity composition of excise revenue shows that a large part of the tax is derived from petroleum products and basic metals. In 1990–91, tax revenue from petroleum products constituted about 13.9 percent of the total, increasing steadily to 41 percent in 2003–04 and then declining to 26 percent in 2009 10 (Table 6) due to a shift to specific tax rates following high international oil prices after 2008–09. Similarly, revenue from basic metals, which was just about 9.6 percent in 1991–92 rose to 19 percent in 2009–10. In contrast, the shares of revenue from textiles,

TABLE 6. Commodity-wise Collection of Union Excise Duties (Percent in Total)

	1990–91	*2000–01*	*2003–04*	*2009–10*
Food Products	4.0	4.5	3.2	1.7
Tobacco Products	8.3	6.7	5.6	5.0
Minerals and Ores	8.4	6.2	6.2	4.2
Petroleum Products	13.9	32.9	41.0	26.1
Chemicals	11.1	10.2	9.3	8.3
Plastics and articles thereof	2.5	2.3	2.4	4.1
Rubber Products	4.9	2.2	1.3	1.3
Leather and Wood Products	0.6	0.2	0.1	0.9
Textiles and Garments	10.8	4.8	3.7	2.9
Basic Metals	9.6	10.4	11.2	19.0
Electrical and Electronic Goods	16.1	8.8	7.8	11.2
Transport Vehicles	8.4	8.9	6.6	12.3
Miscellaneous	1.3	1.8	1.7	3.1
Total	100.0	100.0	100.0	100.0

Source: CBEC, Ministry of Finance, Government of India.

minerals, chemicals and electrical goods all showed declines, reflecting the changing pattern of industrialization and its impact on revenue productivity. To improve the revenue productivity, it is vitally important to broaden the excise duty base by introducing a properly designed GST.

5.4. Low Productivity of the Property Tax

One of the major shortcomings of the Indian tax system is the low productivity of real property taxes. In most multilevel fiscal systems, property tax plays an important role in financing local services. It is also a preferred means of financing local services because it is relatively immobile and, therefore, less distorting, transparent, and simple and easy to administer at the local level. This is an important instrument to link revenue–expenditure decisions at the local level because it is largely a benefit tax and, for that reason, should evoke greater compliance. It is also argued that fiscal differentials at the local level get capitalized into property values (Oates 1969).

Despite its transparency, localized nature, direct link to the beneficiaries of local public services, and progressivity, the tax on immovable properties has not been successful in India. In contrast to the OECD countries which, on average raise about 2 percent of GDP from property taxes, and developing and transitional countries where the average is about 0.6 to 0.7 percent, property taxes in India are negligible. The available estimate based on sample surveys of municipalities for the Thirteenth Finance

Commission for 2006–07 showed that revenue from property tax ranged from a mere 0.16 percent to 0.24 percent of GDP and has remained stagnant over the years.

The most important reason for this disappointing performance is poor coverage and collection efficiency. Poor coverage is due to (a) wide-ranging exemptions; (b) poor information systems and the absence of up-to-date registries of land and properties with municipal bodies; and (c) vacant properties. Exemptions vary from state to state, and from one municipal body to another, but there are some common exemptions. Article 285 of the Constitution provides exemption to all properties belonging to the Union Government. Many metros have large unauthorized buildings, and properties that are not included in the municipal register and as a result do not pay any property tax. Other important exemptions include places of religious worship, educational institutions, charitable institutions, ancient and historical monuments, burial and cremation grounds, government land and buildings set apart for free recreational purposes, offices of trade union associations, buildings and lands of urban development authorities constituted under respective State government acts, institutions providing free medical relief and education, properties owned by ex-servicemen and their families, and certain types of vacant lands and buildings.

Poor information on properties with urban local bodies, lack of clarity on property ownership or tenancy rights and the absence of a cadaster that uniquely identifies properties and their owners, and the inability to adopt market-based valuation all constrain property taxes. Most municipal bodies have not yet sought to update their records relating to property ownership and tenancies, and nor do they coordinate with their own registration departments to obtain information on properties transferred and their values. The Administrative Reforms Commission has noted that only about 60–70 percent of properties in urban areas are actually assessed. The Commission recommended using satellite imagery and geographical information systems to identify properties that are not paying tax.

The problem of low coverage is compounded by poor collection. The assessed values of properties are significantly lower than their market values and do not capture either the increase in value due to improvements or general market conditions. Often assessed values are as low as 8–10 percent of market values; they were found to be on average about 30 percent of market value in the 36 largest municipal corporations in India (Rao 2012). Given these huge gaps, attempts to increase these values are likely to meet with severe opposition.

5.5. Tax Avoidance by Multinational Corporations

The fifth important area needing reform has to do with multinational companies avoiding taxes in a variety of ways— base erosion and profit shifting (BEPS) by such companies is a worldwide phenomenon. Shifting profits to subsidiaries created in low-tax jurisdictions, taking advantage of tax treaties, and manipulating prices in related party transactions through transfer pricing have been commonly used to avoid taxes. Although there are "arm's length pricing rules" to deal with transfer pricing, it is difficult to apply these in practice when intangible assets such as trade names, goodwill, brand recognition and intellectual properties such as patents, copyrights, brands and trademarks, and business methodologies are involved. Multinational companies also act as intermediaries in product sales and distribution, make loans and interest payments to one another, and charge fees from one another for activities such as management services, treasury services, and investment services to reduce tax liability.

Evidence of this, even in developed countries like the United States, United Kingdom, and the European Union, has led the OECD and, in more recent times, the G-20 countries, to seek reforms in the international corporate tax system, which has led to the BEPS Action Plan initiated by OECD in September 2013. The BEPS Plan was approved as a G-20 project and organized through the OECD for delivery by December 2015. In the meantime, the International Commission for the Reform of International Corporate Taxation has made a number of recommendations to deal with this pernicious practice (ICRICT 2015).

In the Indian context, there is considerable anecdotal evidence to show that multinational companies have been indulging in tax avoidance practices. Patnaik and Shah (2011) in their study showed that the effective corporate tax rate on multinational companies was significantly lower than on domestic companies. Rao and Sengupta (2014) in their more detailed study using the Prowess database show that during the period 2006–11, the effective interest rate paid by multinational companies was higher and the amount of tax paid per unit of borrowing was lower. The paper also shows that from 2008 to 2011, while royalty payments by top 25 multinationals doubled, dividend payments increased by just 30 percent. The paper cites specific instances of multinational companies indulging in willful tax avoidance.

The problem is compounded by the fact that while multinational companies have access to resources that they use in hiring the best accountants and lawyers, tax administrations in most developing countries are hamstrung by low resources as well as administrative capacity. It is not surprising that the Ministry of Finance, after putting out the General Anti-avoidance Rules (GAAR), has continuously postponed implementing them.

There is a view that the issue really is more about the poor capacity and incompetence of policy makers and legal drafters than the behavior of multinational companies. While it is legitimate for countries to demand a fair share of taxes, they need to draft their laws better, have more competent staff, and apply laws more evenly. Information exchange among countries may help, but the countries need to have the capability and intentions to use the information better to enforce laws. Given the pressure to meet tax revenue targets, tax departments in India have taken aggressive postures to recover tax from multinational companies, but this has only earned them bad publicity with overseas investors. In India, cases like Vodafone clearly belong to a grey area as transactions were made through subsidiaries located in tax havens, resulting in the Supreme Court in January 2012 overturning the decision of the Bombay High Court and striking down the capital gains tax claims of the Central Board of Direct Taxes (CBDT) from Vodafone.[9] All this, however, does not justify the arbitrary actions of the government in resorting to retrospective changes in tax law purely for revenue reasons.

5.6. Low Capacity of Tax Administrations

Tax administration is a critical element of any tax system. de Jantscher (1990, p. 179) declares that in developing countries "tax administration is tax policy." According to Richard Bird (2004), "The best tax policy is worth little if it cannot be implemented effectively." However, the issue of tax administration is not just about its effective implementation. It has to do with the ability to enforce tax compliance through the complex dealings of taxpayers, the attitude of tax administrations towards taxpayers, the taxpayers' confidence and trust in the tax administration, and clarity in laws to avoid discretion in the hands of tax administrators.

By all accounts, the Indian tax administration does not evoke the confidence and trust that a modern tax administration requires for greater voluntary tax compliance. There have been a number of reports on the reform of tax administration beginning with the report of the Tax Reforms Commission (1991). The careful studies by Das-Gupta and Mookherjee (1998), Bagchi et al. (1995), and more recently, the reports of the Tax Administration Reforms Commission (Government of India

9. Vodafone International Holding B.V. versus the Union of India & ANR; case No: I.A. No. 19 in Civil Appeal No. 733 of 2012.

2014; 2015) have dealt in detail with various aspects of the reform of tax administration. Implementing these reforms requires political will.

Tax administration in India suffers as a result of (a) lack of autonomy; (b) low morale of tax administrators due to their organizational structure, low prospects of career progression, and their subservience to general administrators; (c) the separation, independent functioning, and lack of coordination between direct and indirect tax administration split into the CBDT and the Central Board of Excise and Customs (CBEC); (d) area-based offices rather than functional divisions and poor functional specialization, including on tax intelligence; (e) poor information systems and delayed use of technology for tax administration; (f) perverse incentives for tax administrators by judging performance based on their fulfilment of tax collection targets; (g) poor capacity to forecast revenues and its adverse impact on expenditure management at both Union and State levels; (h) lack of clarity in tax laws, wide discretion to tax officials, and a huge build-up of tax arrears; and (i) tax administrators who see taxpayers as tax evaders and adversaries.

One way in which unclear tax laws and poor administration have manifested themselves is in the buildup of huge tax arrears. At the end of 2013–14, the amount of tax arrears from various taxes amounted to over ₹5.83 lakh crore or 5.1 percent of GDP. Almost 86 percent of this amount is held up in disputes; about 47 percent in disputes of up to 2 years old; and about 76 percent in disputes of up to 5 years old (Table 7).

Another way to see the impact of poor tax administration is the number of non-corporate assessees, which in 2012–13 numbered just about 3.7 million, less than 3.4 percent of the population. Over 75 percent of them had taxable incomes of less than ₹2 lakh.[10] Assessees with an income of more than

TABLE 7. Tax Arrears in 2013–14

	Held in Disputes Rs crore	*Not under Dispute Rs crore*	*Total Rs crore*	*Percent of Total*
Corporate Tax	150,802	41,211	192,013	32.92
Non-corporate Income Tax	259,721	23,985	283,706	48.63
Taxes on Income and Expenditure	410,523	65,196	475,719	81.55
Customs	9,758	4,686	14,444	2.48
Union Excise Duties	41,817	7,978	49,795	8.54
Service Tax	41,245	2,143	43,388	7.44
Total Taxes on Commodities and	97,821	14,807	112,628	19.31
Total	503,344	80,003	583,347	100.00

Source: Report of the Comptroller and Auditor General—Revenue 2013–14.

10. Report No. 10 of 2014 (Direct Taxes), Comptroller and Auditor General, Government of India.

₹10 lakh numbered just about 660 thousand, and those with a reported income of more than ₹1 crore numbered just about 42,800, implying incredibly poor coverage of the income tax in India.

While the problems with both the organizational setup and the functioning of the tax administration are well known, there have been few attempts to address them. An important innovation has been the creation of LTUs, which have helped coordinate the functioning of the CBDT and CBEC and reduce compliance costs for large taxpayers. Another important reform has been the requirement for electronic filing of returns and payment of refunds directly to taxpayer accounts. These are important but small initiatives, and by and large tax administrations have not yet gained the trust and confidence of taxpayers enough to improve voluntary tax compliance, a goal all tax administrations must strive for.

6. The Way Forward: The Need for Urgent Reforms

This analysis of the Indian tax system underlines the need for urgent reform of both direct and indirect taxes at the Union and State levels. An increase in revenue productivity in the least distortionary manner requires expansion in the tax base, rationalization of rates to reasonable levels, simplifying the tax system, and reforming tax administration. Some of these reforms can be taken up immediately, whereas others are medium and long term. While some are not difficult, others are very difficult, and some are formidable in their challenge.

The government will have to evolve a clear strategy of carrying out those reforms in a phased manner, building on the easier ones and progressing to the more difficult ones. The quote from Johnson and Myles (2011) that started this paper goes on to say that "There is always a tension between what is economically desirable and what is politically practical." The major precondition for successful tax reforms is the political appetite for such reforms.

The most formidable task in implementing a comprehensive income tax in India is dealing with the fractured assignment system. While it may not be easy to integrate income from agricultural and non-agricultural sources, the practical solution may be to enter into an agreement with the States and levy income tax according to applicable rates on income declared as agricultural income after allowing deductions for crop insurance premiums, and distributing the proceeds to the States from where the income originates. This will not be easy to do and would still face political opposition, but should nevertheless be in the medium-term reform agenda.

The first discussion paper on the DTC was a well thought-out document, and many of the suggestions contained in it, particularly those relating to grandfathering exemptions and concessions, merit consideration to broaden the base, increase revenue productivity and reduce unintended distortions in resource allocation. It is also important to work on a time-bound plan to effectively apply the general tax anti-avoidance rules on multinational companies and to develop the capacity to administer them. Indeed, there is a need to overhaul the administrative framework to enable functional specialization and coordination among various tax departments including sharing of information. The transition is not likely to be easy and in the short term it would be advisable to create specialized agencies, like the one for administering GAAR, and finally create proper administrative divisions into various functionally specialized groups from the prevailing region-based divisions. Although the Union Finance Minister in his Budget speech stated that the DTC will not be on the reform agenda, there is need to simplify the Income Tax Act of 1961, broaden the base, and reduce compliance costs.

The biggest item in the current reform agenda is of course the introduction of GST at the Union and State levels. The government has shown keenness to implement the reform and has brought in the 122nd Constitution Amendment Bill to hasten the process. The Finance Minister has, on a number of occasions, characterized this reform as a "game changer" and the "reform of the century", and taken several initiatives to persuade State governments to embrace it. The empowered Committee of State Finance Ministers is in broad agreement that the reform is desirable, and has been seeking to arrive at a consensus on a number of issues necessary for its implementation.

The original proposal for the introduction of GST was made in 2008, with implementation planned by April 2010. This has been postponed more than once since then. The Finance Minister in his Budget Speech of 2015–16 had set the date as April 2016, now of course missed. A realistic assessment also shows that the structure and operational details of GST emerging from the compromise agreement reached in the GST Council will be far from being flawless. There is no doubt that the GST replacing a plethora of Union and State indirect taxes is an important reform. This is expected to improve the ease of doing business, enhance efficiency in the supply chain by obviating the need to have branch offices (created to avoid the inter-states sales tax), reduce transaction costs by ensuring seamless trade in commodities and services across the country, and improve export competitiveness by providing comprehensive relief from domestic taxes. The extent to which these objectives can be accomplished will depend upon the ultimate structure and operational details that will emerge. Given the nature of the Indian polity and the fact that the interests of the Union and States, on the one hand, and those of the producing and consuming States, on the other, do not coincide, the consensus solution should be seen only as the next stage of consumption tax reform.

A closer examination of the 122nd Constitution Amendment Bill shows that the GST structure envisaged will not be flawless. First, the Bill provides only a minimalist framework for the levy. The details of the structure and operation of the tax, including exemptions, the rate structure, and thresholds, will be determined through negotiations in the GST Council. Second, keeping petroleum products and natural gas out of the GST chain will not only cause relative price distortions due to cascading, but also create administrative complexities. Both the Union and the State governments want to continue with the high tax rates on petroleum products prevailing at present. Third, the most undesirable compromise is the decision to levy a 1 percent tax on the inter-state supply of goods and services. While the present inter-state sales tax is only on goods, the new levy will be a tax not merely on the sales but also on the supply and not only on goods but on services as well. This will negate a major expected gain from the GST by making the tax partly origin-based, violating the federal principle of providing seamless tax credit, and continuing with the cascading element in the tax by denying input tax credit on this part.

The GST Bill has been stalled in the Rajya Sabha mainly due to differences between the ruling party and the opposition on the structure of the proposed levy, particularly in regard to the levy of 1 percent tax on the inter-state supply of goods, the exclusion of some taxes in the GST, and of the provision for a dispute resolution mechanism. Although the Select Committee of the Rajya Sabha, in its report, diluted the scope of 1 percent tax by confining it to the inter-state sale of goods, the opposition (particularly the Indian National Congress) has demanded dropping of the provision to levy 1 percent tax, fixing the maximum tax rate at 18 percent, and providing for a dispute resolution mechanism. The committee appointed by the Union Government with the Chief Economic Adviser as the Chairman to determine the rate structure of the tax at both the Union and State levels too has recommended that the 1 percent tax on inter-state transactions be dropped from the Bill. It has recommended that with a lower rate of 12 percent and sumptuary items and luxury goods taxed at 40 percent, the general rate of tax should not exceed 18 percent. It, however, suggested that the rate structure should not be a part of the Bill. With political issues taking precedence resulting in the logjam in the Parliament, the Rajya Sabha has not found time to debate and pass the Bill so far. The reform is likely to take time and is not likely to be implemented before 2017. After the Bill is passed, it has to be ratified by one half of the States. Once the amendment comes into effect, the GST Council will have to be formed, which will deliberate and decide on the thresholds, exemption limit, rate structure, special arrangements for the north-eastern States, application of place of supply rule for inter-state sale of services, mechanisms to deal with special arrangements such as works contracts and SEZs, and a dispute resolution mechanism. In addition, tax collectors will have to be trained and technology platforms will have to be put in place, though work is progressing on these already.

In this context, three issues must be noted. First, given the nature of the Indian polity, the GST that will be ultimately adopted will be full of compromises and it would be too ambitious to presume that the GST will be flawless. Second, for the above reason, the implementation of GST should be considered as the next stage of reform. Given the compromises on the structure and operational details, to consider GST as a game changer would be too optimistic. Nevertheless, the reform is important and it should be seen as a process rather than an event. Third, the reform should be preceded by considerable preparation to ensure a smooth transition and that includes the erection of a technology platform, capacity building of the tax administration, and educating taxpayers.

7. Concluding Remarks

The paper has attempted to analyze the Indian tax system from the perspective of the best practice approach to tax policy and reform. Tax policy matters to government, businesses and citizens alike. Governments have to collect taxes to provide public services. People are concerned about parting with their hard-earned money for the services they cannot clearly see and perceive. From the point of view of the economy, tax policy is an important factor in determining the business climate. A simple tax system with a broad base and low rates and differentiation, ease of paying taxes and transparent, non-adversarial administration can help improve the business climate in the country and would be best practice. The revenue productivity of taxes also determines the allocation of resources for providing physical and social infrastructure. Loading tax policy with too many objectives complicates the tax system. The objective of reform should be to reduce administrative, compliance and distortion costs. Thus, a major reform agenda for the government should be to phase out tax preferences to evolve a simple tax system.

The Indian tax system is characterized by low revenue productivity and stagnancy in the tax to GDP ratio. The paper identifies the reasons for low revenue productivity, going back to the Constitutional assignment of income taxes that constrains a comprehensive income tax. Although it is possible to coordinate such a tax between the Union and the States, political difficulties have prevented this. Narrow tax bases of both direct and indirect taxes are also the consequences of wide-ranging exemptions, concessions, and deductions given to pursue a variety of objectives through tax policy. The pursuit of multiple objectives has not only made their attainment difficult but has narrowed the tax base, reduced revenue productivity, and complicated the tax system, resulting in high compliance costs and distortions in resource allocation. The lack of clarity in tax laws and a huge buildup of tax arrears, an overwhelming proportion of which are stuck in tax disputes, is another problem. The paper highlights the problem of base erosion and profit shifting by multinationals and the organizational and functional problems with tax administration, as also the need to build capacity and professionalism in administering tax, including the building and application of information systems and better use of technology.

The paper underlines the need for reforming both direct and indirect tax systems not only to increase revenue productivity but also to improve the business climate in the country. The replacement of a plethora of indirect taxes with the GST is an important reform. However, its structure and operational difficulties will be decided on the basis of the compromise between the Union and the States, on the one hand, and among the States, on the other, with the resulting structure being far from flawless. It is, therefore, important to manage expectations of the GST. It is also important to realize that the Constitution Amendment Bill has some serious shortcomings that should be corrected before it is passed in the Parliament. As far as the reform of direct taxes is concerned, though the Finance Minister has indicated that the implementation of DTC will not be on the agenda, various reforms to simplify the law, phase out tax preferences to broaden the base, and the preparatory measures needed to implement the GAAR should be taken up. Reforms relating to tax administration to professionalize it and make it taxpayer-friendly also need to be pursued with vigor to improve administrative efficiency and voluntary tax compliance.

References

Auerbach, Alan J. 2008. "The Choice Between Income and Consumption Taxes: A Primer," in Alan J. Auerbach and A.D. Shaviro, eds, *Institutional Foundations of Public Finance: Economic and Legal Perspectives* (pp. 13–46). Cambridge. MA: Harvard University Press.

———. 2009. *The Adoption of Tax Reforms*: Raja Chelliah Memorial Lecture. New Delhi: National Institute of Public Finance and Policy.

Auerbach, Alan, M. Devereux, and H. Simpson. 2010. "Taxing Corporate Income," in J. Mirrlees, S. Adam, T. Besley, R. Blundell, S. Bond, R. Chote, M. Gammie, P. Johnson, G. Myles, and J. Porteba, eds, *Dimensions of Tax Design: The Mirrlees Review* (pp. 837–93). Oxford: Oxford University Press for Institute of Fiscal Studies.

Bagchi, Amaresh, Richard Bird, and Arindam Das-Gupta. 1995. "An Economic Approach to Tax Administration Reform," Discussion Paper No. 3. International Centre for Tax Studies, University of Toronto Faculty of Management.

Bird, Richard M. 2004. "Administrative Dimensions of Tax Reform," *Asia–Pacific Tax Bulletin*, 10 (3): 134–50.

Bird, Richard B. 2008. *Tax Challenges Facing Developing Countries*. New Delhi: National Institute of Public Finance and Policy.

Bird, Richard M. and Pierre-Pascal Gendron. 2007. *The VAT in Developing and Transitional Countries*. Cambridge: Cambridge University Press.

Bird, Richard M. and Eric Zolt. 2005. "Redistribution via Taxation: The Limited Role of the Personal Income Tax in Developing Countries," *UCLA Law Review*, 52 (6): 1627–95.

———. 2008. "Tax Policy in Emerging Countries," *Environment and Planning C: Government and Policy*, 26 (1): 73–88.

Das-Gupta, Arindam. 2002. "Central Tax and Administration Reform in the 1990s: An Assessment," in M. Govinda Rao, ed., *Development, Poverty and Fiscal Policy: Decentralization of Institutions* (pp. 139–73). New Delhi: Oxford University Press.

Das-Gupta, Arindam and Dilip Mookherjee. 1998. *Incentives and Institutional Reform in Tax Enforcement*. New Delhi: Oxford University Press.

de Jantscher, Milka Casanegra. 1990. "Administering a VAT," in M. Gills, C.S. Shoup, and G.P. Sikat, eds, *Value Added Taxation in Developing Countries* (pp. 179–90). New York: World Bank.

Emran, M.S. and Joseph Stiglitz. 2005. "On Selective Indirect Reform in Developing Countries," *Journal of Public Economics*, 89 (4): 599–623.

Engel, Eduardo M.R.A., Alexander Galetovic, and Claudio E. Raddatz. 1999. "Taxes and Income Distribution in Chile: Some Unpleasant Redistributive Arithmetic," *Journal of Development Studies*, 59 (3): 155–92.

Feldstein, Martin. 1995. "The Effect of Marginal Tax Rates on Taxable Income: A Panel Study of 1986 Tax Reform Act," *Journal of Political Economy*, 103 (3): 551–72.

Gordon, Roger. 2011. "Commentary on Tax Design: The Mirrlees Review," *Fiscal Studies*, 32 (3): 395–414.

Government of India. 1976. *Report of the Indirect Taxes Enquiry Committee* (Chairman: L.K. Jha). New Delhi: Ministry of Finance, Government of India.

———. 1991 and 1993. *Report of the Tax Reforms Committee* (Chairman: Raja Chelliah). New Delhi: Ministry of Finance, Government of India.

———. 2001a. *Report of the Expert Group on Taxation of Services* (Chairman: M. Govinda. Rao). New Delhi: Ministry of Finance, Government of India.

———. 2001b. *Report of the Advisory Group on Tax Policy and Tax Administration for the Tenth Plan*. New Delhi: Planning Commission, Government of India.

———. 2003a. *Report of the Task Force on Direct Taxes* (Chairman: Vijay Kelkar). New Delhi: Ministry of Finance, Government of India.

———. 2003b. *Report of the Task Force on Indirect Taxes* (Chairman: Vijay Kelkar). New Delhi: Ministry of Finance, Government of India.

———. 2011. *Report of the Expert Group on Taxation of Services* (Chairman: M. Govinda Rao). New Delhi: Ministry of Finance, Government of India.

———. 2014 and 2015. *Report of the Tax Administration Reforms Commission* (Chairman: Parthasarathi Shome). New Delhi: Ministry of Finance, Government of India.

Hahn, Frank. 1973. "On Optimum Taxation," *Journal of Economic Theory*, 6 (1): 96–106.

Harberger, Arnold C. 1990. "Principles of Taxation Applied to Developing Countries: What Have We Learned?" in Michael Boskin and Charles E. McLure, Jr., eds, *World Tax Reform: Case Studies of Developed and Developing Countries* (pp. 25–46). San Francisco: ICS Press.

ICRICT. 2015. *Declaration of the Independent Commission for the Reform of International Corporate Taxation*. New York: Independent Commission for the Reform of International Corporation.

IMF. 2011. *Revenue Mobilization in Developing Countries*. Washington, DC: International Monetary Fund.

Johnson, Paul and Gareth Myles. 2011. "The Mirrlees Review," *Fiscal Studies*, 32 (3): 319–29.

Keen, Michael. 2007. "VAT Attacks! Second Best Perspectives in the Value Added Tax," IMF Working Paper No. WP/07/142. Washington, DC: International Monetary Fund.

Keen, Michael and Ligthart. 2005. "Coordinating Tariff Reduction and Domestic Tax Reform under Imperfect Competition," *Journal of International Economics*, 56 (2): 407–25.

Keynes, John Maynard. 1936. *The General Theory of Employment, Interest and Money*. London: Palgrave Macmillan.

Mirrlees, James. 1971. "An Exploration in the Theory of Optimal Income Taxation," *Review of Economic Studies*, 38 (4): 175–208.

Oates, Wallace E. 1969. "The Effect of Property Taxes on Local Public Spending on Property Values: An Empirical Study of Tax Capitalization and the Tiebout Hypothesis," *Journal of Political Economy*, 77 (4): 957–71.

Patnaik, Ila and Ajay Shah. 2011. *Do Multinationals Pay Lower Taxes?* (Mimeo). New Delhi: National Institute of Public Finance and Policy.

Pechman, Joseph A. 1985. *Who Paid the Taxes, 1966–85?* Washington, DC: The Brookings Institution.

Ramsey, F.P., 1927. "A Contribution to the Theory of Taxation," *Economic Journal*, 37 (1): 47–61.

Rao, Govinda M. 2012. "Property Tax System in India: Problems and Prospects of Reform," *NIPFP Working Paper* No. 114. New Delhi: National Institute of Public Finance and Policy.

———. 2013. "Goods and Services Tax: Challenges of Evolving an Acceptable Structure," in Sameer Kochhar, ed., *An Agenda for India's Growth: Essays in Honour of P. Chidambaram* (pp. 139–53). New Delhi: Academic Foundation.

Rao, Govinda M. and R. Kavita Rao. 2005–06. "Trends and Issues in Tax Policy and Reform in India", *India Policy Forum*, 2: 55–122.

——— 2010. "Tax System Reform in India", in Roger Gordon, ed., *Taxation in Developing Countries* (pp. 109–52). Columbia: Columbia University Press.

Rao, Govinda M. and Tapas K. Sen. 2013. "Federalism and Reform in India," in Stephen Howes and M. Govinda Rao, eds, *Federal Reform Strategies: Lessons from Asia and Australia* (pp. 130–63). New Delhi: Oxford University Press.

Rao, Kavita R. and D.P. Sengupta. 2014. "Action Plan on Base Erosion and Profit Shifting: An Indian Perspective," NIPFP Working Paper No. 2014–133. New Delhi: National Institute of Public Finance and Policy.

———. April 14, 2012. "Direct Taxes Code and Taxation of Agricultural Income," *Economic and Political Weekly*, 47 (15): 51–60.

Stiglitz, Joseph. 2010. "Development Oriented Tax Policy," in Roger H. Gordon, ed., *Taxation in Developing Countries* (pp. 11–36). New York: Columbia University Press.

Slemrod, Joel and Christian Gillitzer. 2014. *Tax Systems*. Cambridge, MA: The MIT Press.

Tanzi, Vito and Howell Zee. 2000. "Tax Policy for Emerging Market and Developing Countries," IMF Staff Working Paper No. 35. Washington, DC: International Monetary Fund.

Comments and Discussion*

Ashok Lahiri
Bandhan Bank

Rao's paper covers a wide canvas on what ails the Indian tax system, the theoretical dimensions of good tax policy, the practical problems of implementing good policies, and the experience of India so far. I will focus only on two issues: the question of the progressivity of personal income tax rates and the assignment issue. On the first, we have done much, and on the second, it is a lot tougher than the paper suggests.

First, Rao emphasizes that direct tax policy, in general, and highly progressive income tax rates, in particular, are blunt instruments, if not counterproductive ones, for achieving redistributive goals. He points out how high marginal tax rates can lead to high economic distortions relative to the revenue raised. Such distortions can be significant when labor supply is relatively inelastic, dampening wage rates and, thereby, defeating the very purpose of reducing inequality.

As some of us will remember, in the 1970–71 Budget speech, Prime Minister Indira Gandhi, also holding charge as the Finance Minister, said "... for the individual who derives his entire income from wealth, the combined effect of income and wealth taxation as now proposed will impose an effective ceiling on income after tax when such income reaches approximately 25,000 rupees per annum." There were 11 tax brackets at that time. We have come a long way. From 11 brackets and a highest marginal tax rate at 97.75 percent in 1973–75, we now have three brackets and the highest rate, including a surcharge of 10 percent and the education cess of 3 percent at 33.99 percent.

The paper also points out studies that highlight the undesirable effects of capital taxation and recommend taxing capital income at lower and less progressive rates, where a flat tax rate could be close to being optimal. India has done precisely that, with a flat rate dividends distribution tax

* To preserve the sense of the discussions at the IPF, these discussants' comments reflect the views expressed at the IPF and do not take into account revisions to the original conference paper in response to these and other comments, even though the IPF Volume itself contains the revised paper. The original conference version of the paper is available on "http://www.ncaer.org".

at the company level from 1997–98 onwards and tax-free dividends for final recipients. The highest marginal tax rate on personal income in India is lower than that in China (45 percent), South Korea (38 percent), Japan (50 percent), USA (45 percent), and most other OECD countries.

The question then that I would like the paper to answer is whether India has reached close enough to its optimal tax structure. There are people who feel that the highest tax rate is too low and that capital gains and dividends are not being taxed in an equitable manner. Is the taxation of capital income close to the optimum?

On my second point, the paper recommends a major overhaul of tax assignment in India, where the constitution assigns agricultural income tax to the states. We all know the two cannons of federal tax devolution assignment: Lower tiers of government are more accountable as own-source revenue increases and relatively immobile tax sources should be assigned to them. We have long followed these canons. But the states have no doubt been very coy in either raising land revenue rates or taxing agricultural income. For the sake of argument, let us consider such an amendment to change the tax assignment, as indeed Pakistan did in 1948. Both the Indian and Pakistani Constitutions were drawn up on the lines of the Government of India Act, 1935. That Act in 1935 had assigned sales tax revenue on goods to state provincial governments and, by exclusion, the sales tax on services to the center. The Pakistan Constituent Assembly changed the assignment of the Pakistan General Sales Tax Act (March 31, 1948) and reassigned it to the federal government. For this reason, among others, the federal structure of Pakistan does not find much acclaim among experts and has come under severe strain over the years. So, I would be careful in amending the constitution and changing tax assignments. I realize that what Rao suggests is not a constitutional amendment but an agreement between the centre and states that the centre will tax agricultural income and give the revenue to the states. But even this tampering may not be a simple matter.

Furthermore, it is important to note that the definition of agricultural income in the Income Tax Act in India is a very limited one. Section 2 of the Income Tax Act makes it clear that agricultural income includes rent or revenue from agricultural land that must be cultivated. It is a fairly restrictive definition. For example, poultry, livestock, dairy farming, and beekeeping are not part of agricultural income. To that extent, the revenue loss because of the tax exemption of agricultural income is not as large. For the time being, I am ignoring the loophole of non-agricultural income passing off as agricultural income. I will come to that later.

My own back-of-the-envelope calculation, based on rather heroic assumptions that I am happy to share with anyone interested in my method, also suggests that revenue loss for not having a perfectly good agricultural income tax is about ₹63,000 crores, or about 0.5 percent of GDP, very close to the 0.6 percent that Rao and Sengupta (2011) came up with.

Rao's paper rightly points out that "a tax policy is only as good as it can be administered." Trying to tax agricultural income spread over some 0.6 million villages can be challenging and may end up increasing black money in the economy. Let me suggest two alternatives to mobilize revenue and combine equity with administrative feasibility. First, the 1972 report of the Committee on Taxation of Agricultural Wealth and Income headed by Dr K. N. Raj recommended a progressive agricultural holdings tax to be levied by the states as a good substitute for an agricultural income tax imposed by the center. A land tax is likely not to be administratively more difficult than an agricultural income tax because the asset is there for all to see, though land titles would need to be cleared first, which itself is not an easy task. But it would not require a constitutional amendment and would strengthen fiscal federalism by augmenting the own-source revenue of the states, enhancing their accountability. What is needed is an all-India incentivized effort under the Center's leadership to encourage the States to introduce such a tax.

Second, agricultural income is indeed exempt from income tax, but there has been a twist post-2014. Agricultural income is considered for determining the tax rate while computing income tax liability if net agricultural income exceeds ₹5,000 and the total income, excluding net agricultural income, exceeds the basic exemption limit. There is a complicated, three-step process if an assessee's total income, excluding net agricultural income, exceeds his or her applicable basic exemption limit. It is a complex process of the partial integration of agricultural and non-agricultural incomes, with more taxable income in the higher tax slabs and the same non-agricultural income taxed at a higher rate, so I will not go into the details.

My overall argument is that because of informational problems and lacuna in tax administration, we have not been able to stop non-agricultural income being declared as agricultural income, leave alone to properly implement the partial integration that was envisaged at the beginning of the 1974–75 assessment year as recommended in 1972 by the Raj Committee. Perhaps we should first try and plug these loopholes in declaring nonagricultural income as agricultural income and implement partial integration. It has been more than 40 years since, and we still have not done it. Learning to walk before running may be a safer strategy.

Mihir Desai
Harvard Business School

It is a pleasure to be here and I would like to thank Govinda for this excellent paper.

I want to start by saying that the first section on what makes for a sound tax system is very hard to pull off. It is a compression of a hundred years of research on optimal taxation, and, notwithstanding how capable one is, it would be hard to do justice to it. So, for example, one can always quarrel with the paper's characterization of the latest developments in optimal tax theory. I wonder if it is even necessary here, because (a) it is relatively generic and (b) I would consider staying instead with the data, which is extremely interesting and doing more with it. So, let me a give you a couple of straightforward comments and ask for more from what is already an extremely rich paper.

The first is more distillation. Sometimes, the most important points were unclear in the paper, and I will try to give my version of them. Second, the paper seems a bit depressing, and so perhaps it could highlight the success stories a little more as being instructive. Third, I think it is difficult to make the argument the paper is making without talking about India in a comparative perspective, because otherwise we run the risk of "Indian tax exceptionalism", which is a very dangerous path to traverse. Finally, I want to talk about the theory of reform, push the paper a little bit on the emphasis on revenue, discuss how an IPF paper can effectively use emerging ideas to lay out a research agenda, and suggest why the paper should list out the concrete proposals that should be implemented.

On distilling key messages, it is not entirely clear what the big lessons are, and, in particular, a lot of the problems cited, the Johnson and Myles quote, the political economy carve-outs are quite generic. One could say exactly the same thing about the US tax system. It would be nice to know what is wrong with the Indian tax system that is not so generic. In my opinion, the assignment problem—which level of government should tax what—is the original sin.

I think it would also be useful to distill some of the striking things that have gone well and organize them around the key ideas of the paper. For instance, there was a remarkable 5–6-year period in the early 2000s when revenues grew considerably. Since the paper is very worried about the level of revenues, one would want to dig into that period and understand it. A second significant, almost startling, success is the basic structure of personal income tax, the reduced numbers of brackets, and the relatively low marginal rates compared to several other countries. A third big success, which the paper underplays considerably, is corporate taxation, which has tripled as a share of the GDP over the last 20 years, has been very resilient, and is now a stable source of revenue at 3.5 percent of GDP. The fourth big success, which the paper notes, but could cover more substantially, is service tax and its growth from zero to close to 2 percent of GDP. It would be useful to know more about how and why these things happened. I think all these developments are reasons for optimism, and the paper could highlight them. In fact, the paper could have been organized around tax successes and failures, rather than focusing just on the "bads."

The big failures of the Indian tax system are covered well in the paper. The first is the coverage of personal income tax, where the paper reports two mindboggling numbers. The number of people reporting incomes of more than 10 million is only about 40,000. Taxpayers comprise only 3 percent of the population, and, even there, 75 percent of them are reporting an annual income of less than ₹2 lakh. This is a remarkable failure. The second failure, as you suggest, is a decline in the tax/GDP ratio after the 2008 global financial crisis, which I think is mainly in indirect taxes. Why did that happen? The paper could say more. My own instinct is that the tax assignment issues around agriculture are the problem. It would be useful to get a definitive picture. The final, mindboggling, failure number in the paper relates to tax arrears at 5.1 percent of GDP. Thinking a little more about that would be useful.

It is difficult to talk about these issues without country comparisons, and the paper refers to the Bird and Zolt (2003) and the IMF (2011) papers. From these, it is not entirely clear that India is so much of an outlier, not appearing to be very different from the other large emerging markets such as Turkey, Brazil, or China. These comparisons are hard to make, but I do not know how to assess failure or success without that. If we are worried about India, then there is no more powerful motivator than putting the Indian experience in relief. That way, we also avoid falling prey to Indian tax exceptionalism.

Although the paper talks about the importance of tax reforms in India, I did not quite understand its theory of reform. Tax reforms are politically difficult everywhere—winners do not pay, losers are vengeful—but it is not exactly clear why this is more difficult in India than anywhere else. The paper suggests that tax reform in India is a very slow process that gets bogged down in the details. I think that perhaps the opposite is also true, that very significant tax reforms are not really a process but sudden events that happen quickly through an alignment of significant political forces and actors. That was certainly true for the 1986 US tax reforms, and it is certainly true for VAT reforms in most countries that happened quickly as part of an IMF program.

I am deeply skeptical of the OECD initiative on base erosion and profit shifting (BEPS), which the paper talks about, though it is not a big part. I think there is a lot of hand wringing about multinational firms, which is strange because corporate tax revenues have been robust, the most robust in emerging markets, and an increasing share of overall revenues. It also does not seem particularly relevant in the Indian setting, where underinvestment in the manufacturing sector and capital investment, in general, are the first-order priority.

What is driving the state heterogeneity flagged here? Some research on that would be fascinating. Economic growth in the early 2000s and the role of IT in it is a huge question mark, and if we could demonstrate something about that through research, it would be an enormously valuable contribution.

Finally, when tax arrears get as big as over 5 percent of GDP, how does that distort the behavior of taxpayers? We do not know much about this, and research on this would be very helpful. Also, I did not get a strong sense of what the key policy proposals on this should be. May be it is time to think about amnesties and how they can be implemented if arrears get really large. Overall, personal income tax inclusion would seem to be the first-order thing to be addressed rather than pursuing BEPS or trying to alleviate poverty alleviation through the tax code. Finally, it is a great paper, and it is unfair to ask for something more of a paper as rich as this.

General Discussion

Pranab Bardhan conjectured that the unbelievably small number of high taxpayers in India could have more to do with the gaps in taxation of real estate and property. Carrying further Mihir Desai's implied argument that the inaccurate determination of real estate wealth influences the structure of capital taxation, he said that India does not adequately cover property taxation or take into account real estate wealth. He pointed out that wealth tax had been abolished very recently in India on the grounds that the amount collected was not significant enough to justify the costs (the same reason given for abolishing estate duty in 1983). This was ironical. While India is doing this, the world is sitting up and taking note of Thomas Piketty's proposal for a global system of progressive wealth taxes to reduce inequality. It is time to rethink property and wealth taxation and the estate duty in India.

Nirvikar Singh suggested that the paper could focus a little more on the effect of tax policy on growth, particularly on the tax policy designed to encourage investments, especially start-ups and early stage firms. Sudipto Mundle talked about Mihir Desai's comment on the birth defect in GST, the levy of a 1 percent tax not only on the sale but also on the interstate supply of goods, which implies that a commodity passing through four or five states would attract a levy in each state, defeating the purpose of GST. He hoped that the final version of the GST bill would not include this birth defect. On tax administration, he abhorred the prevalence of silo behavior between CBDT and CBCE and wondered if the paper could discuss the feasibility and desirability of the Parthasarathy Shome Committee's proposal recommending the consolidation of CBDT and CBEC, which had been opposed by the Revenue Service officers as jeopardizing their careers.

Karthik Muralidharan supported Bardhan's plea for more attention to property taxes, noting the core principle of property values going up sufficiently to yield a discounted cash flow of increased tax revenues that could then pay for urban infrastructure. Not having a good property tax system in place would make it difficult to generate the funds for the massive urban infrastructure that India needs.

Thomas Richardson felt that following the 2013 Tax Administration Reform Commission's report, India's tax rates are broadly fine, but what is of course shocking is the small number of taxpayers in India, only 30 million compared to, say, China's 300 million. He felt that keeping agriculture outside the tax net also contributes to this since many are allegedly only nominally engaged in agriculture with the bulk of their income coming from construction or other activities. Hence, there is a lot of scope to improve tax administration, enhance taxpayer services, and change the way in which the administration approaches and interacts with the taxpayer. Whichever way one looks at it, tax revenue of 18–19 percent of GDP is really low by emerging market standards. Tax modernization would boost not only revenues but also India's 'Ease of Doing Business' ranking.

Devesh Kapur noted that taxing agriculture is politically very contentious. Following Ashok Lahiri, he asserted that the revenue could be substantially enhanced by taxing land whose use has been converted from agricultural to non-agricultural purposes, resulting in a real windfall gain. This would be much less controversial politically since the tax would fall not on farmers but on land not being used by them. On large tax arrears, Kapur blamed it on the lack of incentives for tax officials to settle tax claims quickly out of fear of being accused of taking kickbacks. Tax cases continue for years, often reaching the Supreme Court, with major adverse implications for India's tax system.

Surjit Bhalla remarked that like Mihir, there is a success story on personal income tax that should be acknowledged. And, keeping morality out of it, we should think of tax rates that balance revenue maximization without distorting incentives. The huge unaddressed problem in personal income tax, however, is the missing middle, comprising tens of millions of Indian residents outside the top and the bottom tax brackets who do not pay taxes. While 60 percent each of those in the highest and low income tax brackets are paying taxes, 40 percent of the population in each of the two categories are not paying any taxes. This group comprises professionals, doctors, and others, whose tax compliance rate is about 20–25 percent, as opposed to 60–65 percent among the high and low income categories of urban taxpayers. Only salaried people have taxes regularly deducted at source. On corporate tax, Bhalla emphasized that although tax rates in the country are in the competitive range, the problem is that it is not the nominal rate that matters but the effective tax rate, and that India is second after Japan, globally.

Jeffrey Hammer said on tax administration capacity that what is important is to figure out the nature and frequency of information needed by the authorities and how then to put it to best use. He thought that it might be absolutely necessary to conduct cadastral surveys, though they are expensive to undertake and difficult to update. He suggested that policy makers should focus on the technology of tax administration that is needed to balance the costs and benefits of identifying specific targets for taxation. There were large declines in revenue after the 1991 reforms, mostly due to reducing tariffs that were highly distortionary but easy to reduce. There was a trade-off, and the subsequent recovery of revenue was perhaps due to the tax authorities learning to do the more difficult taxes.

Tarun Ramadorai asked whether research could be done to estimate the extent of tax evasion in India. He cited an interesting paper on Greece (Artavanis et al. 2015) that measures income tax evasion through loans to tax-evading individuals from banks that assess the individual's true income. Using microdata on household credit from a Greek bank, they replicated the bank's underwriting model to infer the bank's estimate of individuals' true income. They estimated that some 43–45 percent of self-employed income goes unreported and, thus, untaxed. For 2009, this implied foregone tax revenues of over 30 percent of the fiscal deficit. The primary tax-evading sectors were the professional services—medicine, law, engineering, education, and media. Ramadorai suggested that a similar analysis of tax evasion in India would be extremely revealing if the data were available.

Reference

Artavanis, Nikolaos T., Adair Morse, and Margarita Tsoutsoura. 2015. "Measuring Income Tax Evasion Using Bank Credit: Evidence from Greece," Chicago Booth Research Paper No. 12–25, Chicago: University of Chicago-Booth School of Business, September 25.

KAUSHIK DEB*
Group Economics, BP plc
PAUL APPLEBY†
Group Economics, BP plc

India's Primary Energy Evolution: Past Trends and Future Prospects

ABSTRACT This paper assesses India's primary energy mix and changes in consumption and production to identify factors causing these changes and their likely economic and emission impacts. A rising GDP growth rate and the changing structure of the economy during 1980–2013 resulted in a significant growth in energy consumption, though with little apparent impact on the primary energy mix, with coal and oil dominating at unchanged levels. Despite growth in energy consumption, India's primary energy consumption per capita remains low as compared to the world averages. Industrialization, urbanization, and the energy mix are key factors that will influence growth in India's energy demand. Going forward, India's primary energy consumption is expected to grow at a rate outpacing China's. Coal will continue to dominate the energy mix, though it will lose some market share to gas and renewables. India's energy and emission intensities have declined over time but mostly due to improving energy efficiency and not due to a change in the energy mix. With the energy mix not changing, the gains from greater shares of more energy- and carbon-efficient fuels are likely to remain limited. Significantly for India, domestic production has been sluggish in responding to energy demand growth, and imports are likely to continue rising, placing a significant burden on the macro economy. A higher GDP growth path and a green growth path are explored to understand their implications for the energy policy environment, improvements in energy and carbon intensities, import dependency, and domestic production.

Keywords: *India, Energy Demand, Energy Production, Energy Intensity, Energy Forecasts, Carbon Emissions, Energy Imports, Green Growth*

JEL Classification: *Q47*

* *kaushik.deb@se1.bp.com*
† *paul.appleby@uk.bp.com*

The large increases in energy consumption that have accompanied rising population and economic growth in India have been shaped by a variety of environmental factors and policy choices. India faces a stubborn energy mix that seems unlikely to change very much over the next two decades, with growth in population and GDP driving up energy consumption. This growth in demand calls for increased consumption of fossil fuels. In addition, despite growing domestic production of both fossil and non-fossil fuels, imports will continue to rise. This is likely despite an expected, rapid ramp-up in renewable energy and nuclear power generation, apart from gains in energy intensity.

This paper presents a forecast of India's energy demand and future based on the results of the *BP Energy Outlook 2035* (BP 2015a). Section 1 briefly describes the growth in India's primary energy demand and supply since 1980. Section 2 is a brief review of the prevalent energy demand modeling techniques and the existing forecasts of energy demand in India and the world. Section 3 presents the approach and methodology used in the *BP Energy Outlook 2035*, followed by the results for India in a reference, base case. Section 4 presents two alternative scenarios, constructed to assess the impact of higher GDP growth and that of a greater penetration of renewable energy and higher energy efficiency. The impact of the three scenarios is described in terms of energy demand, carbon emissions, and import dependency. Section 5 concludes the paper.

1. Growth of Energy Demand and Supply in India

India's energy consumption has grown by 5.5 percent per annum since 1980, on par with the fastest growing economies in the world, particularly in Asia. Amongst fossil fuels, consumption of oil has grown by 5.3 percent per annum, coal by 5.6 percent per annum, and gas by 11.7 percent per annum during 1980–2014. Growth in non-fossil fuels has been led by renewables, which started from almost negligible generation in 1990 to 61.5 terawatt-hours (TWh) by 2014, while nuclear generation in the power sector has grown by 8.1 percent per annum and hydro by 2.6 percent per annum during this period. In all, 93 percent of the total increase in consumption was met by fossil fuels, with coal contributing the largest at 57 percent of the total increase between 1980 and 2014, followed by oil at 28 percent and gas at 8 percent (Figure 1). Non-fossil fuels together added just 7 percent of the increase in consumption during this period.

FIGURE 1. India: Increase in Energy Consumption, 1980–2014 (Mtoe)

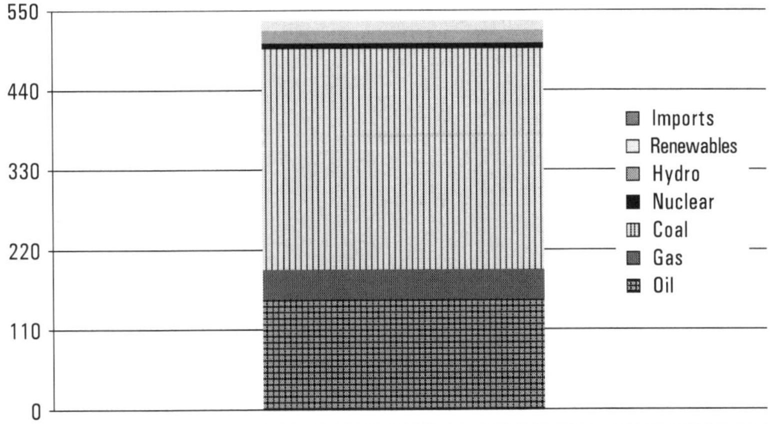

Source: BP (2015b). Mtoe = million tons of oil equivalent.

India's share of global demand during these 34 years has risen from 1.5 percent of the global energy consumption in 1980 to 4.9 percent by 2014, making its way from the tenth largest energy consumer in the world in 1980 to the fourth largest by 2014. India still remains the second largest non-OECD (Organization for Economic Cooperation and Development) energy consumer, behind China.

India's energy production, however, has grown only by 4.2 percent per annum during this period. As a result, 36 percent of the increase in domestic consumption has been met by rising fossil fuel imports (Figure 2). Fossil fuels account for 89 percent of the increase in domestic production, with coal accounting for 71 percent of the total increase between 1980 and 2014. This is followed by oil accounting for 10 percent and gas accounting for another 8 percent. Non-fossil fuels together add a total of 11 percent to the increment in domestic energy production during 1980 and 2014.

1.1. Energy Demand and Energy Mix Implications

Over the last few years, even with economic growth slowing down in India, energy consumption has remained robust. GDP growth slowed down from 7.4 percent per annum during 2000–10 to 6.1 percent per annum during 2010–14, but energy consumption growth went up from 5.6 percent per annum to 5.8 percent per annum. As a result, improvements in the energy intensity of GDP also slowed down. The fuel mix had implications for CO_2 emissions from energy use. More significantly, the sharper slowdown in

FIGURE 2. India: Increase in Energy Production and Imports, 1980–2014 (Mtoe)

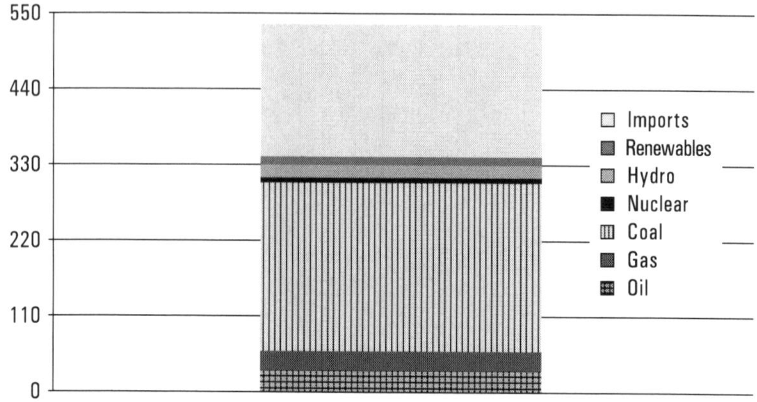

Source: BP (2015b).

domestic production as compared to consumption implied that the share of India's energy consumption met by domestic sources fell to 57 percent by 2014, the lowest on record.

The energy sector is generally slow-moving, and changes in consumption and production are a result of lumpy investment decisions and only gradual improvements in efficiency. As a result, India's energy sector at one level appears largely unchanged since 1980, with coal and oil still dominating the energy mix. The broad averages, however, mask a significant shift away from coal and toward oil until 2000, and the subsequent recovery in coal's share in the early part of this century (Figure 3). The competition between coal and oil in the last century has now been played out between coal and gas over a much shorter period. A rapid rise in gas consumption during 2005–10, followed by a decline during 2010–14, was offset by equivalent changes in coal consumption. However, an increase followed by a decline in gas production during the same intervals was not matched by an equivalent trend in coal production.

In comparison, the global energy mix has evolved gradually but definitively away from fossils (Figure 4). Oil has steadily lost market share since the first oil crisis in the 1970s, and continues to do so by the virtue of its consumption growth lagging overall primary energy consumption growth. The market share of coal, which seemed to have peaked in the mid-1980s as industrial growth in OECD slowed down, has had a renaissance on the back of China's rapid industrial growth before peaking at the beginning of this decade. Gas and nuclear have slowly gained market share with rapid

FIGURE 3. **India: Primary Energy Shares, 1980–2014 (%)**

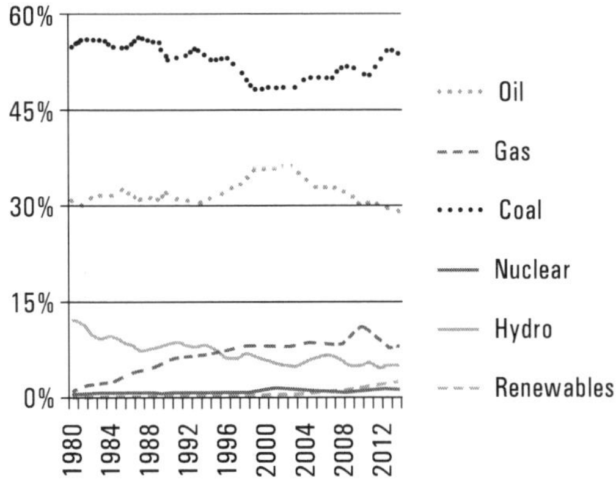

Source: BP (2015b).

FIGURE 4. **Global: Primary Energy Shares, 1980–2014 (%)**

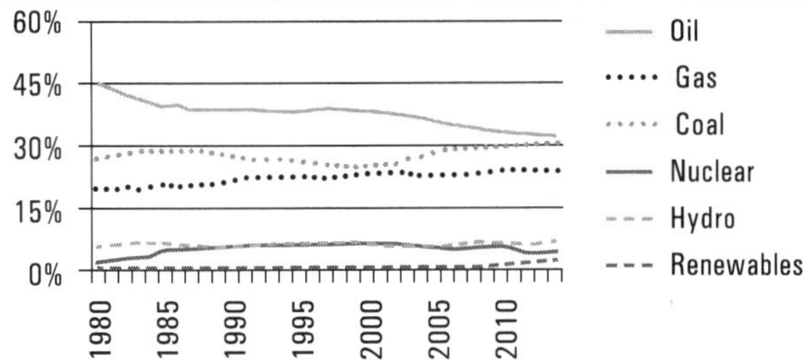

Source: BP (2015b).

growth rates, albeit in very small volumes. In general, the share of fossil fuels appears to be converging, with the current shares varying between 23 percent of the total primary energy for gas and 33 percent for oil, while the share of non-fossil fuel energy forms varies between 2.5 and 7 percent.

1.2. Rising Import Dependency

India's net energy imports increased by 5.5 percent per annum during 2010–14, as compared to 4.8 percent per annum in the first decade of the century. While coal led the trend, with imports rising by 28.6 percent per annum during this period, gas and oil imports rose by 12.4 percent per annum and 4.9 percent per annum, respectively. Underlying this rapid increase in coal imports were developments in domestic gas production during this period and the tight Asian liquid natural gas (LNG) market. As domestic gas production collapsed in India in 2010, energy demand shifted to imports (Figures 5 and 6). LNG, on the other hand, entered a three-year lull in supply growth in 2011 and, along with the 2011 Fukushima nuclear disaster, pushed Asian LNG demand (and prices) to record highs, making gas imports much more expensive than coal imports. The result was the dramatic increase in coal imports by India during 2010–14.

1.3. Higher Energy Intensity and Emissions

Energy markets are sluggish in their response to economic drivers. Consequently, while GDP growth slowed down, energy consumption growth remained stable, thus slowing down improvements in India's energy intensity

FIGURE 5. India: Coal and Gas Imports, 1985–2014

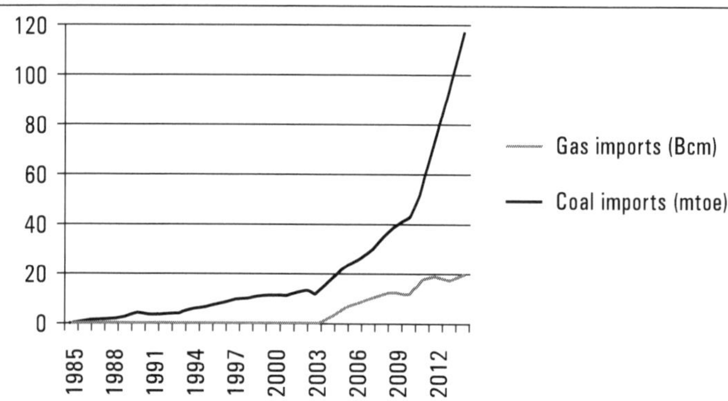

Source: BP (2015b); Bcm = billion cubic meters.

FIGURE 6. India: Oil Imports, 1985–2014 (thousand barrels/day)

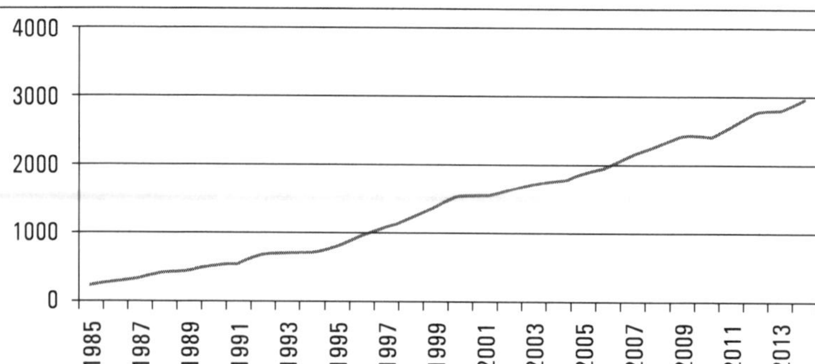

Source: BP (2015b).

(measured as units of energy per unit of GDP) as well. From a reduction of 1.6 percent per annum during 2000–10, energy intensity fell by only 0.3 percent per annum during 2010–14 (Figure 7). These gains in the first period occurred when GDP growth was much faster than the increase in energy consumption; GDP rose by 7.4 percent per annum during 2000–10, while energy consumption increased by 5.6 percent per annum. In the following four years (2010–14), GDP growth came down to 6.1 percent per annum, while energy consumption growth increased to 5.8 percent per annum, leading to a much slower decline in energy intensity per annum.

The growth in CO_2 emissions from energy consumption accelerated in India—from 5.6 percent per annum during 2000–10 to 6.2 percent per annum during 2010–14 (Figure 8). This implies that the carbon intensity of energy

FIGURE 7. India: Energy Intensity, 1980–2014 (tons of oil equivalent (toe) per million $ of 2010 PPP GDP)

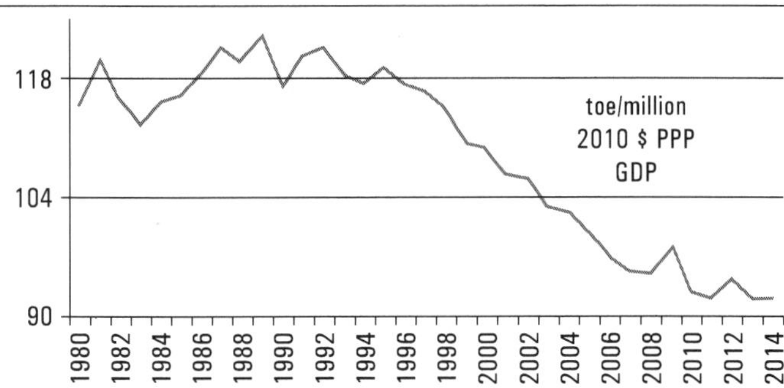

Source: BP (2015b).

FIGURE 8. India: CO_2 from Energy Use, 1980–2014 (metric tons)

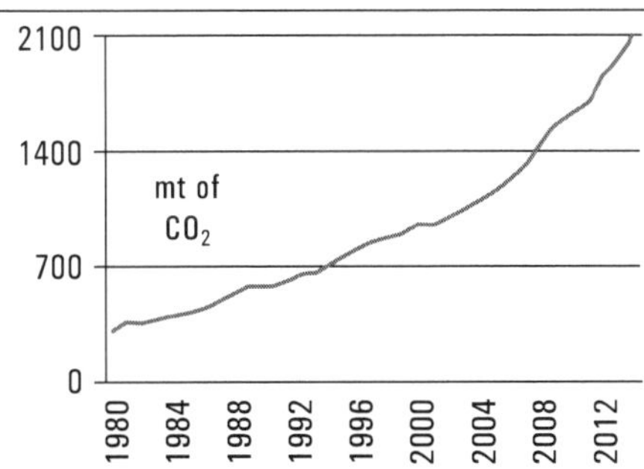

Source: BP (2015b).

consumption was broadly unchanged during 2000–10, but then increased over the period 2010–14 as coal gained shares from gas rapidly.

2. Energy Modeling Approaches

Modeling techniques in the energy sector are mostly applied to modeling energy demand, while energy supply models are usually simple aggregations of individual supply sources. Each supply source, in turn, is usually projected on the basis of resource availability and likely utilization rates. The likely decline rate of the supply source of fossil fuels also brings another factor to a supply forecast model.

The literature on energy demand modeling is rich and varied. Econometric, top-down modeling and bottom-up, end-use modeling are the two prevalent approaches for modeling in the energy sector. The end-use or engineering models taking a bottom-up approach estimate demand based on equipment saturation, efficiencies, and usage. This section provides a very brief description of the more widely applied energy demand modeling techniques, followed by a review of the recent energy sector modeling exercises in India, with the latter using the survey reported by Navroz Dubash et al. (2015).

2.1. Econometric Modeling of Energy

Top-down econometric models are aggregate models of the economy based on past trends used to predict relationships between the sectors of the economy (IPCC 2001). Technological change is usually incorporated exogenously in the model, rather than explaining it within it. For example, autonomous energy efficiency improvement describes the rate at which sectors require less energy over time to produce a given level of output (MIT 1997). Econometric models then apply differing rates of change among sectors and regions based on historic data or future assumptions. In general, top-down models are useful for forecasting in cases where historical development patterns and relationships among key underlying variables hold constant for the projection period (Hourcade et al. 1996).

Top-down models are often used when there is little information available on equipment stocks (Zarnikau 2003). The econometric methods require a consistent set of information over a reasonably long duration and are hence easier to execute for individual sectors. There is a large literature on specific functional forms for econometric analysis of short-run electricity demand (Batancourt 1981). Other papers have examined the demand for electricity in India by developing a logarithmic linear econometric model, wherein a relationship between electricity consumption and variables such as income, price of electricity, and price of diesel, among others, was developed to estimate short-run and long-run elasticities (Bose and Shukla 1999). Systems-based approaches include residential, industrial, and total electricity demand estimation in the United States using both a partial adjustment approach and a simultaneous equations approach (Kamerschen and Porter 2004). In estimating residential energy demand, energy prices, disposable income, and other attributes of the consumers are usually incorporated. Crucial here is having a long enough data series that allows for a sufficiently large number of variables and rich functional forms to be used.

2.2. Bottom-up Energy Modeling

Bottom-up modeling focuses on counting equipment and stocks and adding up energy consumption by analyzing the efficiency and frequency of use of the equipment. These models allow for more comprehensive analysis by aggregating demand across sectors, regions, and fuels. Total energy demand is then a product of activity levels and energy intensity (energy used per unit of economic output) or process efficiency (energy demand per physical output). These models incorporate the development of new technology and processes that improve the efficiency of energy-using equipment and usually forecast demand based on the engineering costs of a wide range of technologies (IEA 1997; IPCC 2001).

Bottom-up models often make use of the vintage stock concept to project demand or supply into the future. In other words, they model future energy use based on costs, timing, and the market shares of technologies or the vintages of equipment and stocks. These models often use simulation and back-casting to project into the future and are most suited in cases where new technologies are penetrating the market or new policies are changing preferences and behavioral patterns.

However, such models are weak in incorporating feedback between the structural evolution of a particular sector and overall economic development patterns, such as the influence of consumer non-energy behavior and changes in the size and spread of various sectors of the economy.

2.3. Energy Modeling in India

Energy modeling and analysis in India have largely been based on a bottom-up, optimization approach (Pandey 1998; Sengupta 1993; Shukla and Kanudia 1997). Several bottom-up and input–output studies, though aggregate in nature, have modeled energy at the sector level (Table 1) (Pachauri 2002; Pandey 1998; Shukla and Kanudia 1997; Tiwari 2000).

The Asian-Pacific Integrated Model or AIM-end-use model (Shukla 1996) was set up for a 40-year horizon from 1995 onwards by minimizing discounted energy system costs at the end-use, sub-sector level. The Market Allocation (MARKAL) model, originally developed for Canada (Berger et al. 1992), has also been adopted for India (Pandey 1998; Shukla and Kanudia 1997). Garg et al. integrate the top-down AIM-end-use model with the bottom-up MARKAL model to provide insights into the implications of mitigation commitments on the energy and technology mix, energy costs, mitigation costs, and the competitiveness of Indian industries (Garg et al. 2001). A stochastic Indian MARKAL model (Loulou et al. 1997) reflects long-term uncertainties in technology and fuel substitution within the Indian context. Most studies focus only on technical and economic variables influencing energy use, without including other social, demographic, and structural and transitional dynamics at the household level that impact energy use and development, particularly in a developing country (Pandey 2002).

The Dubash review quoted earlier and most other studies have been motivated by climate change and environmental considerations. A number of these studies also highlight issues around energy security, both nationally and in the form of household access to energy. For instance, the objectives of the modeling elements of studies from the World Bank (2011) and

TABLE 1. Recent Energy Modeling Studies in India

Study	*Approach*	*Type*	*Reference*
Expert Group on Low Carbon Strategies	Activity analysis model	Top-down	Planning Commission (2014)
The Energy Report—India	MARKAL location model	Bottom-up	TERI (2013)
Energy Emissions—Trends and Policy Landscape	Integrated assessment model	Hybrid	Shukla et al. (2015)
A Sustainable Development Framework for India's Climate Policy	Integrated energy model	Bottom-up	CSTEP (2015)
Energy Intensive Sectors of the Indian Economy	World Energy model	Bottom-up	World Bank (2011)
India Energy Security Scenarios	Excel-based simulation	Bottom-up	NITI Aayog (2015)

the Delhi-based TERI (2013) are to quantify the impact of sector-specific mitigation activities on greenhouse gas (GHG) emissions. Energy security and the rising share of imports in meeting domestic energy demand are considered in the Planning Commission's work (2014).

2.4. Other Global Energy Models

There are a number of other global energy projects that present energy consumption and supply forecasts, differentiated by regions and fuels, using the same approach as this paper. Key amongst these are the International Energy Agency's (IEA) annual *World Energy Outlook*, the US Energy Information Administration's (EIA) annual *International Energy Outlook*, and the Shell Scenarios. Again, this list is only indicative of the vast literature and products available to researchers and analysts.

The Shell Scenarios are described as "ask(ing) 'what if?' questions to explore alternative views of the future and create plausible stories around them. They consider long-term trends in economics, energy supply and demand, geopolitical shifts and social change, as well as the motivating factors that drive change" (Shell 2014). The Scenarios present alternative narratives of how and where the demand and supply of energy are driven by a complex interplay of politics, economics, social development, and technology change. More significant than the demand and supply forecasts that result from the exercise is the impact that these alternative narratives have on energy growth paths and the way they help identify the fault lines in the world energy situation that governments and businesses need to be cognizant of.

As compared to the Shell Scenarios, the forecasts from the IEA and EIA are closer in approach to this paper. The *International Energy Outlook* of the US Government's EIA presented two oil prices and two global GDP growth cases in its recent edition to examine a range of potential interactions of supply, demand, and prices in world energy markets. The model adjusts energy demand and supply growth to balance the market in each scenario (EIA 2013). The *World Energy Outlook* of the IEA available at the time of writing this paper contains three scenarios. The IEA emphasizes that none of the scenarios is a forecast—they are not designed to predict likely outcomes but to explore possibilities under different policy assumptions (IEA 2014). The "New Policies Scenario" (NPS) assumes that announced national policy objectives are fully implemented, while the "Current Policies Scenario" assumes very little change in policy. An aspiration forecast is also presented in the "450 Scenario" that sets out an energy pathway consistent with the goal of limiting the global increase in temperature to 2°C by limiting the concentration of GHGs in the atmosphere to around 450 parts per million of CO_2. IEA identifies the NPS as its central case.

3. India's Energy Future: Approach, Methodology, and Results

This paper and its assessment of India's energy future differ from previous studies in three ways. First, being prescriptive in nature, most of the studies cited earlier develop baseline and alternative scenarios as different cases, with the baseline being a "more-of-the-same" type projection based on the past, while alternative scenarios build in more aggressive policy reforms. One outcome of such a distinction is that each policy reform can be evaluated in terms of its impact. The baseline forecast in this paper, on the other hand, takes into account the likely policy reform process and builds in autonomous technology development, recognizing that policies do change and evolve over time, and that the natural progression of technology development works through the system. Thus, for example, the government's targets for wind, solar, and coal production in India are recognized while making policy assumptions for the future.

Second, the paper contextualizes India's energy demand, especially energy imports, against the overall global demand and supply of energy. This allows for adjusting demand on a yearly basis depending on the excess demand volumes for oil, gas, and coal, and the availability of these resources for import in regional markets. For the oil market, this assessment is based on the global oil balance, while for coal and gas, the regional supply scenario provides a boundary for import volumes. Although energy prices are not explicitly taken into account in the country-level forecasts, this balance provides an indication of the tightness of the market.

Finally, the India-centric studies listed earlier account for efficiency improvements and technology changes based on domestic industrial conditions and best-in-class experiences from the rest of the world. This forecast is global by design and approaches efficiency improvements and technology changes based on global trends and their transmission through global trade. For instance, improvements in vehicle efficiencies are reproduced around the world, with the automobile industry meeting demand in the OECD countries from manufacturing facilities in the non-OECD countries that allows for countries like India to benefit from these efficiency improvements. Similarly, policy developments in the OECD countries, such as strengthening

Euro emission standards in the European Union (EU), imply that non-OECD manufacturing facilities also need to improve product efficiencies.

3.1. Methodology

The forecast presented in this paper does not rely on a single, all-encompassing, general equilibrium model of the global energy economy. Such models do exist and can be very useful in highlighting the interdependencies within the energy system and identifying some of the potential unintended consequences of policy interventions. However, their complexity and high maintenance cost (in terms of the time and data required to keep them up-to-date and calibrated against the real world) limit their usefulness as tools for forecasting a "most likely" outcome.

The approach taken here, which is similar to that taken by the IEA and EIA work (IEA 2014; EIA 2013), is to apply a range of modeling strategies across different sectors and geographies and then aggregate the results in an accounting framework that ensures that everything balances. On the demand side, the forecast comes from a hybrid of top-down, econometric modeling and activity-level models applied in conjunction with a bottom-up aggregation of energy consumption in individual units based on their utilization rates. The final outcome relies heavily on expert judgment, applied to the most up-to-date data that is available, with modeling tools used, where possible, to inform and support that judgment.

The transport sector's demand for fuels is modeled in two different ways. First, a technology-rich, "bottom-up" model is used to simulate the evolution of vehicle fleets, based on a range of parameters that enter into vehicle choice decisions, including importantly the constraints imposed on auto manufacturers in the environmental performance of their vehicles (for example, Corporate Average Fuel Economy Standards in the United States, tailpipe CO_2 per km emission standards in the EU). Second, an econometric analysis of the relationship between transport fuel demand and incomes and fuel prices provides the basis for a "top-down" projection, given assumptions about the growth of income and changes in prices. The results from these two different modeling strategies are compared and expert judgment is applied through an iterative process of discussion to agree on a final set of numbers for the projection of transport fuel demand. Some of the key results from the modeling exercise are the following:

- The global vehicle fleet (commercial vehicles and passenger cars) more than doubles from around 1.2 billion today to 2.4 billion by

2035. Most of that growth is in the developing world (88 percent), since some OECD markets are already at saturation levels.

- Fuel economy gains are likely to accelerate over the period to 2035, with vehicle fleet fuel economy forecast to improve by 2.1 percent per annum between 2013 and 2035, having improved by about 1.5 percent per annum over the past decade of 2003–13.
- Transport fuel demand will continue to be dominated by oil (89 percent share in 2035), but the share of non-oil alternatives will increase from 5 percent in 2013 to 11 percent in 2035, with natural gas being the fastest growing transport fuel (6.3 percent per annum).

Industrial demand is based on the levels of economic activity represented by GDP, an assessment of the energy-intensive sectors within each region, and availability and competition between alternative fuels. For instance, China's industrial demand is based on likely trends in the share of industry in GDP in China, competition between coal and gas for market share, and likely trends in meeting energy intensity and GHG reduction targets in the economy. The fading impact of industrialization is apparent in the split of primary energy consumption by sector. Industry has been the fastest growing sector since 2000, averaging at 2.7 percent per annum, but projected growth slows to 1.4 percent per annum.

Power generation is the one sector where all fuels compete, and so it plays a major role in how the global fuel mix evolves. The demand for primary fuels for power generation is based on generation-capacity augmentation in all regions and for all fuels, on policy trends, and on regulatory changes likely to comply with GHG targets and technology improvements in electricity generation. The last factor is especially important for forecasting the generation of electricity from renewable sources, where reduction in the cost of generation through achieving economies of scale, learning by doing, and autonomous efficiency improvements result in significant achievements. The outcome by 2035 is a more balanced and diversified portfolio of fuels for power generation. Coal remains the dominant fuel, accounting for more than a third of the inputs to power generation, but that share is down from 44 percent today and the gap between the shares of coal and of other fuels narrows significantly.

Supply forecasts are more bottom-up. The projection of nuclear power in India is a good example. This is based on current data on projects under construction and planned, and on announced policy targets, all subject to expert overview of the likelihood of plans being implemented and targets being met. Forecasts for the supply of fossil fuels are based on adding up likely decline rates of existing producing regions, balanced with the likely demand for each fuel so as to be able to mimic price effects. These are then moderated by the proved reserves base[1] and expectations of changes in market structure due to policy reforms that may encourage greater exploration and production activity. For instance, the confluence in the United States of abundant resources with supportive policy and market structure—the world's largest rig fleet, access to extensive pipeline networks, and deep financial markets—that led to the rapid growth in energy production in the United States is unlikely to be replicated as widely anywhere else in our forecasts.

Given the considerable inertia in the global energy system, the long life of assets, and the long lead times on new builds, the key ingredients for a good forecast are the most up-to-date data to establish the starting point and initial momentum of the system and people with deep knowledge of how the individual parts of the system work and how they connect with one another.

3.2. Forecasts and Comparison with Other Studies

Table 2 contains the details of the BP forecast and comparisons with other publicly available projections over the period 2013–35. The BP Energy Outlook forecasts are within the range of these publicly available forecasts.

TABLE 2. BP Forecast Compared with Other Global Forecasts, 2013–35

	Primary energy consumption annual growth rate during 2013–35 (%)				*Shares in 2035 (%)*			
	BP	*IEA New Policies*	*IEA Current Policies*	*EIA*	*BP*	*IEA New Policies*	*IEA Current Policies*	*EIA**
World	1.5	1.2	1.5	1.6	100.0	100.0	100.0	100.0
Oil	0.8	0.5	0.9	0.9	27.4	28.0	29.1	28.5
Biofuels	3.2	1.5	1.4		0.7	10.7	10.0	0.0
Gas	1.9	1.6	1.8	1.7	26.4	22.7	21.6	22.8
Coal	1.1	0.5	1.6	1.6	27.1	26.0	29.2	27.9
Nuclear	1.9	2.5	1.9	2.7	4.9	6.3	5.4	6.9
Hydro	1.8	2.0	1.8		7.1	2.8	2.5	0.0
Renewables	7.0	7.5	1.8	2.7	6.4	3.5	2.3	14.0

Sources: Authors' estimates, BP (2015a), IEA (2014), EIA (2013).

Note: EIA forecasts are for 2010–35. Biofuels are included in renewables here.

1. The BP *Statistical Review of World Energy* defines "proved reserves" as "Generally taken to be those quantities that geological and engineering information indicates with reasonable certainty can be recovered in the future from known reservoirs under existing conditions."

We see weaker growth in OECD energy demand than others, while our projections for non-OECD growth are stronger than most. Compared to the IEA scenarios (which are not forecasts but assessments of potential outcomes based on defined sets of policy assumptions), our outlook lies above the IEA's "New Policies Scenario," which assumes that the announced national energy conservation and efficiency policy objectives are fully implemented, and close to the "Current Policies Scenario," which assumes no change in existing polices. This probably reflects our differing views on the outlook for rapidly industrializing economies and the speed with which China, in particular, can move to a less energy-intensive growth path.

3.3. Building Blocks for Policy Analysis for India

Population growth and increases in income per capita are the key drivers behind growing demand for energy, so the assumed path for these variables is a critical input for our forecasts. The population projections are taken directly from the United Nations Population Division, Revision 2010. By 2035, India's population will exceed 1.5 billion, which means an additional 250 million people will need energy.

The economic growth assumptions are based on projections provided by Oxford Economic Forecasting and sit well within the range of forecasts for the global economy that are available. The GDP numbers are expressed in real 2011 US dollars and Purchasing Power Parity (PPP) exchange rates. Using PPPs instead of market exchange rates, to convert currencies makes it possible to compare the output of economies and the welfare of population in real terms (using the same prices for the same goods in all countries and all years).

Over the outlook period, the global GDP is expected to more than treble, with India contributing nearly 13 percent of the total world's GDP growth. India's per capita GDP is assumed to increase by 166 percent over 2013–35, growing at an average of 4.6 percent per annum. On this measure, by 2035, India's per capita income would be just above where China's is today, and less than half of the current EU level.

Given these assumptions for population and income growth, both the level of energy demand and the fuel mix are heavily influenced by policy. The primary focus of India's policy throughout the 2013–35 period is assumed to remain the securing of affordable and reliable energy to support economic development. But there is also an increasing emphasis on clean energy, driven both by local environmental concerns and India's desire to play its

TABLE 3. Energy Policy Assumptions for India, 2013–35

	Current status	*Policy assumption*
Gas	Administered prices with some incentives for exploration and production	Gradual price deregulation by 2025
Coal	Target of 1 billion tons of production by 2020	Coal production reaches 1 billion tons by 2027
Solar	Target of 100 GW by 2022	80 GW by 2035
Wind	Target of 100 GW by 2022	110 GW by 2035
Nuclear	Target of 63 GW by 2032	27 GW by 2035

Source: Authors' estimates. GW = gigawatt.

TABLE 4. India: Energy Demand Elasticities

	Elasticity with respect to GDP		*Annual Growth Rate (%)*	
Demand	*2015–25*	*2025–35*	*2015–25*	*2025–35*
Oil	0.67	0.62	4	3
Gas	0.98	0.44	6	2
Coal	0.63	0.63	4	3
Nuclear	1.48	0.75	9	4
Hydro	0.50	0.68	3	4
Renewables	1.76	1.28	10	7
Total	**0.72**	**0.65**	**4**	**3**
GDP (PPP)			6	5

Source: Authors' estimates.

appropriate part in addressing global climate change issues. Some specific policy assumptions are illustrated in Table 3.

Given India's stage of economic development, energy demand is expected to remain closely linked to economic growth. That linkage weakens gradually as the economy matures, and this weakening is reinforced by policy efforts to improve efficiency (including, for example, the removal of energy subsidies). The effects can be seen in the elasticity of energy consumption with respect to GDP (that is, the ratio of energy growth to GDP growth), which has averaged 0.85 over the past decade and is assumed to decline to 0.72 over the next decade and to 0.65 in the final decade to 2035. Table 4 provides more detail by fuel type.

The potential for India's own fossil fuel production to meet energy demand growth is constrained by its resource endowments. The forecasts of production are based on existing proved reserves, likely extraction and decline rates, and the prospects for finding and developing new reserves—all conditional on expected policy reforms (Table 5).

TABLE 5. India: Growth of Energy Supply

	Proved Reserves	*2015–25 Annual Growth Rate (%)*	*2025–35 Annual Growth Rate (%)*
Oil (billion barrels)	5.74	–2	0
Gas (trillion cubic meters)	1.43	1	5
Coal (billion tons)	60.60	4	3
Total		**5**	**3**

Source: BP (2015a).

3.4. Reference Case

Based on these assumptions, India's primary energy consumption is expected to grow by 128 percent between 2013 and 2035, achieving an average growth rate of 3.8 percent per annum (Figure 9). That is almost double the average rate of growth for non-OECD energy markets; India's share of global energy demand would rise to 8 percent in 2035, still some way behind China (at 26 percent), but ahead of Russia (5 percent) and Brazil (3 percent).

Despite the rapid growth in total energy consumption, India's per capita consumption of energy will remain relatively low in 2035; less than half the global average. To put this in perspective, in terms of per capita energy use, India, in 2035, will be roughly where South Korea was in 1978 or Thailand in 1995. India's energy intensity (the amount of energy consumed per unit

FIGURE 9. India: Projected Growth of Energy Consumption, 2013–35 (Mtoe)

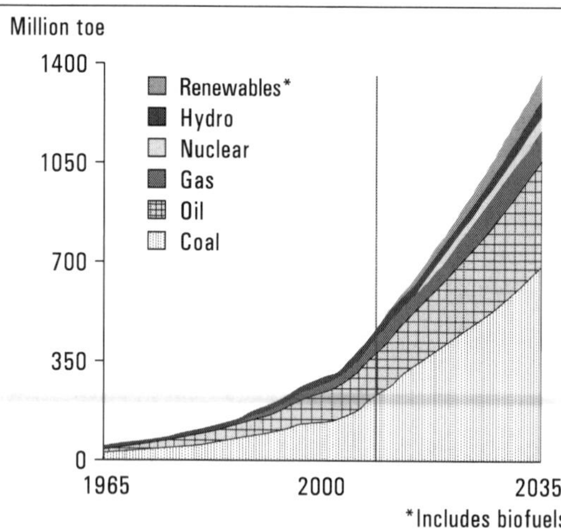

Source: BP (2015a).

of GDP) will also remain low, declining by 1.6 percent per annum. India's economic development is expected to be much less energy-intensive than China's recent experience.

In these projections, India's energy mix continues to evolve slowly, with fossil fuels accounting for 87 percent of the demand in 2035, down from 92 percent today (and compared to a global average of 81 percent in 2035). Coal continues to dominate the energy mix, accounting for 51 percent of the energy consumption in 2035, though it does lose some market share, notably to renewables and nuclear (Figure 10). Coal would account for nearly half of the growth in India's energy consumption by 2035.

The consumption of fossil fuels more than doubles over 2013–35, with natural gas up 145 percent, oil up 117 percent, and coal up 112 percent. Renewables and nuclear grow even more rapidly, expanding by 564 percent and 363 percent, respectively. Large-scale hydroelectricity shows the slowest growth, but still achieves a very respectable 98 percent increase in output.

India's own energy production meets just over half of the increase in energy consumption, growing by 117 percent (3.6 percent per annum). Amongst fossil fuels, only coal is able to keep up with the growth rate of demand, with production expanding by 119 percent. Gas production also grows (by 78 percent) but less rapidly than consumption, and oil production declines. Coal remains the dominant fuel produced in India with a 66 percent market share in 2035. Renewables in power overtake oil as the second largest, increasing from 3 percent to 11 percent in 2035, as oil drops from 12 percent to 4 percent. India would contribute the third largest increment to renewable energy generation during 2013–35 in the world (Figures 10 and 11).

FIGURE 10. India: Projected Primary Energy Shares, 1965–2035 (%)

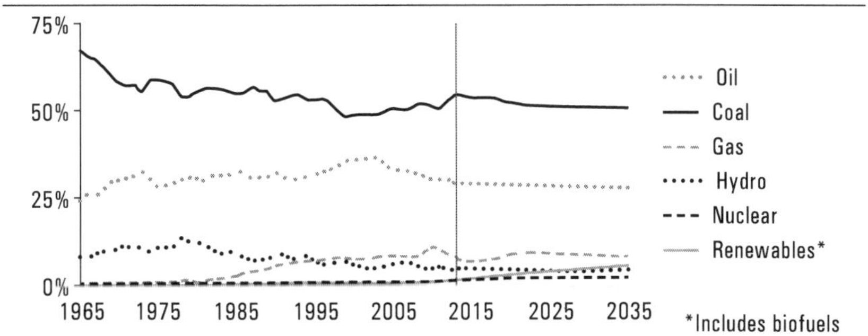

Source: BP (2015a).

FIGURE 11. Projected Renewable Energy Growth, China, the United States, India, 2013–35 (TWh)

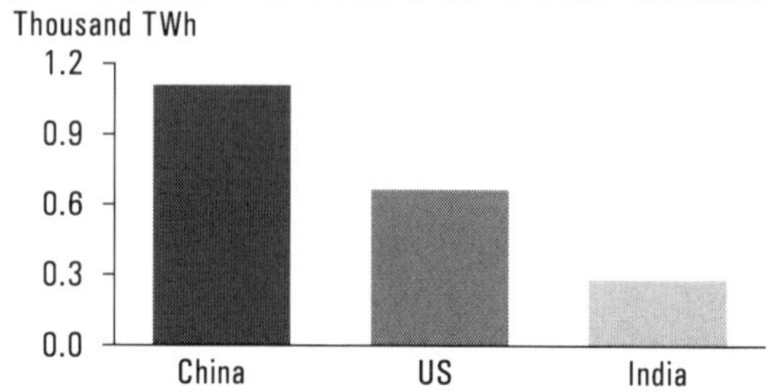

Source: BP (2015a). TWh = terawatt-hours.

3.5. Policy Implications

The projections described earlier pose two key policy challenges. First, with energy demand growth outpacing the expansion of domestic energy supply, India's dependence on imported energy increases. India's energy production as a share of consumption would decline from 59 percent today to 56 percent by 2035 as imports would rise by 143 percent. Oil imports would rise by 161 percent and account for 61 percent of the net increase in imports, followed in volumetric terms by increasing imports of coal (by 96 percent) and gas (by 270 percent). This would place a significant burden on the macro economy as India currently consumes 4.3 percent of the total world oil consumption and 7 percent of the total trade in oil. By 2035, India's share of the world's oil consumption would rise to 7 percent, while it would account for 11 percent of the total imports. India's share of the global LNG trade would increase from 6 percent today to 8 percent in 2035.

The second key challenge is the growth of carbon emissions. While India's energy intensity of GDP would decline by 1.6 percent per annum by 2035, India's slow-moving energy mix means that the carbon intensity of India's energy consumption would decline only modestly by 0.3 percent per annum by 2035. The net result is that CO_2 emissions from energy use would more than double, averaging a growth of 3.5 percent per annum. Over the final decade of the projection, from 2025 to 2035, India would account for more than a third of the growth in global GHG emissions, adding more than twice as much CO_2 as China during that decade. However, this would still allow India to meet its stated goal of reducing CO_2 intensity of GDP by 20 percent by 2021, a year later than the target date (UNFCCC 2011).

4. Alternate Cases

There are, of course, many uncertainties surrounding any projection of India's energy future. To illustrate this, two alternative cases are described in the following subsections. One explores the implications of assuming a higher GDP growth path. The other examines the possibility of a "greener" growth path with greater gains in energy efficiency and a stronger push on renewables. Neither of these examples is a full-blown scenario. They represent a rough form of sensitivity analysis in which we adjust a few key parameters relative to our reference case. We do not attempt to assign any probabilities to these cases—they are simply designed to illustrate the range of possibilities for India.

4.1. Implications of a Higher GDP Growth Path

If India aspires to higher GDP growth than the assumed growth rates in the base case described earlier, what might happen? What would be the impact of assuming GDP growth of, say, 7.5 percent per annum during 2013–35 while keeping the relationship between economic growth and sectoral energy demand the same as in the reference case? Total energy demand growth would increase to around 5 percent per annum (Table 6, "High" case). Both oil and gas would grow slightly faster than 5 percent, and coal slightly slower.

This case results in CO_2 emissions growing at 4.7 percent per annum, which would be a concern in a world that is increasingly likely to be carbon-constrained. Moreover, if India's own production of fossil fuels remains at

TABLE 6. India: Energy Consumption Growth and Shares, 2013–35 (%)

	Annual average growth, 2013–35 (%)			*Share of primary energy (%)*			
	Base	*High*	*Green*	*2013*	*Base*	*High*	*Green*
Oil	3.6	5.2	2.2	29	28	31	28
Gas	4.1	5.4	3.6	8	8	9	10
Coal	3.5	4.4	–2.0	55	51	49	21
Nuclear	7.2	8.0	7.6	1	3	2	4
Hydro	3.1	3.9	3.5	5	4	4	6
Renewables	9.0	9.8	16.0	2	6	5	31
Total	**3.8**	**5.0**	**2.4**	**100**	**100**	**100**	**100**

Source: BP (2015a) and authors' calculations.

the reference case level, higher domestic demand in this higher GDP growth case would result in a significant increase in energy imports.

Today, India imports a little over 40 percent of its energy consumption. By 2035, that would have risen to 44 percent in the base case and to 54 percent in the high GDP growth case. In volume terms, the net imports of fossil fuels would exceed to 900 Mtoe in 2035 in the high case, as compared to around 600 Mtoe in the reference base case. That level of imports is not infeasible—global supply flows could accommodate India's requirements, albeit with pressure on fuel prices. In this high growth case for India, China and India together would be importing around a quarter of the world's oil production and more than 40 percent of the world's LNG. In terms of oil trade, 16 percent of the global oil exports would find their way to India. The major challenge for this alternative case would, of course, be the question of whether the Indian economy could afford the import bill.

4.2. Implications of Green Growth

India is committed to playing its part in addressing the risk of climate change. Under what conditions is it possible that India's carbon emissions in 2035 would be no higher than they are today? The arithmetic of this case is relatively simple; finding a feasible policy set that could credibly deliver it is much more challenging. As compared to the reference base case, this greener alternative requires a much faster decline in energy intensity and a much more rapid shift from fossil to non-fossil fuels.[2]

The "green" case assumes that energy intensity declines at 3 percent per annum. This is quite a stretch for India, given that it starts already at a relatively low level, but similar rates of decline sustained for at least ten years have been seen in other rapidly developing Asian economies (for example, Taiwan, the Philippines). The result is total energy demand growing at just 2.4 percent per annum (Table 6).

This case also assumes that India's renewables grow at the same rate (16 percent per year) as in the EU over the past 20 years, and that both nuclear and hydroelectricity achieve production growth rates that sit between the base case and high case rates. Finally, among fossil fuels, gas is assumed to gain a larger share of primary energy, while oil maintains the same share as in the base case. That leaves coal being squeezed out, with quite a dramatic decline in its share of energy to just over 20 percent by 2035.

2. To keep the analysis simple, we have ignored the potential for carbon capture and sequestration in this case. If that technology were available to be deployed at scale, it would allow a larger share for coal to be consistent with the goal of stabilizing carbon emissions.

This case delivers zero growth in carbon emissions from energy use. It also sharply reduces net energy import requirements. The decline in coal demand leaves the level of coal consumption in 2035 below the current level of coal production, thereby eliminating the need for net coal imports. There would still be a requirement to import oil and gas, but overall, net energy imports in 2035 would be about half the base-case level and a third of the high-case level.

This alternative "green" case has much to commend it in terms of outcomes. However, it is clearly built on some very challenging assumptions. To illustrate the challenge, consider the policy interventions that have been required in the EU to secure the rapid and sustained growth of renewables. The Renewable Energy Directive 2009 established a binding target of 20 percent for the share of renewables in EU's final energy consumption by 2020. Individual EU countries then committed to a range of differentiated targets to achieve this EU aggregate goal and submitted National Renewable Energy Action Plans, which laid out sectoral targets and policy measures. A simple measure of the degree of policy support for renewables is the estimated amount of subsidy that has been paid to renewable energy sources. The most recent report for the European Commission (De Vos et al. 2014) cites a figure of €40 billion for renewable energy support in 2012.

5. Conclusion

Rising GDP and the changing structure of the economy in India have resulted in a significant growth in energy consumption over the past 30 years, even as the energy mix appears to be stubbornly dominated by fossil fuels. However, the significant shifts in the energy mix, away from coal and toward oil until the 2000s and the subsequent recovery in coal's share, followed by a period of competition between coal and gas, illustrates the potential for change. This change is most affected by the changes in domestic production, especially of gas and renewables.

Going forward, India's primary energy consumption is expected to grow at a rate outpacing most large developing countries. Coal will continue to dominate the energy mix, though it will lose some market share to gas and renewables. Other implications of this slow-moving energy mix are observed in overall energy intensity and carbon emissions. While India's energy intensity and emissions have declined over time, these gains are mostly due to improving energy efficiency. However, with a relatively inflexible energy mix, the gains from improving the share of more energy- and carbon-efficient fuels would remain limited. More significantly for India, domestic production has been sluggish in responding to energy demand growth, and imports are likely to continue rising. This increased share of energy imports as a percentage of GDP would place a significant burden on the economy.

References

Batancourt, R.R. 1981. "An Econometric Analysis of Peak Electricity Demand in the Short Run," *Energy Economics*, 3(1): 14–29.

BP. 2015a. *BP Energy Outlook 2035*. London: BP.

———. 2015b. *Statistical Review of World Energy 2015*, June. London: BP.

Berger, C., R. Dubois, A. Haurie, E. Lessard, R. Loulou, and J.P. Waaub (1992). "Canadian MARKAL: An Advanced Linear Programming System for Energy and Environmental Modelling," *INFOR* 30(3): 222–39.

Bose, R.K. and M. Shukla. 1999. "Elasticities of Electricity Demand in India," *Energy Policy*, 27(3): 137–46.

CSTEP. 2015. *A Sustainable Development Framework for India's Climate Policy: Interim Report*. Bangalore: Centre for Study of Science, Technology and Policy.

De Vos, Rolf, Pieter van Breevoort, Niklas Höhne, Thomas Winkel, and Catherine Sachweh. 2014. "Assessing the EU 2030 Climate and Energy Targets." A Briefing Paper. Available online at: http://www. ecofys. com/files/files/ecofys-2014-assessing-the-eu-2030-targets.pdf (accessed on August 12, 2014).

Dubash, Navroz K., Radhika Khosla, Narasimha D. Rao, and K. Rahul Sharma. 2015. *Informing India's Energy and Climate Debate: Policy Lessons from Modelling Studies*. Climate Initiative Research Report. New Delhi: Centre for Policy Research.

EIA. 2013. *International Energy Outlook 2013*. Washington, DC: U.S. Energy Information Administration.

Garg, A., D. Ghosh, and P.R. Shukla. 2001. "Integrated Energy and Environment Modelling System and Application for India," *OPSEARCH (Special Issue on Energy and Environment Modelling)*, 38(1).

Hourcade, J.C. 1996. "Estimating the Cost of Mitigating Greenhouse Gases," in *Climate Change 1995: Economic and Social Dimensions of Climate Change*. Cambridge, MA: Cambridge University Press.

IEA. 1997. *Mapping the Energy Future—Energy Modelling and Climate Change Policy (Energy and Environment Policy Analysis Series)*. Paris: International Energy Agency.

———. 2014. *World Energy Outlook 2014*. Paris: International Energy Agency.

IPCC. 2001. *Climate Change 2001: Mitigation, Report of Working Group III to the Third Assessment Report of the IPCC*. Cambridge, MA: Cambridge University Press.

Kamerschen, D.R. and D.V. Porter. 2004. "The Demand for Residential, Industrial and Total Electricity, 1973–1998," *Energy Economics,* 26(1): 87–100.

Loulou, R., P.R. Shukla, and A. Kanudia. 1997. *Energy and Environment Policies for a Sustainable Future.* New Delhi: Allied Publishers Ltd.

MIT (Massachusetts Institute of Technology). 1997. *Energy Technology Availability: Review of Longer Term Scenarios for Development and Deployment of Climate-Friendly Technologies.* Cambridge, MA: MIT Energy Laboratory.

NITI Aayog. 2015. *India Energy Security Scenarios (IESS) 2047.* New Delhi: NITI Aayog.

Pachauri, S. 2002. *An Energy Analysis of Household Consumption in India.* Zurich: The Swiss Federal Institute of Technology.

Pandey, R. 1998. *Integrated Energy Systems Modelling for Policy Analysis and Operational Planning.* Ahmedabad: Indian Institute of Management.

———. 2002. "Energy Policy Modelling: Agenda for Developing Countries," *Energy Policy,* 30(2): 97–106.

Planning Commission. 2014. *Low Carbon Strategies for Inclusive Growth.* New Delhi: Planning Commission, Government of India.

Sengupta, R. 1993. *Energy Modelling for India: Towards a Policy for Commercial Energy.* New Delhi: Planning Commission, Government of India.

Shell. 2014. "Shell Scenarios."Available online at http://www.shell.com/energy-and-innovation/the-energy-future/scenarios.html (accessed on May 17, 2016).

Shukla, P.R. (1996). "Greenhouse Gas Mitigation for India: Future Emissions, Policy Analysis and Perspectives on Modelling." AIM Interim Paper. Tsukuba, Japan.

Shukla, P.R., Amit Garg, and Hem H. Dholakia. 2015. *Energy—Emissions Trends and Policy Landscape for India.* New Delhi: Allied Publishers.

Shukla, P.R. and A. Kanudia. 1997. "Future Energy and Greenhouse Gas Emissions Modelling from India: Modelling and Analysis," in *Energy Strategies and Greenhouse Gas Mitigation.* New Delhi: Allied Publishers Ltd.

TERI. 2013. *The Energy Report—India: 100 Renewable Energy by 2050.* New Delhi: WWF India.

Tiwari, P. (2000). "An Analysis of Sectoral Energy Intensity in India," *Energy Policy*, 20(11): 549–66.

UNFCCC. 2011. *Compilation of Information on Nationally Appropriate Mitigation Actions to be Implemented by Parties Not Included in Annex I to the Convention.* New York: United Nations Framework Convention on Climate Change, United Nations.

World Bank. 2011. *Energy Intensive Sectors of the Indian Economy.* Washington, DC: Energy, Environment, Water Resources and Climate Change Units Sustainable Development Department, South Asia Region, The World Bank.

Zarnikau, J. 2003. "Functional Forms in Energy Demand Modeling," *Energy Economics,* 25(6): 603–13.

Comments and Discussion*

Navroz K. Dubash
Centre for Policy Research

I have three sets of points I would like to make. The first looks at the alternative causal narratives of different trends—the first part of Kaushik's paper. What is behind the elevator description of this going up and coming down? The second is to reflect a little bit on the models. I am not a modeler. I think that they are useful and constructive to engage with, but in general, I also remain skeptical. Anupam and I have done a little division of labor, and he will deal with models. And third, what are the big questions we are trying to answer and how?

First on the elevator part. Kaushik's presentation was quite rich and did better justice to the material than the paper, because the paper went into a lot of detail about trends in different time periods but you did not really get a sense of the larger narrative. What are the explanatory factors? Why do we see something going up at this point and going down at the other point? The narratives are important because that is what really sticks in your mind and it also signals the policy direction. It is what allows a policy conversation, and a lot of my comments are going to be about how we use analysis like this for policy because that is, presumably, the interest of this forum.

First, the paper has some really great stories, but I would like to actually see more of these. My favorite was the one about how post-Fukushima we saw a spike in gas prices, driving gas up to unaffordable levels and, therefore, an increase in coal imports. In another presentation by Kaushik, I heard him tell a fascinating story a couple of years ago: While the Europeans pumped a lot of money into renewable energy, the Americans instead invested in shale, essentially driving down the price of coal in the United States, which then went in and undercut all the renewables in Europe. That kind of story is actually what makes these trends really interesting, and I would encourage the revision of this paper to bring about some of those larger storylines a little bit better.

* To preserve the sense of the discussions at the IPF, these discussants' comments reflect the views expressed at the IPF and do not take into account revisions to the original conference paper in response to these and other comments, even though the IPF Volume itself contains the revised paper. The original conference version of the paper is available on www.ncaer.org.

In addition, I felt there was a bit too much of reliance on unicausal stories. So, for example, oil or gas goes down because there is a decreased investment without actually explaining why that is. But, of course, there is a complex political economy behind that, which anybody who reads even the front page of the financial papers in India knows. For example, there is a story about the credibility of governance and pricing arrangements in gas and the sanctity of contracts: What kind of price is obtained for gas and what is the basis for that price? Something similar is now going on in power purchase agreements based on coal power. Moreover, if you want to think about coal in India, you cannot really think about coal prices without thinking about the implicit subsidy that the railways provide to passenger rail on the back of freight cost, which then has implications for the competitiveness of our coal. These kinds of larger stories could, thus, at least be alluded to, even in a secondary way, that is, what lies behind this lack of investment.

An overarching point: early in the paper, it would be nice to get a little bit more of a sense of what are the big questions we are trying to answer. Are we saying it is really about imports of fuels? Are we saying it is about the mechanisms of encouraging investment? I did not really feel that I got that from the beginning of the paper.

Turning on to the models, my issue with a lot of modeling studies is that they sort of quite blithely embrace the fallacy of false concreteness. There is a number that is put out there, and you are not really sure how credible that number is. By way of example, I am going to take up with Kaushik an issue on one number related to the "green scenario" that Kaushik put out. Under the "green scenario" of the BP study, the per capita energy consumption rises by only 1.5 percent as compared to a 4.5 percent increase in the base case. That, *a priori*, makes it sound like India should be very wary of the climate negotiations. But if you dig into it a little bit, it turns out that the green scenario has been constructed to assume zero growth in carbon from energy over the next 20 years! That is not a realistic scenario which anybody talks about, nor is it on the table for India in climate negotiations. So, you have to have the context and assumptions right, otherwise scenarios and model results can be misleading.

One reason I find it hard to engage with a lot of modeling studies is perhaps that they are so complex; it is very difficult to get a sense of the reasoning behind various assumptions. So, I benchmarked this study against seven studies we looked at in a CPR analysis[1] to get a sense of some of the differences in the underlying assumptions and how well they are explained.

1. http://www.cprindia.org/research/reports/informing-india%E2%80%99s-energy-and-climate-debate-policy-lessons-modelling-studies.

The most important assumption, of course, is about GDP growth rates. Depending on the nature of the model, GDP is either endogenously or exogenously assumed. The studies we looked at, which are domestic studies, assume that over the next 15 years, the average GDP growth will be somewhere between 7 and 8.75 percent a year, with no lower end cases below 7 percent. I think that actually the BP paper is much more sensible with a GDP growth rate assumption of around 4.6 percent. Interestingly, nobody is really occupying the middle ground, which is probably where we will end up if we are lucky. So, that obviously makes a huge difference. There is an interesting sidebar here: International studies uniformly have lower growth rate assumptions than national studies because the national studies feel they have to shoot for an aspirational target. Of course, in the process, we might be shooting ourselves in the foot in climate negotiations because it looks like we are going to be a huge share of the future problem, because high GDP growth typically requires higher emissions, when, in fact, we are going to be a much smaller share of the problem if we have more reasonable assumptions.

Then there are policy assumptions. A lot of these numbers are just extremely hard to defend. Why does BP assume 80 gigawatts of solar energy by 2035? India's low carbon study projects 3 gigawatts of solar energy by 2030 in its baseline scenario, presumably based on current capacity, which is, frankly, ridiculous, and 110 gigawatts of solar by 2030 in its low carbon policy scenario. Which of these numbers do we take seriously and why? There has to be a much more of a reasoned process, and I think that the paper has to spend a little bit more time explaining why particular numbers are used and the rationale behind them, and contextualize them a little bit more.

Another example related to the assumptions is that the elasticity of energy consumption falls from 0.85 to 0.65 percent by 2035 in the BP paper. Now, what if we actually manage to get manufacturing to increase? Will we then see this decline in energy elasticity? It is not really clear.

So, where do these modeling results take us? I put the BP paper up on the left with CPR's summary of primary energy on the right from the model scenario comparative analysis that we undertook. I scaled this so the scale is approximately the same, and you will see that the primary energy required according to BP is of the order of about 1100 million tons of oil equivalent or MTOE (in 2035), that is, well below even the lowest case in the modeling comparison study, which is between 1200 and 1600 (by 2030–32). That is a pretty big difference. How does a policy maker take this seriously? What does he or she do with it? This point is underscored when you look at a single number like carbon. CPR's model comparison basically shows that

Indian emissions might double or triple by 2030. Again, a pretty big range. How do you enter a negotiation space or plan domestic policy if you do not know whether your emissions will double or triple during a 15-year period?

Hence, how do we move beyond this? I think the paper really needs to dig into some of these underlying assumptions and give some sense of what the outcomes really turn on. All the analysts are doing their work in silos. Let us have some common assumptions leading to common reference cases and then you can build some sensible policy cases. When this paper is revisited, we could best use this enormous amount of material and really world-class modeling to extract some of the stories perhaps a little better than the authors currently do, tell us a little bit more about the assumptions, and focus it better around a few key questions.

Let me just end with one last point. Energy policy debates are no longer just about supply side issues, such as can we increase our coal to 1,000 million tons or not? They are also about achieving different objectives, such as energy access, energy security, assured energy for growth, local environmental quality (in particular air pollution, which is becoming a big deal), and global environmental protection. There are potential synergies and tradeoffs across all these things. Until the models get to the point where they can start helping you think about those synergies and tradeoffs, their utility is going to be limited. Maybe the paper can reflect upon that too.

Anupam Khanna

Former Chief Economist, Shell and NASSCOM

I would like to thank Shekhar and NCAER for inviting me to discuss this paper. I want to state right away that my comments will be on the draft paper itself, which is slightly different from the presentation Kaushik just delivered. I think the presentation addresses one or two of my earlier concerns, so I will skip those. I also want to congratulate NCAER for including this topic in the IPF because it addresses, or at least I hope it will by the time we are done with it, the "missing middle" problem that Dr Bardhan referred to in his talk earlier. Over the last six years since my return to India, I find that about 80 to 90 percent of the research seminars and analytic work that I read coming out of India is on either macro–macro or micro–micro and very little on the middle where the policy tyre hits the road. A lot of events I have attended are full of aims and exhortations, with zero analysis about the instruments in the middle, including policy incentives and programs where public money is actually being spent.

I will list very quickly the paper's contents and my take on them. The first topic, which Navroz has already talked about, covers the demand and supply of primary energy since 1980. The discussion in the paper is mainly descriptive. The authors have got some proximate correlates about oil and gas, but these provide no insight and the implications that are drawn out are pretty obvious. There is no model or any analysis which relates energy mix, import dependence, or energy intensity. There is no counterfactual or any drilling down on their drivers. The Indian energy system is, in some ways, very, very simple because we are so starved of energy. We have a demand side, which is pretty much going with a certain set of drivers; a supply side, which is essentially autonomous; and then we have a huge import trade to bridge the gap. I found the paper somewhat confusing wherein the authors ascribe the production levels to the consumption because I do not think there is any direct relationship and almost all the analytic work that has been done to date does not really make that connection.

There is another big omission in the first part of the paper about what went up and what went down, what Navroz called "the elevator story." The authors need to talk about what has been happening to the international markets. While one slide describes the status of all commodity markets for the past decade, the next one is about what has been happening to the energy market. So, if one is going to talk about oil versus gas, he needs to know what happened to the relative prices of oil and gas which substitute for each other in many ways. Not only that; one has to worry about what happened to oil and gas globally versus what happened in Asia. We all know that while the oil market is global, the gas market is actually still regionally fragmented, with at least three different regions showing distinctive pricing. Another part that was somewhat confusing in the paper relates to the demand side, though I think the elements are there and perhaps a little more work can rectify the problem. The story that the table tells in five-year segments is that the drivers of consumption seem to be changing, resulting in big changes and shares of primary energy. Some of this had to do with prices. Another part had to do with other factors. What were they? For example, the point that is made here, if you compare what happened in the late 1990s versus the early 1990s, is that coal only contributed about a third to the increment in primary fuel consumption in the latter period, as opposed to typically what had been its incremental contribution (about half). Why was that? Why did oil come in so high? Is it all about the transport demand, the point noted by Kaushik?

The other big problem with all of this is the huge data inconsistencies. I am not talking just about the assumptions and estimates of elasticities, for instance, which even in the best of studies have wide differences.

There appears to be a limited factual basis even on very fundamental questions such as what has the consumption been in recent years and what is actually the power demand? Does the electricity consumption data include all the varieties of captive power or not? What are motor vehicles contributing in terms of the demand for oil? All these are highly variable. If you give me a result you want, I can pretty much derive it with suitable methodological frameworks and assumptions and rig the model in a way to give you that. So, I think there is a basic issue with both overly simple and overly complex models. This type of model is good for exploratory purposes, but when one is doing serious policy analysis, he needs to think about the analytic framework and choose an approach to fit the purpose.

There are two or three well-established approaches in this regard. The paper refers to the scenario approach, for example, what the other global energy major Shell does, or what the security agencies in the United States versus what the energy agencies (for example, IEA or US Department of Energy) do, which tend to go more along this route, albeit with key differences in the details. The other big tendency today in terms of modeling is that most of the models that Kaushik referred to tend to be highly mechanistic and very deterministic in terms of economic mechanisms, even though they have certain stochastic elements in terms of either parameters or economic shocks. The shortcomings of this approach have been amply documented, and there is a new trend which is trying to get a better fix on the reality by incorporating two things, technology and behavioral change, into these models. I believe that would make a big difference in terms of some of the policy conclusions.

Navroz has already expressed his skepticism about energy models. I think I have also pointed out that there are so many moving parts and assumptions that you have to be careful about how you interpret these results or how seriously you take them. But, at the same time, one does need some way of making decisions or at least getting comfort from these decisions. One may not know what might happen in a particular area but he might want to pose the question: "What if?" For this, I mentioned that one option was the scenario approach, but there are other complementary ways as well. Consider what occurred in the United States. In the late 1970s, that is, during the time immediately after the first energy crisis, there was a lot of preoccupation with numbers. On going back and reading the literature, one discovers that after some time, they realized that this preoccupation with numbers was actually getting in the way of serious policy. So, I think one of the most innovative things that occurred was the establishment of the Energy Modelling Forum. Many of the well-known names in energy policy analysis today, such as

Jim Sweeney, Bill Hogan, John Weyant, and many others from different institutions, were participating actively in the discussion. The idea here was to get all the modelers to engage with each other and basically make them talk not about "computerese" and numbers but key issues, and find out the differences. Of course, to make that a serious exercise, given the vastness and complexity of the US energy system, they ended up having to take up particular themes. I went back and looked at the papers from 1982 onwards, which describe the first seven years of the forum, and I was amazed by the relevance for us of the six or seven topics in another age on another continent that were actually used as a way of getting the models to talk to each other so that one could offer consistent advice to policymakers. The topics I have shown in the slide—energy in the economy, coal in transition, electricity demand, aggregate elasticity of energy demand, and oil and gas supply—are what I have been trying to persuade Navroz and a couple of other people, including Gireesh, to work on seriously.

I want to highlight just a few more major gaps. One of the biggest gaps in energy modeling for a geographically large country such as India, which applies to other countries too, is the issue of transport of energy. I just want to point out that two years ago, the biggest issue in terms of energy in India was the fact that we could not get coal to our power stations. I do not think anybody would disagree with that. This problem has, in fact, been persisting for at least 20 years, and we have not dealt with it. It is not that other countries have not had this problem. China faced exactly the same sort of situation in 1989. But their government dealt with it. The point is that unless one delves into the requisite analysis in some depth, many of the things that we talk about, including imports and moving coal to these power stations (50 percent of our rail freight today just entails moving coal for power), cannot be meaningfully framed in policy terms. Even if we say simplistically that we can import all the power and supply it to power stations, we will find it impossible to do so. The energy policy goes totally haywire. Gireesh can take this up in his remarks and perhaps also address the transmission dimension.

Finally, I want to say that the energy agenda is much wider. This includes issues not just on the supply side but also on the demand side. I think the biggest bank for the buck of national effort comes from energy efficiency, not just technical but also allocative efficiency economy-wide. The issues of transport, renewable energy, and technology development also need to be considered. The imperative of energy access lies at the core of this. Lastly, there is an entire dimension that we have not talked about, which relates to many initiatives being taken by the government to promote energy efficiency and the use of renewables. A lot of money is being spent or programmed to spend, but there is hardly a single study which actually looks at the effectiveness of such programs. I could only find one study done by Anand Sudarshan only recently. In other countries, many innovative programs continue to be introduced and evaluated, such as "cash for coolers" (and refrigerators and air conditioners) in Mexico, rationing to affect long-term behavior in Brazil, the CFL distribution process, and better information on energy labels. All these are highly pertinent to India, but I think we need to look seriously at what works and what does not before we pour a lot of money into such programs.

General Discussion

Vijay Joshi asked Navroz Dubash his view on the conclusion of the Indian Planning Commission's 2005 study on "Low Carbon Strategies for Inclusive Growth," that a low carbon growth strategy would reduce India's average GDP growth rate to 2030 by only 0.15 percentage points below the study's baseline growth scenario. Was that credible?

Navroz Dubash replied that the exact number was lower GDP growth over 2007 to 2030 by 0.16 percentage points, resulting in the 2030 GDP being lower by 3.33 percent. This was not particularly credible, though it would be a wonderful result if it were to come true. Deeper analysis of the work suggests that the low carbon strategy involves a series of questionable assumptions including about energy efficiency gains from appliances and the growth rate of renewable energy. There appear to be only five or six concrete changes between the two scenarios, but it was not clear if the model was fully accounting for either their costs or their gains. For example, it does not account for cobenefit gains in air pollution reduction, which should ideally be assessed. He was not sure how far policy should be based on it exclusively.

Rajnish Mehra noted that in a general equilibrium model, a change in the GDP growth rate also changes the discount rate, which is a function of the growth rate. So we get this small change in GDP that the Planning Commission study got if we keep the cost of capital constant. Mehra also wondered, referring to the graph on nuclear energy in India in the paper, why a country that is highly dependent on imported energy and has access to fairly good nuclear technology does not generate more of its power through fission.

Kaushik Deb replied that every additional nuclear power plant built anywhere has been more expensive than the last one. At its best, when it was about 6–7 percent of the global energy mix, nuclear energy was present in only nine countries, but has been losing market share since then. When renewables accounted for 6 percent of the global energy mix, they were present in 93 countries, with costs declining constantly with increasing deployment scale. Similarly in India, renewables have turned out to be much more cost effective and less challenging. Mehra commented that taking into account the imputed cost of global warming would improve the relative cost comparison of nuclear technology, at least with fossils. France had shown that.

Agreeing with Mehra, Deb commented that nuclear works best where governments are able to execute challenging decisions, and perhaps not that much attention is paid to the difference between financial and economic rates of return. So, countries like China and Russia have achieved renewables growth, but India, characterized by considerable reliance on the private sector for generation, finds it difficult to bridge these rates of return. Since no private insurer is typically willing to insure a nuclear power plant, this has to be socialized, which makes nuclear difficult in countries that depend largely on markets and where execution of top-down mandated targets is difficult. Nuclear power has been declining in every OECD country, including France and Japan, though the latter is rebooting some plants that were operational before the Fukushima disaster, but at a much lower scale of operation. These, and similarly the US nuclear plants, are unlikely to be replaced, though their life may be extended for a couple of decades.

Anupam Khanna noted that nuclear is typically never an integral part of economic or financial modeling but is incorporated exogenously in almost every energy model, except very specifically in determining conditions under which nuclear energy would be competitive. Similarly, renewables in India typically tend not to be part of energy models, and these are exogenously brought in with one set of results if market clearing mechanisms are used and another when social goals are sought to be achieved such as accelerating the process of adopting renewables. Energy modeling is heavily guided by the heavy reliance on "expert inputs," also the case for this paper. Dubash added that all the domestic Indian models overproject the nuclear capacity to be between 15 and 42 gigawatts of nuclear power by 2030, though only 2 gigawatts have been added in the last decade. There appears to be an official number for nuclear power, basically 60 gigawatts, and it seems that no official pronouncement can go down below that.

Shekhar Shah asked Dubash to comment on the future of renewables in India, given the survey he had done. Can India achieve the government's recent target of adding 100 gigawatts of solar energy by 2022?

Gireesh Pradhan (chair) averred that he was thoroughly in awe of economists but wanted to point out that India is currently in a state of scarcity amidst plenty. Installed capacity is almost 270,000 MW against a peak demand yesterday of 127,000 MW, and yet we had a shortage of 2 percent. We have concentrated a lot on the supply side, mostly using coal, and this will remain the focus in the short and medium terms. So, the capacity is there, but we are not able to meet the current demand, and, furthermore, 36 percent of Indians have no access to electricity, so there is a big question of India's energy security. The other problem that the government needs to tackle is the poor financial health of distribution companies, which makes the entire power sector extremely shaky. The power sector has a huge debt overhang and is adding losses of some ₹40,000 crores every year.

On climate change, Pradhan felt that there was no need to be defensive, with India being at just 920 KWh per capita as against a global average of 2,800 KWh and its CO_2 emission far less than China's. On solar, the present government increased the previous goal of 20,000 MW of grid connected solar to 100 GW by 2022, part of an overall goal of 175 GW of renewables by then, comprising in addition to solar, 60 GW from wind, 10 GW from biomass, and 5 GW from small hydro. The approach on solar is to take advantage of short gestation lags and install large plants, assuming that the substantial funding and land acquisition needed will be available. The problem will be when large amounts of renewable power have to be integrated into the grid, requiring ancillary services and balancing to transmit power from multiple sellers to multiple buyers in a complex environment where service reliability must be assured and the standards for the actual grid connection must be established and maintained.

Shah picked up on Khanna's mention of the Energy Modeling Forum (EMF) at Stanford University and suggested setting up a similar forum in India to bring together leading experts and decision-makers from government, industry, universities, and other research organizations to study important energy and environmental issues. Would that be doable?

Khanna added the Stanford EMF remains very active, though it has moved on to next generation issues. He felt that Dubash had already started framing the key issues for such a forum in India by reviewing six or seven significant studies in this area. But maintaining such a forum necessitates a lot of commitment from the members beyond just meeting at regular conclaves. It requires a serious commitment to putting data together and ensuring its authenticity and availability, some of the things that also came out during the first few rounds of the EMF.

Dubash fully agreed that something like the Stanford EMF was needed in India, though his own group was more an intelligent consumer of models not a producer. Even consumption was not easy, which is why they had done the review of models. And there would be serious institutional and other challenges in setting up a forum, since there are a handful of organizations in India who do these models, and the utility of these models entails some kind of a U-curve. South Africa has only one serious modeling group, which nobody really contests, so it is at one end of the U. We are somewhere in the middle with the multiplicity of Indian models, but none quite at the definitive level required to build a serious dialogue, and also not yet at the point at the other end of the U when we can ensure the sensible use and value of the multiple models. Dubash said that they had requested NITI Aayog to play a strategic, cross-ministerial, long-term role in energy modeling and policy dialogue—they already have an in-house spreadsheet-based model that can form the foundation for such dialogue. He felt that setting up this kind of a forum would not come about automatically and would need a sustained and systematic collective action.

Khanna felt that the NITI spreadsheet model was good for some dialogue but was not really a model. He mentioned that the US Department of Energy's Pacific Northwest National Laboratory (PNNL) in Washington State had undertaken some work on an Asian energy forum, but the problem was the scarcity of people. And international efforts may be crowding out others. At the very least, this will require considerable leadership, commitment, and buy-in.

Shah noted that Arvind Panagariya would be delivering the IPF lecture that evening, and the suggestion about an energy forum at NITI could be conveyed to him. He referred to a similar exercise in a forum on growth macro-modeling undertaken by the erstwhile Planning Commission that was run by Commission Member Kirit Parekh with several institutions involved whose work was also funded by the Commission. These met regularly to present their model results and to build a dialogue around them. He mentioned that this forum added considerably to NCAER's capacities in macro-modeling.

ILA PATNAIK*
Ministry of Finance, Government of India

AJAY SHAH†
NIPFP

NIRVIKAR SINGH‡
University of California, Santa Cruz, and *NCAER*

Foreign Currency Borrowing by Indian Firms: Toward a New Policy Framework§

ABSTRACT India has a complex multidimensional system of capital controls for foreign currency borrowing by firms. In this paper, we summarize existing regulations, review the outcomes, and discuss areas of concern and recent policy changes. Unhedged foreign currency exposure for firms, the complexity and uncertainty in the policy framework as it has evolved, and questions about regulation-making processes are highlighted. In an emerging economy with a managed exchange rate and incomplete markets, foreign currency borrowing poses systemic risks when left unhedged by large firms that constitute a significant part of the gross domestic product. We identify policy directions to help address these concerns.

Keywords: *Capital Controls, External Debt, Market Failure*

JEL Classification: *F3, G1, D6*

1. Introduction

A well-established concept in the field of international capital flows is the problem of "original sin": where governments or firms have currency mismatches with foreign borrowing that is typically in dollars. When such exposures exist, there is the possibility of substantial balance sheet effects in the event of a large depreciation. In India, foreign currency

* *ilapatnaik@gmail.com*
† *ajay.shah@nipfp.org.in*
‡ *boxjenk@ucsc.edu*
§ We thank Radhika Pandey, Apoorva Gupta, Pramod Sinha, Mohit Desai, Shekhar Hari Kumar and Sanhita Sapatnekar for valuable inputs into this work.

borrowing (FCB) has grown sevenfold, from $20 billion in 2004 to $140 billion in 2014. This has generated concerns about systemic risk.

Rational firms are conscious about the destruction of wealth that comes with a large depreciation and unhedged exposure, and are likely to avoid currency mismatches. The moral hazard hypothesis suggests that firms *choose* to have unhedged FCB because governments and central banks communicate their intent to manage the exchange rate when faced with large depreciations. Concerns about unhedged FCB by firms are a greater issue in emerging markets where the monetary policy regime targets the exchange rate, as compared with mature market economies with floating exchange rates.

Capital controls are proposed as a way of avoiding moral hazard associated with FCB under pegged exchange rates. The puzzle lies in designing a capital control system that interferes with unhedged FCB but not with foreign borrowing by firms with hedges. For firms which have natural hedges, unhedged FCB is a valuable source of low cost capital. These firms include not just net exporters, but net producers of tradeables where domestic output prices are set by import parity pricing.

What is a policy framework where hedged firms are able to obtain the economic benefits of unhedged FCB, while avoiding it? One strategy is to combat the moral hazard at the root cause: the monetary policy framework. A monetary policy framework which enshrines inflation as the target, and not the exchange rate, would remove the moral hazard. Inflation targeting central banks are, in general, associated with greater exchange rate flexibility.

The second element of the policy question is the capital control regime. The Indian strategy for capital controls on FCB presently involves many kinds of restrictions. The dominant form of currency borrowing is "External Commercial Borrowing" (ECB) by companies.[1] Rules restrict who can borrow, who can lend, how much can be borrowed, at what price, what end-use the borrowed resources can be applied for, who can offer a credit guarantee, when borrowed proceeds must be brought into India, when loans can be prepaid, when loans can be refinanced, procedural rules for all these activities, and rules for banks to force all borrowers to hedge currency exposure. Further, loans above a certain amount require approval.

1. The term ECB has a specific meaning in the context of Indian regulations on borrowing from abroad, and is different from the term "foreign currency borrowing" in several respects. The differences will be made clear later in the paper.

The present policy framework is highly complex, uncertain, and, as has been suggested by the Sahoo Committee, *Report III* that was set up by the government to review the existing framework, fails to address some of the concerns of policy makers. For example, policy makers are concerned about the level of unhedged foreign currency exposure (FCE) in the economy, issues of discretion and transparency, and policy uncertainty in the framework. Further, the recent focus on modern regulation-making processes and rule of law has raised questions about the appropriateness of the existing policy framework. We compare the present distribution of FCB among firms against a normative ideal (foreign borrowing by naturally hedged firms), and find large deviations.

In recognition of these problems, in recent times, some policy changes have been introduced in the capital controls that may help reduce currency mismatch. These include allowing firms to undertake rupee-denominated ECB, an increase in the caps on FII investment in rupee-denominated corporate bonds (the cap has increased slowly to USD 51 billion in 2015), monitoring of the hedge ratio for ECB by requiring firms to report these, requiring infrastructure firms to fully hedge their ECB, and prudential requirements for banks when lending to companies with unhedged FCE.

For Indian firms, markets for derivatives are illiquid and costly owing to restrictive regulations, making it unattractive to hedge explicitly through these markets. On the other hand, while some borrowers may have natural hedges, the policy framework for ECB does not take this into account. This helps explain why firms with natural hedges, such as domestic makers of tradeables, are not strongly present in FCB.

The current restrictions on ECBs raise concerns about engaging in ill-defined or poorly justified industrial policy, about the scale of economic knowledge required to write down the detailed prescriptive regulations, the impact upon the cost of business, and about rule of law. Recent research suggests that the large number of changes in the capital controls governing ECB are motivated by exchange rate policy and not systemic risk regulation. This raises questions about the process through which regulations are being made.

In the international discourse, there is renewed interest in capital controls, in particular in order to address the systemic risk associated with large-scale unhedged FCB by firms in countries with pegged exchange rates. The careful examination of the Indian capital controls on FCB suggests that the Indian framework has not been effective in permitting safe activities while reducing systemic risk.

2. The Existing Regulatory Framework

We now describe the present arrangements for capital controls against foreign borrowing by Indian firms. The present policy framework governing foreign borrowing by firms offers two alternative routes:

1. **Foreign currency borrowing:** Firms borrow in foreign currency denominated debt through ECB and trade credit.
2. **Rupee-denominated borrowing:** This route allows foreign investors to buy bonds issued locally, denominated in rupees. In this paper, we focus on the policy framework for FCB. Neither total borrowing shown in Figure 2 nor financial borrowing shows these figures. Recently, ECB in rupees has also been allowed.[2]

2.1. Foreign Currency Borrowing

Firms can access foreign borrowing primarily through two routes: Trade Credit and ECB. Trade credit includes suppliers' credit or buyers' credit.

ECB is foreign borrowing that is not trade credit, with a maturity greater than 3 years. There are two routes for doing ECB. Some classes of firms are permitted to borrow under certain conditions through an "automatic" route. When the loan size is above a prescribed limit, firms have to apply for "approval."

On November 30, 2015, RBI announced a revised framework of ECB. The revised ECB framework comprises three tracks with varying degrees of restrictions:[3]

1. Foreign currency denominated ECB with minimum average maturity of 3–5 years.
2. Long term foreign currency denominated ECB with minimum average maturity of 10 years.
3. Indian rupee-denominated ECB with minimum average maturity of 3–5 years.

2. Both foreign purchases of rupee-denominated bonds and rupee-denominated ECB involve foreigners lending money to Indian firms with accounting in rupee terms—only the channel for the transaction is different, but this entails parallel regulations. Of course, in either of these cases, currency mismatch or risk is not an issue.

3. See Reserve Bank of India (2015b).

Table 1 summarizes the following key elements of control on foreign borrowing:

1. *Eligible borrowers*: The regulatory framework specifies the entities that are allowed to access ECB under Track I, Track II and Track III. As an example, real estate investment trusts (REITs) and investment trusts (INVITs) are allowed to borrow under Track II but are not allowed under Track I. Further, non-bank financial companies (NBFCs) and NBFCs-micro finance institutions are allowed under Track III but are not allowed to borrow foreign currency denominated ECB under Track I and Track II.
2. *Eligible lenders*: The regulatory framework places restrictions on who can lend to Indian firms. Here also we see differential restrictions under the three tracks. As an example, overseas branches/subsidiaries of Indian banks are allowed to lend under Track I but not under Track II and Track III.[4]

TABLE 1. Regulatory Sub-categories for ECB and Trade Credits

Sub-category	*ECB**	*Trade credits automatic route*
Eligibility criteria to borrow	Eligible borrowers	
Controls on eligible lenders	Recognized lenders	
Quantitative caps and maturity restrictions	Amount and maturity	Amount and maturity
Price ceiling	All-in-cost ceiling	All-in-cost ceiling
Permitted activities with foreign exchange	End-use	End-use
Activities not permitted with foreign exchange	End-uses not permitted	
Guarantees by financial institutions	Guarantees	Guarantees
Remittance of borrowed funds into India	Parking of ECB proceeds	
Early repayment of ECB	Prepayment	
Additional ECB for repayment of ECB	Refinancing of an existing ECB	
Legal process	Procedure	Reporting arrangements

Source: RBI: Master Circular on ECBs and Trade Credits, July 2014.
Note: * Loans up to a certain ceiling can be automatically approved but need approval thereafter.

4. Obviously, restrictions on who can lend are not motivated by concerns about the risks incurred by borrowers, but rather (presumably) by issues such as money laundering and tax evasion.

3. *Cap on maximum amount that can be borrowed*: The framework specifies the maximum amount that can be borrowed under the automatic route. In addition, there are separate caps based on the category of eligible borrowers. The cap has increased from USD 500 million in 2006 to USD 750 million at present. If the loan is above this amount, it has to go through the approval route.
4. *All-in-cost ceilings*: An additional dimension of control is the all-in-cost ceiling. The regulator specifies a maximum level for the overall interest cost at which the borrowing occurs. Only potential borrowers who are able to access funds within this interest cost ceiling are allowed to do so; others may not borrow. At present, the all-in-cost ceiling is 300 basis points over the six-month London Interbank Offered Rate (LIBOR) for foreign currency denominated ECB with minimum average maturity of 3–5 years (Track I). The cost ceiling is 500 basis points over six-month LIBOR for tenor of more than 10 years (Track II). For Track III, the all-in-cost is determined on market conditions.
5. *End-use requirements*: The revised framework of ECB prescribes separate end-use requirements for the three tracks of ECB. For Track I, the framework lists the purposes for which ECB can be accessed. Track II offers a comparatively liberalized framework with a negative list of purposes for which ECB access is not allowed. Track III offers a marginally liberalized negative list.
6. *Hedging requirements*: There is no mandatory requirement to hedge. The framework maintains that entities raising ECB under Track I and Track II are required to follow the guidelines issued, *if any*, by the concerned sectoral or prudential regulator.
7. *Parking of borrowed proceeds abroad*: If funds are borrowed for rupee expenditure, they are required to be repatriated immediately. In the case of foreign currency expenditure, ECB proceeds may be retained abroad pending utilization. When retained abroad, the funds may be invested in prescribed assets.
8. *Issuance of guarantee*: The framework prohibits issuance of guarantee, standby letter of credit, letter of undertaking, or letter of comfort by banks, financial institutions, and non-banking financial companies from India relating to ECB.
9. *Prepayment*: The framework allows prepayment subject to compliance with the stipulated minimum maturity restrictions.
10. *Refinancing of existing ECB*: Borrowers are allowed to refinance their existing ECB by raising a fresh ECB, subject to the condition

that the fresh ECB is raised at a lower all-in-cost ceiling, and provided the residual maturity is not reduced. Such refinancing is not permitted by raising fresh ECB from overseas branches or subsidiaries of Indian banks.

11. *Procedural complexities*: The regulatory framework prescribes a detailed framework for raising funds through ECB. Entities desirous to raise ECB under the automatic route are required to approach an authorized dealer bank with their proposal along with a duly filled form. The authorized dealer shall ensure that the ECB is in compliance with applicable guidelines. For cases involving approval, the borrowers may approach the RBI with an application in prescribed format through the authorized dealer bank. Such cases are considered by an empowered committee set up by RBI.
12. *Hedging requirements implemented through banking regulation*: On January 15, 2014, India issued a set of guidelines or recommendations in the form of an informal "regulation" titled *Capital and provisioning requirements for exposures to entities with unhedged FCE*. In this, banks are asked to provision more, and hold more capital, when faced with a borrower who has unhedged currency exposure. This "regulation" features a certain approach on defining and measuring unhedged currency exposure.

3. Broad Facts about Firm Foreign Borrowing

In this section, we show broad empirical facts about foreign borrowing by Indian firms, and descriptive statistics about foreign borrowing that are obtained from firm-level data. In some respects, especially size, the characteristics of firms that avail of FCB are different from their counterparts, which do not (or perhaps cannot) do so. In other characteristics, FCB and non-FCB firms are not very different.

3.1. Time Series Aggregates

Figure 1 shows the ratio of outstanding ECB to gross domestic product (GDP).[5] ECB as a ratio of GDP stood at 7.9 percent at the end of 2013–14. There is some year-to-year variability in this ratio, but we do not wish to

5. ECB data has been sourced from *India's External Debt: A Status Report*, which is released by the Ministry of Finance (Department of Economic Affairs 2014).

FIGURE 1. External Commercial Borrowing as percent of GDP

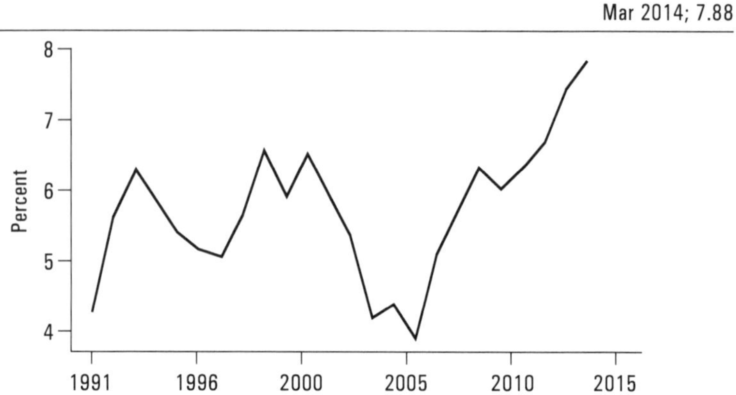

Source: *India's External Debt: A Status Report* (Various editions, Department of Economic Affairs 2014), and National Income Account statistics.

speculate as to the causes, and there are not enough years of data to claim any trend.

3.2. Firm-level Borrowing

We now describe FCB using firm-level data, drawing upon the CMIE database. We focus on non-financial firms only, in order to avoid non-comparability of accounting information between financial firms and non-financial firms. ECB is not directly visible in the data. We observe FCB, which measures debt taken by a company denominated in a currency other than the Indian rupee, from any source.[6]

This definition includes trade credit. In other words, we observe FCB which is the sum of ECB and trade credit.[7] We are not able to disentangle

6. The definition of FCB in the CMIE database is: Any loan taken by the company in a currency other than in Indian rupees is a foreign currency loan. Examples of such loans are loans taken from foreign banks, foreign currency loans taken from foreign branches of Indian banks, foreign currency loans taken from Indian banks, loans taken from EXIM banks, loans taken from multinational lending institutions such as World Bank, IBRD and Asian Development Bank, ECB, suppliers/buyers credit, global depository receipts, and American depositary receipts.

7. A further caveat should be noted, namely that the accounting of both ECB and trade credit in the data is not quite complete. For example, firms may receive and pay off trade credit within a period short enough for it not to appear in a year-end balance sheet. Another possibility is that some ECB is received in tranches, and, if paid off early, may also not appear in the observed balance sheet. In some sense, while it would be ideal to measure these more transitory instances of borrowing, they are of less concern precisely because they do not show up on balance sheets.

FIGURE 2. Aggregate Prowess Firm-level Foreign Currency Borrowing Versus Total External Commercial Borrowing

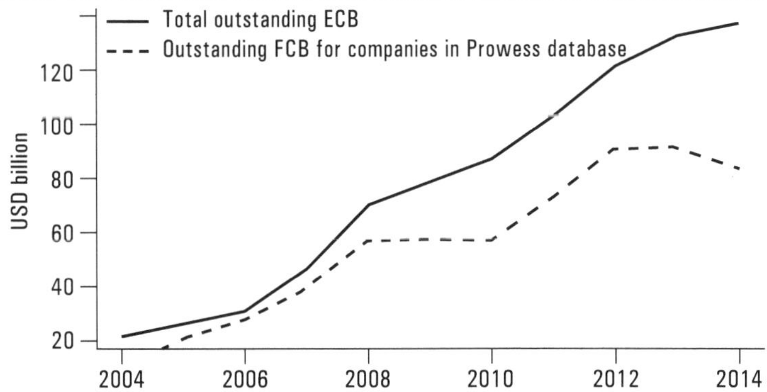

Source: *India's External Debt: A Status Report* (Various editions, Department of Economic Affairs, 2014) and CMIE Prowess.

ECB from trade credit. We examine the period from 2004 to 2015, which yields a dataset consisting of 127,963 firm-years.

Figure 2 juxtaposes the FCB of the firms in our dataset against the total ECB of the country. Borrowing by the firms in our dataset is overstated to the extent that it also contains trade credit. This graph suggests that our dataset captures a significant portion of the country's foreign borrowing.

Table 2 shows summary statistics at one point in time—the financial year 2011–12—for which 10,869 firms are observed. One can immediately see that less than 10 percent of the firms in that year's sample have documented FCB.

The firms which borrow abroad are, on average, much larger than those which do not. The median size of firms with foreign borrowing is measured as ₹5518.50 million, while the median size of firms without foreign borrowing is measured as ₹218.00 million; the firms that borrow abroad are, on average, more than 25 times bigger than the firms that do not. Information asymmetries and other factors captured in the home bias literature suggest that foreign investors are likely to favor large, internationally active, and low-credit risk firms. This is likely to be exacerbated by Indian capital controls, where all-in-cost ceilings impose interest rate caps and thereby limit foreign borrowing to firms with low-credit risk. These two issues may be coming together to restrict FCB to much bigger firms.

We examine three internationalization measures, namely exporting, importing, and foreign institutional investment. Firms that borrow abroad are much more internationalized, by all three measures. Half of the non-FCB

TABLE 2. Descriptive Statistics for Firms with and without Foreign Currency Borrowing in Companies in Prowess Database. 2011–12

*Variable**	*Category*	*Mean*	*SD*	*Min*	*25th*	*Median*	*75th*	*Max*	*Observed*
Size (Rs. Million)	FCB firms	32790.49	153958.44	7.80	1672.40	5518.50	17105.05	2757054.80	907
	Non-FCB firms	3300.65	23200.35	0.10	30.10	218.00	1181.30	1322338.00	9962
FII holding (%)	FCB firms	7.95	8.75	0.00	0.86	4.87	12.63	52.99	368
	Non-FCB firms	6.21	8.30	0.00	0.27	2.69	9.18	58.45	843
Exports to sales (%)	FCB firms	22.39	33.59	0.00	0.03	6.86	35.10	453.97	877
	Non-FCB firms	10.89	72.61	0.00	0.00	0.00	3.06	5000.00	7598
Imports to sales (%)	FCB firms	37.38	511.42	0.00	1.17	7.93	23.35	15007.69	877
	Non-FCB firms	69.47	3399.70	0.00	0.00	0.00	1.96	273240.00	7598
Debt-to-equity ratio	FCB firms	6.25	69.30	−616.84	0.99	1.81	3.08	1714.47	907
	Non-FCB firms	30.56	930.24	−14915.00	0.05	0.83	2.67	65291.00	9857
Interest cover ratio	FCB firms	29.16	382.16	−173.00	2.03	3.83	8.86	10851.06	874
	Non-FCB firms	72.65	691.24	−4024.00	1.31	2.87	8.88	22238.00	5928
Total trade to sales (%)	FCB firms	59.77	511.74	0.00	6.91	26.11	60.27	15007.69	877
	Non-FCB firms	80.36	3408.47	0.00	0.00	0.00	14.55	273240.00	7598

Source: CMIE Prowess

* Size is defined as the three-year average of the total income and total assets of a company. *FII holding* is defined as the percentage of shares of a company held by non-promoter foreign institutional investors. *Export to sales* is the percentage of export of goods and services in total sales. *Import to sales* is the percentage of import of raw materials, stores and spares, finished goods, and capital goods, in total sales of a company. *Debt-to-equity* is defined as the difference between total assets and net-worth of a company, divided by its net worth. *Interest cover* is ratio of Profit before Tax and Depreciation (PBDITA) to the interest expenses of a company. *Total trade to sales* is the sum of exports and imports as a percentage of total sales.

firms have zero exports, while the median value of exports for FCB firms is 6.86 percent of sales. The median value for imports as a percentage of sales is 7.93 percent for FCB firms, and negligible for non-FCB firms. In terms of foreign institutional investment, the median value for FCB firms is 4.87 percent, while the median value for non-FCB firms is 2.69 percent.

Turning to leverage, the median debt equity ratio[8] of FCB firms is 1.81 while for non-FCB firms it is 0.83. Hence, FCB firms are much more leveraged. At the same time, in 2011–12, according to the standard corporate finance rule-of-thumb measure, the FCB firms were relatively comfortable in managing this borrowing: the median interest cover ratio of FCB firms is 3.83, while for non-FCB firms it is 2.87. At this point, in light of our subsequent discussion, it is important to note that the standard interest cover ratio does not account for the additional risk posed for FCB firms by potential currency fluctuations.

To summarize, evidence suggests that FCB firms are much larger than non-FCB firms,[9] have more debt financing, are more internationalized, and were more comfortable servicing their debt in 2011–12 subject to the caveat about currency risk noted in the previous paragraph.

Table 3 provides some information on changes in the characteristics of FCB and non-FCB firms by documenting median values and inter-quartile ranges for the years 2004, 2008, and 2012. The size variable is in nominal terms, while the other variables are unit-free ratios. With one exception, there are no strong trends; the exception is in the size variable. Using the change in nominal GDP over this period—which was roughly a tripling of magnitude—as a benchmark, one can note that the change in the size of the median non-FCB firm was less than this, while the change in size of the median FCB firm was much larger. It may also be noted that the measures of internationalization for the median FCB firm—FII holdings and total trade-to-sales—also change substantially in the first part of this period.

8. Debt equity ratio has been defined as total assets minus net worth, divided by net worth. In other words, the firm's equity on the balance sheet is represented by net worth, and the residual from total assets is debt.

9. The concentration of FCB among larger firms can also be illustrated by the following two additional facts gleaned from the data. First, almost all FCB is concentrated among the top size quartile of firms in our sample. Second, the top thirty firms by FCB amounts account for about two-thirds of the total FCB in the sample.

TABLE 3. Trend in FCB Firms Versus Non-FCB Firms

	Units	Non-FCB firms			FCB firms		
		2004	*2008*	*2012*	*2004*	*2008*	*2012*
Size	Rs. (Million)	128	117.6	218	696.9	2292.4	5518.5
		(475.1)	(563.55)	(1151.02)	(2617.2)	(7203.4)	(15432.65)
FII holding	Percent	0.49	3.07	2.69	1.86	6.66	4.87
		(4.3)	(9.54)	(8.91)	(8.69)	(11.25)	(11.73)
Exports to sales	Percent	0	0	0	2.71	7.62	6.86
		(6.81)	(3.92)	(3.05)	(27.65)	(38.49)	(35.07)
Imports to sales	Percent	0	0	0	3.52	7.73	7.93
		(4.04)	(3.25)	(1.96)	(15.69)	(20.79)	(22.18)
Debt equity	Times	0.88	0.88	0.83	1.63	1.9	1.81
		(2.43)	(2.59)	(2.62)	(2.36)	(2.13)	(2.08)
Interest cover	Times	3.48	3.8	2.87	4.09	4.47	3.83
		(8.04)	(8.53)	(7.57)	(6.33)	(6.84)	(6.82)
Total trade to sales	Percent	0.32	0	0	15.73	25.95	26.11
		(20.91)	(17.77)	(14.55)	(46.74)	(55.69)	(53.36)
Number of Obs.	Number	10115	12331	9962	535	1027	907

Source: CMIE Prowess.

Note: The table reports the median values for each variable in 2004, 2008, and 2012. The numbers in the brackets represent the inter-quartile range.

4. Areas of Concern

In this section, we describe the areas of concern associated with FCB by firms in India. The main area of concern is, of course, currency mismatch, with the underlying problems of moral hazard and incompleteness of markets being highlighted. This section then briefly considers the somewhat independent problem of policy uncertainty, and finally brings out the challenges of policy design in this area in the context of more general issues of rule of law and governance quality.

4.1. Currency Mismatch

During the East Asian Crisis of 1997, many countries experienced a breakdown in pegged exchange rate regimes, with large depreciations and subsequent greater exchange rate flexibility. Prior to the crisis, financial and non-financial firms in many of these countries had accumulated large stocks of unhedged FCB. These firms experienced credit distress resulting from large unexpected depreciation. Similar problems were also seen in the Tequila Crisis of 1994 in Mexico. In the 2008 Global Financial Crisis, many East European firms and households were adversely affected through currency mismatch.

Following on the crises of the 1990s, the literature has emphasized the problems of currency mismatch deriving from the "original sin" of borrowing in foreign currency (Aghion et al. 2001; C´espedes et al. 2002; Jeanne 2002; Krugman 1999; Razin and Sadka 2001). Isolated mistakes in commercial judgment made by a few firms are not a cause for concern. However, if a large fraction of a country's corporate balance sheets are denominated in foreign currency and if a significant fraction of firms face credit distress when a large depreciation takes place, there is an adverse impact upon the country as a whole. Firms facing credit distress may go bankrupt, which induces bankruptcy costs. Even if they do not, distressed firms may have reduced ability to finance investment and, if there are enough distressed firms, there are adverse effects on macroeconomic conditions. Hence, there can be a market failure in the form of externalities imposed upon innocent bystanders, when a large fraction of a country's corporate balance sheets have a substantial currency mismatch.

In the early decades of the international finance literature, a simplistic approach gained prominence, where it was argued that debt flows are dangerous while equity flows are safe. In recent decades, understanding of the topic has been clarified, and a more nuanced position has gained ground.

The understanding today emphasizes the dangers that arise out of a combination of the following three elements:

1. *A managed exchange rate.* This can potentially yield a large and sudden depreciation.
2. *A class of firms which have large unhedged foreign borrowing and low ability to absorb shocks.* Vulnerable firms are those with two characteristics: (a) they have substantial FCB, and (b) they have small amounts of equity capital which can absorb these shocks.
3. *This class of firms must be large when compared with GDP.* If this condition is not satisfied, then FCE is just an ordinary business risk that some firms bear.

For example, if 20 percent of firms (by balance sheet size) stand to lose 20 percent of their equity capital in the event of a large and sudden 20 percent depreciation, there is little cause for concern. If, however, 50 percent of the firms (by balance sheet size) stand to lose 50 percent of their equity capital in the event of a sudden 20 percent depreciation, there is cause for concern. Similarly, large sudden depreciations are less frequent if the exchange rate is more flexible.

Consequently, concerns arise when faced with the combination of a pegged exchange rate and large-scale unhedged FCB by firms in the presence of small equity buffers.

We now turn to the question of why a large number of firms carry unhedged currency exposure.

4.1.1. Mismatch Owing to Moral Hazard

The "moral hazard" hypothesis (Eichengreen et al. 2007) argues that firms fail to hedge currency exposure, as they believe that the government will manage the exchange rate. When the government makes explicit or implicit promises about currency policy, it encourages firms to leave their exposure unhedged.

If the exchange rate regime were to feature a market-determined exchange rate for small changes in the exchange rate, while preventing large changes from coming about, firm optimization would lead them to hedge against small changes but not against large changes.

For example, a firm may use a currency futures contract as a linear hedge, but simultaneously derive revenues from selling options with strikes at ±5 percent, to express the view that the government will not permit the exchange rate to change by more than 5 percent. This would reduce the cost of the hedge.

The moral hazard hypothesis relies on rational and sophisticated firms that understand the de facto exchange rate regime (which may differ from the de jure exchange rate regime) to make decisions about taking on or laying off exposure. These conditions are more likely to be met in large, financially complex and internationally active firms.

Under the moral hazard hypothesis, currency policy is the root cause of currency mismatch; reducing exposure would, therefore, involve removing the explicit or implicit promises to protect firms from exchange rate fluctuations.

A feedback loop can potentially arise, where currency policy gives rise to currency mismatch (owing to moral hazard) and, once a large number of firms leave their exposure unhedged, they mobilize themselves politically to perpetuate the currency regime. This can generate a "fear of floating" trap where a country finds it hard to reform the exchange rate regime in favor of a market-determined exchange rate.

4.1.2. Mismatch Owing to Incomplete Markets

An alternative hypothesis emphasizes the difficulties faced by firms when trying to hedge. The "incomplete markets" hypothesis asserts that it is in the self-interest of firms to not hold currency exposure, but that attempts by firms to hedge are hampered by the inadequacies of the currency derivatives market. In particular, long-dated borrowing would call for long-dated derivatives contracts. These contracts are often not traded on the market, and have to be constructed either through rolling over (for linear exposure) or through a dynamic trading strategy (for non-linear exposure). In an illiquid market, the transaction costs incurred may be prohibitive.

Under the incomplete markets hypothesis, firms are victims of exchange rate fluctuations that they are unable to hedge against. This suggests a policy response grounded in the exchange rate policy (in order to protect firms) and market development (in order to obtain a more liquid currency derivatives market). Of course, a managed exchange rate policy will introduce the problem of moral hazard discussed earlier.

4.1.3. Evidence from India

RBI officials have time and again warned companies about unhedged foreign currency exposure. According to a speech by RBI Deputy Governor, H.R. Khan, on October 4, 2014, the hedge ratio for ECBs and foreign currency convertible bonds came down from 35 percent in 2013–14 to just 15 percent in July–August 2014. The Deputy Governor expressed the concern that:

> Large scale currency mismatches could pose serious threat to the financial stability in case exchange rate encounters sudden depreciation pressure. It is absolutely essential that corporates should continue to be guided by sound hedging policies and the financing banks factor the risk of unhedged exposures in their credit assessment framework.

RBI's Executive Director G. Mahalingam, in his address as keynote speaker on February 27, 2015, reiterated that unhedged corporate exposure remains a major risk factor. He remarked that:

> The outstanding US dollar credit to non-bank borrowers outside the US has jumped from USD 6 trillion to USD 9 trillion since the Global Financial Crisis. This could expose the corporates in EMEs with large forex exposure to significant interest rate and currency risks unless these positions are adequately hedged....
>
> A point of comfort for India is that the Indian corporates do not contribute significantly to this increased exposure (basically because of the macro prudential measures put in place in India); however, if a wave of corporate defaults happen in other EMEs, this can lead to some cascading impact on India and its financial markets.

The RBI Governor in his post policy briefing on April 7, 2015, warned companies against keeping their FCEs unhedged, saying they might face "big risk" in the event of change in the monetary policy globally.

Patnaik and Shah (2010) use a natural experiment in changes of the exchange rate regime, to explore the moral hazard versus the incomplete markets hypothesis on the currency exposure of firms. Table 4 shows that India's exchange rate regime went through structural change, with low flexibility (January 4, 1993–February 17, 1995); followed by high flexibility (February 17, 1995–August 21, 1998); followed by low flexibility

TABLE 4. The Four Periods of Varying Exchange Rate Flexibility

	Dates	*INR/USD weekly vol.*	β_2
1	1993-04-01 to 1995-02-17	0.16	5.899
2	1995-02-17 to 1998-08-21	0.93	0.540
3	1998-08-21 to 2004-03-19	0.29	3.753
4	2004-03-19 to 2008-03-31	0.64	2.066

Source: Patnaik and Shah (2010).

(August 21, 1998–March 19, 2004); followed by high flexibility (March 19, 2004–March 31, 2008). This offers an opportunity to examine changes in the currency exposure of firms. The paper finds that the currency exposure of large firms was high, low, high and then low through these four periods.

Using an "augmented market model," where the sensitivity of the valuation of firm to changes in the exchange rate is measured, the paper finds that in Period 1, starting from April 1, 1993 to February 17, 1995, where currency flexibility was limited, the exposure of firms was considerable. In Period 2 from February 17, 1995 to August 21, 1998, where high currency volatility was observed, the exposure of firms fell dramatically. In Period 3, starting from August 21, 1998 to March 19, 2004, where currency flexibility again dropped, the exposure of firms rose. Finally, in Period 4, starting from March 19, 2004 to March 31, 2008, where greater currency volatility came about, the currency risk dropped sharply (see third column of Table 4).

This is consistent with the moral hazard hypothesis: firms changed their exposure when the de facto exchange rate regime changed. This is also inconsistent with the incomplete markets hypothesis: firms *were* able to execute the changes in exposure in response to changes in the exchange rate regime.

4.2. Policy Uncertainty

The Indian authorities have, on many occasions, used tightening and easing of capital controls on foreign borrowing. Pandey et al. (2015) examine the causes and consequences of these actions. This paper analyses 76 capital flow measures (CFMs) that were observed from 2003 to 2013. Of a total of 76 events, 68 were easing and 8 were tightening.

In terms of the causes of these CFMs, the main finding concerns exchange rate movements. It appears that capital controls against ECB were eased after significant exchange rate depreciation. This suggests that the authorities may have been using capital controls against foreign borrowing as a tool for currency policy.

In order to obtain causal identification of the consequences of CFMs, the paper identifies pairs of periods with similar conditions (through propensity score matching), where in one case the CFM was employed but in another case it was not. This permits a matched event study methodology which would measure the causal impact of the CFM. The main finding of the paper is that there was little causal impact upon various outcomes, including the level of the exchange rate.

4.3. Sound Practices in Governance and the Rule of Law

Section 2 describes the existing policy framework and the processes through which this policy framework is implemented. This raises the following concerns:

Industrial policy: When the law favors certain industries over others, without a clear and explicit economic rationale, it constitutes an ill-defined industrial policy. As an example, foreign borrowing is allowed for working capital requirements for the civil aviation sector but not for other sectors.

Economic knowledge required to write down detail: When the law gives detailed and bright line regulations, it raises concern about the foundations of economic knowledge that are required. For example, the law permits firms to borrow when their all-in-cost is below LIBOR + 300 basis points, but blocks firms when their all-in-cost is above LIBOR + 300 basis points. Such detailed regulations would need to be backed by sophisticated economic reasoning that demonstrates the presence of a market failure, and that the intervention in the form of detailed regulation addresses this market failure.

The cost of doing business: The complex policy framework induces delays, uncertainty, and costs of compliance, including legal fees.

Rule of law: Under the rule of law, six features should hold: (a) the law should be comprehensible and known to all citizens; (b) identically placed persons should be treated equally; (c) outcomes of prospective transactions should be predictable to practitioners; (d) there should be no arbitrary discretion in the hands of officials; (e) reasoned orders should be given out for all actions; and (f) the orders should be subject to efficacious appeal. There is currently work underway to improve the financial sector regulation on all these areas through the implementation of the Financial Sector Legislative Reforms Commission (FSLRC) non-legislative handbook, as discussed in Section 5.2.5.

5. Recent Evolution of Policy

This section offers a description of recent policy initiatives in the arena of FCB. Of course, any changes in one area have to be in concordance with, and coordinated with, other aspects of the policy with respect to engagement with the international financial system, as the earlier discussion of ECB policy and exchange rate policy illustrates.

5.1. The Sahoo Committee Report on the ECB Framework

The Sahoo Committee was set up in 2013, to develop a framework for access to domestic and overseas capital markets. The third report of the Committee focused on rationalizing the framework for FCB in India. The Committee recommended that regulatory interventions must be guided by an analysis of potential market failures, and must seek to target and correct those failures. The most critical market failure associated with ECB was identified to be externalities arising from systemic risk, on account of currency exposure.[10]

The key observation of the report is that if there are numerous firms that undertake FCB, but do not hedge their currency exposure, there is a possibility of correlated failure of these firms if there is a large exchange rate movement. The negative impact of this movement on their balance sheets could then hamper investment and the country's GDP. This imposes negative externalities which constitute a market failure.

The Committee observed that, at present, there is an array of other interventions aimed at addressing the process of FCB. Most of these interventions were brought in to meet the specific needs of the hour, and have arguably outlived their utility. None seem to address any identified market failure today. The Committee, therefore, recommended removing these interventions. It noted that the possibility of market failure can be ameliorated, by requiring firms that borrow in foreign currency to hedge their exchange risk exposure. There can be two kinds of hedges: (a) natural hedges, or (b) hedging using financial derivatives. Natural hedges arise when firms sell more tradeables than they consume. This generates the net economic exposure of an exporter. Ownership of real or financial assets abroad also provides firms with some natural hedging, although the liquidity of those assets will be important for the degree of protection offered. Firms may also use financial derivatives (such as currency futures, currency options, etc.) to hedge their currency exposure.

The Committee made an assessment of the currency risk by Indian firms undertaking ECB. Using data from the Prowess database of the Centre for Monitoring Indian Economy, the Committee developed a measure of firms' natural hedge level. For all firms that reported FCB, the annuity payable at the end of a financial year based on their quantum of borrowing at an

10. See *Sahoo Committee, Report III.*

average rate of interest was calculated. This imputed liability arising out of ECB was matched with the firms' receivables arising out of their net exports. This gave a measure of the level of a firm's natural hedge. Based on this measure, all foreign borrowing firms were divided into three categories of hedge coverage:

- *High*: Net exports for the year are more than 80 percent of the annual repayment of ECB for the year.
- *Low*: Net exports for the year are less than 80 percent but more than 20 percent of the annual repayment of ECB for the year.
- *None*: Net exports for the year are less than 20 percent of the annual repayment of ECB for the year.

The analysis by the Committee showed that in 2013 more than 50 percent of the firms that undertook ECB had small or no foreign currency receivables to naturally hedge the foreign currency liability arising from ECB. Additionally, the value of naturally unhedged borrowing far exceeded the value of naturally hedged borrowing. The quantum of naturally unhedged ECB was 3–4 times the amount of borrowings that are naturally hedged. The analysis by the Committee showed that around 50 percent of the firms undertaking ECB, which constitute over 70 percent of the ECB amount borrowed in a year, are in need of financial hedging to cover their risks arising out of FCB.

The main recommendation of the Committee was that Indian firms should be able to borrow abroad through foreign currency debt, while requiring them to substantially hedge their FCE, whether through financial derivatives or natural hedges.

The Committee examined the framework in comparable jurisdictions to hedge FCE. The Committee noted that recently Bank Indonesia introduced hedging requirement to address the systemic risk concerns emanating from FCB. Their approach is to prescribe a certain percentage of the negative balance between foreign currency assets and liabilities to be hedged. The percentage applies to all sectors irrespective of the net exchange rate exposure of a sector.

The regulation states: "Non-Bank Corporation holding External Debt in Foreign Currency is required to fulfil a specified minimum Hedging Ratio by Hedging the Foreign Currency against the Rupiah."[11]

11. In addition to prescribing a minimum hedging ratio, the regulations also prescribe liquidity ratio and credit rating related requirements.

The minimum hedging ratio is set at 25 percent of:

1. The negative balance between foreign currency assets and foreign currency liabilities with a maturity period of up to three months from the end of the quarter; and
2. The negative balance between foreign currency assets and foreign currency liabilities with a maturity period of between three and six months from the end of the quarter.

Similarly, the Committee observed that the South African exchange control framework prescribes a checklist of requirements to enable the authorities to assess the adequacy of hedging. Some of the key requirements prescribed are as follows:

- Are the facilities required to cover a firm's exposure to possible losses arising from adverse movements in foreign exchange rates?
- Is the transaction clearly identifiable as a hedge?
- Does it reduce the exposure to risk?
- Is there a high correlation between the price of the hedge contract and the underlying asset, liability, or commitment (the underlying transaction)?

Based on a review of the current framework and policy directions in comparable jurisdictions, the key recommendations of the Committee can be summarized as follows:

1. The present complex array of controls on FCB should be done away with.
2. Irrespective of the nature and purpose of foreign borrowing, every borrower must hedge a minimum specified percentage of its currency exposure. Such percentage must be uniform across sectors or borrowers.[12]
3. Every firm wishing to borrow abroad must demonstrate hedging of currency exposure either through natural hedge or commitment to hedge through derivatives transactions. This means that a borrower

12. Nothing in this recommendation obviates policy reforms that might improve corporate governance and best practice in the sphere of risk management. The point of a minimum specific requirement on FCB is that there are specific externalities and systemic risks associated with this source of debt exposure.

may meet the hedge requirement through natural hedge and/or through currency derivatives.

4. It is necessary to develop the on-shore currency derivatives market. The government and regulators must make a concerted effort to make the currency derivatives market deep and liquid. This would reduce the cost of hedging and make hedging facilities available to firms.
5. The minimum hedge ratio may be decided by the authorities keeping in view the financing needs of the firms and of the economy, the development of onshore currency derivatives markets and any other systemic concern such as volatility in global risk tolerance. The ratio may be modified by the authorities periodically depending on the exigencies.
6. The board of every borrowing company must be obliged to certify at least once a year that the company fulfils the hedging requirement. In addition, supervision may include powers to inspect books of borrowers to confirm adherence to hedging norms.
7. The Indian domestic rupee debt market is a viable alternative to foreign borrowing for financing Indian firms and does not entail any market failure. The policy should aim at removal of all impediments to the development of the domestic rupee debt market.

In Section 6, we discuss the feasibility, including specific challenges, as well as the desirability of implementing the above recommendations of the Sahoo Committee. However, this is a dynamic area of policy making and several changes have already been undertaken. These recent policy changes are discussed in Section 5.2.

5.2. Recent Policy Changes

Recent policy changes in the framework for foreign borrowing in India have moved in the direction of addressing some of the issues raised above. These changes pertain to rupee-denominated borrowing, monitoring and regulating direct and indirect unhedged exposures, and foundational reforms in financial sector laws and regulations.

5.2.1. Increasing Access to Rupee-denominated Borrowing

Foreign participation in rupee-denominated corporate bonds is being gradually liberalized. At present, foreign investors are allowed to invest in rupee-denominated corporate bonds up to USD 51 billion. Till April 1, 2013, there were sub-limits within the overall cap of USD 51 billion, these have now been merged. Subsequently, the authorities announced a rationalization of foreign investment in corporate bonds. The ceiling of USD 1 billion for qualified foreign investors (QFIs), USD 25 billion for foreign portfolio investors (FPIs), and USD 25 billion for FPIs in long-term infrastructure bonds were merged within the overall cap for corporate bonds at USD 51 billion.[13]

Further, the process of allocation of limits to individual entities within the aggregate debt ceiling has been liberalized. A previously used auction mechanism for allocating debt limits to individual firms has been largely replaced by an "on-tap system." The auction mechanism would be initiated only when the aggregate of individual firm borrowings reaches 90 percent of the overall debt limit, for allocation of the remaining 10 percent of possible borrowing to individual firms. These measures aim at simplifying the norms for foreign investment and can play a role in encouraging development of the debt market in India.[14]

Increasing access to foreign participation in rupee-denominated bonds avoids the problem of currency mismatch for borrowers who use this alternative. Of course, when foreign investors buy rupee-denominated bonds, they are exposed to fluctuations of inflation and interest rates in India, as well as currency risk. A well-functioning, liquid corporate bond market can reduce transactions costs and make the risk–reward tradeoffs more transparent for all participants, including foreign investors. In turn, increased foreign participation can help to further increase liquidity.

5.2.2. Steps to Monitor Unhedged Currency Exposure

The regulator has initiated steps to improve the reporting framework for currency exposure by requiring companies to disclose information on hedging. The format of ECB-2 Return (the form for monthly reporting by ECB firms) has been modified. A new part has been added which requires firms to disclose details of financial hedging contracted if any. The reporting firms are also required to provide details of average annual foreign exchange earnings and expenditure for the last three financial years to RBI.[15] Such reporting enables RBI to monitor unhedged currency exposure of borrowers.

5.2.3. Guidelines on Capital and Provisioning Requirements

In order to discourage banks from providing credit facilities to companies that refrain from adequate hedging against currency risk, the RBI has prescribed guidelines on incremental capital and provisioning requirements

13. See RBI (2013).

14. However, foreign participation is restricted to rupee-denominated corporate bonds having a minimum residual maturity of three years. See Reserve Bank of India (2015c).

15. See RBI (2014a).

for banks with exposures to entities with the so-called unhedged foreign currency exposure (UFCE). RBI has also prescribed the manner in which losses incurred on UFCE should be calculated.[16]

The methodology used by RBI has the following key elements:

1. *Ascertain the amount of unhedged FCE*: RBI defines FCE as the gross sum of all items on the balance sheet that have impact on profit and loss account due to movement in foreign exchange rates, where only items maturing or having cash flows over the period of the next five years are considered.

   UFCE excludes items which are effective hedge of each other. Financial hedging through derivatives is only considered where the entity at the inception of the derivative contract has documented the purpose and the strategy for hedging and assessed its effectiveness as a hedging instrument at periodic intervals. Natural hedges are considered when cash flows arising out of the operations of the company offset the risk arising out of the FCE defined above. For the purpose of computing UFCE, an exposure is considered naturally hedged if the offsetting exposure has the maturity/cash flow within the same accounting year.[17]
2. *Estimate the extent of likely loss*: The loss to an entity in case of movement in USD–INR exchange rate is calculated using the annualized volatilities. The largest annual volatility seen in the USD–INR rates during the period of last ten years is taken as the movement of the USD–INR rate in the adverse direction.
3. *Estimate the riskiness of unhedged position and provide appropriately*: Once the loss figure is calculated, it is compared with the annual EBID as per the latest quarterly results certified by the statutory auditors. This loss may be computed as a percentage of EBID. EBID is defined as: Profit After Tax + Depreciation + Interest on debt + Lease Rentals, if any. As this percentage increases, the susceptibility of the entity to adverse exchange rate movements increases. Up to 15 percent, there is no incremental provisioning requirement on the total credit exposures over and above extant standard asset provisioning. After 15 percent, provisioning requirements apply.[18]

16. See RBI (2014b).
17. Ibid.
18. Ibid.

5.2.4. Initiatives to Liberalize Issuance of Rupee-Denominated Bonds

On September 29, 2015, the RBI allowed Indian corporates eligible to raise ECB to issue rupee-denominated bonds within the overarching ECB policy.[19]

The salient features of the framework for Indian corporates are:

1. Any corporate or body corporate is eligible to issue rupee-denominated bonds overseas. REITs and INVITs coming under the regulatory jurisdiction are also eligible.
2. The bonds may be floated in any jurisdiction that is Financial Action Task Force (FATF) compliant.
3. Only plain vanilla bonds either privately placed or listed in exchanges as per host country regulations are allowed.
4. The bonds will be issued with a minimum maturity of 5 years.
5. The all-in-cost ceilings will be commensurate with prevailing market conditions.
6. The proceeds can be used for all purposes except for a small negative list including investment in capital market and real estate activities.
7. Up to USD 750 million is allowed under the automatic route; beyond this limit, regulatory approval would be required.

The effectiveness of this framework remains to be seen. While addressing currency exposure, the rationale for the remaining ECB framework restrictions is not entirely clear. Due to larger currency restrictions, we may not see a larger number of private firms moving from dollar bonds to rupee bonds in the immediate future.

5.2.5. Addressing the Foundations of Sound Governance

As argued in Section 4.3, the present arrangements have many problems, including concerns about the ill-defined or non-transparent industrial policy, the economic knowledge required to write down detail for practical implementation, the cost of doing business, and the rule of law. Recall that the last characteristic has very precise components, as described in the earlier section. The FSLRC has drafted a concrete framework for the rule of law in finance in the draft "Indian Financial Code," a unified modern law covering all aspects of Indian finance. The Ministry of Finance has drafted an *FSLRC Handbook* of elements of this framework that are being adopted by regulators as good practices.

19. See RBI (2015a; 2015b).

Reforms that shift the economic foundations as described above and emphasize the rule of law by adopting the procedures of the *FSLRC Handbook* are required in the field of FCB. This would involve the following changes in the regulatory framework of foreign borrowing in India:

1. All draft subordinate legislation governing foreign borrowing would be published with a statement of objectives, the problem it seeks to solve, and a cost-benefit analysis (using best practices).
2. The draft subordinate legislation would be accompanied by a statement of the problem or market failure that the regulator seeks to address through the proposed regulations, which will be used to test the effectiveness with which the regulations address the stated problem.
3. Any proposed change in regulations would be preceded by inviting comments from the public. All comments would be published on the website of the regulator. The process of soliciting public comments would enhance the legitimacy of regulatory intervention by engaging with stakeholders. It would enable the regulator to seek external views and advice in a cost-effective manner.
4. The board would approve the final regulations after considering comments from the public and modifications of the regulation consequent to the comments.
5. All the approved regulations would be published on the website within 24 hours of their coming into force. If all the relevant information were to be published, it would become easier for firms to understand what they are, and are not, allowed to do. As a result, they will be able to operate with clarity and confidence.
6. A key reform would involve requiring the regulator and government to develop a detailed legal process governing approvals. This would imply that all applications for borrowing under the approval route would be accepted or rejected within a specified time. In the event of rejection of an application, reasons for rejection would be provided. This would substantially reduce the discretion that the regulator possesses in the current arrangement. If administrative orders were freely and publicly available, a rich jurisprudence could develop around the process of approvals, bringing legal clarity and predictability to the system.

6. Remaining Challenges

The measures elaborated in the previous section are incomplete and, in some cases, transitional responses to the issue of managing aggregate risks associated with FCB by Indian firms. This section presents some remaining issues and challenges relating to foreign borrowing in the context of the current and evolving regulatory and economic reform landscape. As was discussed earlier in the paper, addressing challenges relating to foreign borrowing can also involve broader issues of financial sector reform. In many cases, taking a more comprehensive view of reform can provide potentially more robust policy changes.

6.1. Addressing Moral Hazards

The issue of moral hazard as a source of currency mismatch, and therefore, of risk associated with foreign borrowing, was highlighted in Section 4. The moral hazard for firms engaged in such borrowing arises from exchange rate management. Over recent years, however, the Indian exchange rate regime has evolved substantially, away from an administered rate towards a market-determined rate. The Monetary Policy Framework Agreement of February 20, 2015, has enshrined price stability as RBI's objective. This would be consistent with a greater movement towards exchange rate flexibility, since trying to manage the exchange rate can undermine domestic monetary policy control (part of the classic trilemma). To the extent that the rupee is a floating exchange rate, there would be reduced moral hazard; firms would hedge out of their own self-interest.

6.2. Addressing Incomplete Markets

Incomplete markets for currency hedging were also highlighted in Section 4, as a source of currency mismatch. At present, the Indian currency derivatives market is relatively illiquid and only gives choices to firms for short-term hedging. Furthermore, a substantial part of this market trades at overseas locations, and capital controls prevent Indian firms from accessing this market.

Financial development, in the form of building the "bond–currency–derivatives (BCD) nexus," would help create sophisticated markets onshore, through which access to hedging would improve. The term "BCD Nexus" has been used in the Indian context to highlight the interconnectedness of different financial markets. The regulation of markets for corporate and government bonds, foreign currencies, and financial derivatives tied to them has often been piecemeal, failing to take account of their interconnectedness. In particular, greater liquidity in a subset of these markets can enhance liquidity in other markets, making it optimal to develop different markets together. Of course, the key underlying idea is that such overall financial development is likely to be beneficial from India's current starting point, in terms of improving opportunities for risk management as well as channeling of funds to productive uses. In addition to this broader reform for financial development, very specific reforms of capital controls would also need to be considered, in order to give Indian firms the choice of using rupee derivatives which trade at overseas locations. In all cases, the overarching goal would be to reduce the costs of hedging by reducing the severe effective incompleteness of financial markets that enable such forms of risk management.

6.3. Measuring Exposure and Hedging

As discussed in Section 5, the Sahoo Committee report discussed both explicit and natural hedges by firms engaging in FCB, as well as offering some estimates of the then-current extent of natural hedging by such firms. As discussed in Section 5, the RBI announced regulations for banks requiring them to measure and provision for the FCE of firms borrowing from them. This section discusses some of the practical challenges in measuring currency exposure and natural hedging levels.

6.3.1. Import Parity Pricing

In the traditional literature, currency mismatch is seen to arise from mismatches between the stream of net exports and the stream of payments required owing to debt servicing. A possible refinement in this approach is rooted in the concept of import parity pricing.[20] When trade barriers decline and when the infrastructure of transportation improves, more types of goods and services become tradeable. In the limit, when the value of the goods is large compared with the total transactions costs (including tariffs), arbitrage becomes efficient and the domestic price closely tracks the global price.

In the intuition of arbitrage with financial derivatives, a "no-arbitrage band" is seen around the world price expressed in rupees. If the domestic price rises and goes outside the no-arbitrage band, rational arbitrageurs will make a profit by importing and selling into the domestic market. If the domestic price drops and goes outside the no-arbitrage band, rational

20. For example, see Patnaik and Shah 2008, for a discussion of currency exposure and import parity pricing, as well as further references.

arbitrageurs will make a profit by exporting. Actions by multiple arbitrageurs will ensure that the domestic price stays within the no-arbitrage band, that is, the zone where international trade is not profitable, net of transactions costs. Under these conditions, the domestic price is approximately equal to the world price, expressed in rupees. The presence of raw materials or outputs which are priced by such "import parity pricing" has potential implications for currency exposure.

For example, a firm which switches from importing steel to buying imported steel from a domestic dealer does not change anything about its exposure to the world price of steel, expressed in rupees.[21] An Indian firm may buy or sell steel against a domestic counterparty, but it experiences currency exposure exactly as if it were importing or exporting steel. When import parity pricing holds, product prices fluctuate with the exchange rate. These transactions[22] are influenced by the exchange rate, even if the buyer and seller are both domestic firms. The ordinary business activities of such firms involve currency exposure, even if there is no direct export or import.

In order to fix intuition, a stylized version of a representative Indian non-financial firm in 2013–14 is considered. The key facts from its income and expenditure statement are presented in Table 5. Some firms make tradeables; some firms consume tradeables; some firms buy and sell tradeables. In this illustrative tradeable–firm case, a typical engineering firm, which may buy steel and sell ball bearings, is used for expositional purposes. In this case, the raw materials and the finished goods are priced by import parity pricing.

TABLE 5. The Income and Expenditure Statement of the Typical Large Indian Non-financial Firm (2013–14)

Total revenue	100
Raw materials purchased	57.87
Other operating expenses	27.98
Operating profit	14.15

Source: An illustration.

21. Indeed, the same argument applies if the firm switches to buying domestic steel, if the price of domestic steel is fully subject to import parity conditions. In this context, one can see that just as exchange rate management distorts corporate risk and risk management relative to external shocks, so does domestic-administered pricing or price controls for tradeables.

22. Simplifying assumptions have been used in constructing Table 5:

1. The purchase of finished goods is merged into the "raw materials purchased;"
2. All energy expenses are merged into "other operating expenses" even though some of these are tradeable.

By the logic of import parity pricing, for all practical purposes, this firm imports ₹57.87 and exports ₹100. Goods arbitrage for ball bearings is feasible; ball bearings are tradeable. Hence, the Indian price of ball bearings is the same as the world price of ball bearings. There is, therefore, no difference between selling ₹100 of ball bearings on the domestic market and exporting ₹100 of ball bearings in terms of the impact of currency fluctuations on the variability of the firm's revenue. Even though other operating expenses may be non-tradeable, and therefore not subject to import parity pricing, operating profit will vary in the same way for the exporter and the firm that sells only domestically.

Such a firm has currency exposure owing to its effective net exports; its exposure is equivalent to a firm that actually exports ₹42.13. If the rupee depreciates by 10 percent, the total revenue of the firm increases to ₹110 and the raw materials cost increases to ₹63.66 as a result of import parity pricing. Other operating expenses are non-tradeable and do not change, in partial equilibrium. Hence, the operating profit is ₹18.36. This is an increase of ₹4.21, that is, 10 percent of the net exposure of ₹42.13. For all practical purposes, the firm is an exporter with exports of ₹42.13.

In practice, most firms buy a mix of tradeable raw materials (for example, steel) and non-tradeable raw materials (for example, cement). Similarly most firms sell some mix of tradeable and non-tradeable goods and services. Detailed analysis would be required to uncover the actual currency exposure; a simple analysis of imports and exports would be inadequate.

6.3.2. Evidence of Natural Hedging

As described in Section 5, the Sahoo Committee report estimated the degree of natural hedging by Indian firms in the Prowess database, using net exports as the indicator of natural hedging. In this section, a similar exercise is conducted allowing for the risk implications of import parity pricing, in addition to net exports. As discussed earlier, if firms that borrow in foreign currency are hedged (naturally or through derivative markets) and have low leverage, they are individually well-placed to absorb currency shocks, and therefore systemic risk is unlikely to arise from this particular source.

As noted earlier in the paper, neither of the above two characteristics (natural hedges and low leverage) is taken into account in the current regulations. Hence, changing the regulatory framework to allow firms that meet these criteria to borrow, where they are currently unable to, has the potential to bring down their cost of capital and improve their competitiveness and performance. In a companion paper (Patnaik et al. 2014) we found that firms that borrow abroad under existing regulations (all relatively large firms, as noted earlier) do slightly better than firms that do not, in terms of asset growth and sales growth. The measured impacts are not strong, and are partly consistent with the substitution of foreign for domestic borrowing rather than increased access to capital. Ultimately, market judgments would determine which additional firms could borrow if allowed to do so, and what the impacts on their performance would be. The central point is that loosening the restrictions on firms with low leverage and natural hedges is unlikely to increase systemic risk in this dimension. The existence of natural hedges also implies that such firms do not have to use derivatives to reduce the currency risk associated with their borrowing abroad.

Table 6 examines the present situation from this point of view. All industries are classified into two groups: tradeables and non-tradeables. In each industry, firms are broken into three groups with low, medium, or high

TABLE 6. Mean FCB to Total Borrowing by Debt–Equity Ratio

Tradeable sectors			
	Debt Equity		
	Low	*Medium*	*High*
Chemicals	0.17	0.36	0.25
Consumer goods	0.31	0.11	0.01
IT services	0.12	0.26	0.22
Machinery	0.15	0.06	0.04
Metal products	0.00	0.17	0.15
Minerals	0.59	0.01	0.15
Textiles	0.05	0.05	0.07
Transport equipment	0.14	0.16	0.09
Median	0.15	0.13	0.12

Non-tradeable sectors			
	Debt Equity		
	Low	*Medium*	*High*
Communication services	0.00	0.32	0.11
Construction materials	0.47	0.12	0.01
Electricity distribution	0.00	0.18	0.06
Electricity generation	0.30	0.10	0.01
Food and agriculture	0.26	0.09	0.05
Hotel tourism	0.00	0.12	0.17
Infrastructure construction	0.00	0.14	0.05
Real estate	0.00	0.03	0.00
Transport services	0.19	0.21	0.14
Wholesale-retail trading	0.10	0.12	0.01
Median	0.05	0.12	0.05

Source: CMIE Prowess.

leverage. The value shown in each cell is the average share of FCB in the total borrowing of all firms.

The discussion above suggests that large values for FCB should preferably be seen in the "low" and "medium" columns for tradeables and nowhere else, assuming, of course, that there is no other characteristic of firms that is positively correlated with being non-tradeable or having high leverage which also makes such firms more attractive borrowers (for example, superior management). Large values for FCB, relative to industry averages, are found in many cells for non-tradeable firms. Hence, the evidence suggests that ECB is currently not dominated by firms who are exporters, or those with the currency exposure of exporters. Following this logic would, therefore, suggest reforms of capital controls, whereby:

1. The exposure of the firm is computed correctly, after taking into account import parity pricing; and
2. Firms which do not have natural hedges must use currency derivatives for some minimum level of hedging.[23]

Recent policy approach to hedging has begun to incorporate considerations of the degree of natural hedging, for example, the language of the RBI's guidelines to banks for assessing the UFCE of their borrowers speaks of fluctuations of cash flows in general terms, potentially encompassing those due to exporting as well as import parity pricing. Nevertheless, how to measure natural hedging and how to set a minimum level of explicit hedging for firms without natural hedges are complex issues, and some of the challenges are discussed in the next sub-section.

6.3.3. Challenges in Assessing Currency Exposure and Hedging

There are several practical challenges in developing a policy framework that incorporates measures of natural hedging as well as overall risk management of firms, as an input into risk management standards such as minimum hedging requirements for currency risk. Since tradeable and non-tradeable components of a firm's revenues and expenditures cannot be observed directly from income statements and balance sheets, and the degree to which input and output prices satisfy import pricing parity can also be difficult to

23. A minor caveat is that inferring the normative direction of improvement in the distribution of FCB from the current situation where large FCB firms do not have natural hedges assumes that these firms are not otherwise hedged, and that they do not have other characteristics that make them systematically "better" borrowers. Both these assumptions seem reasonable from our knowledge of the overall situation of the FCB firms.

determine in practice, regulations with respect to hedging standards would not be easy to implement in an optimal manner. The RBI regulations for banks represent one attempt to tackle the practical challenges.

In another conceptual approach, Patnaik and Shah (2010) use stock prices to infer currency exposures, by estimating the response of stock prices to changes in the exchange rate. They examine various models, including first estimating unanticipated changes in the exchange rate, and then estimating the lagged response of stock prices over time to these unanticipated changes. This method of measuring currency exposure of firms is feasible, but it may not be sufficiently simple and robust to serve as a reliable and practical policy tool.

The practical issues with respect to estimating firms' currency exposure are even more complex than what the Patnaik and Shah (2010) analysis allows for. Their procedure uses the rupee–US dollar exchange rate, but the relevant trade-weighted exchange rate might differ across different firms, depending on their patterns of production and sales. In the RBI guidelines, a simplified approach is used, wherein the riskiness of UFCE for non-USD currencies is to be ascertained by converting them to USD using current market rates, but this may not be an accurate method of assessing true currency risks. Furthermore, firms' currency risk is only a part of their overall risks, and is not likely to be independent of other risks. For example, currency risk for firms that borrow abroad contributes to the overall default risk, and appropriate risk management standards should also focus on the latter and not just the former.[24]

On the one hand, therefore, one can argue that prescribing hedging, measuring exposure, and monitoring the extent of hedged exposure at the individual firm level are very challenging tasks for a central regulator. Ideally, these tasks are best left to the firm that undertakes hedging as a business decision, provided corporate governance and overall risk management standards are themselves adequate. Certainly, there is a role for regulatory standards in those broader contexts. A second line of defense is monitoring by lenders, who will be concerned about their own bottom lines. One could take the policy approach that lenders will do appropriate due diligence; so if a firm has lined up access to FCB, its default risks and its risk management efforts have already been assessed and passed muster.

24. For example, Goedhart et al. (2015) have provided a lucid discussion of some of the complexities of management of currency risks, including some basic references to the literature on corporate risk management and a discussion of different types of risks.

However, as the global financial crisis revealed, market judgments on individual firm risks are not sufficient to ensure optimal management of systemic risks. The problem of overall mitigation of systemic risks is a complicated one, and beyond the scope of this paper. Here we merely suggest that, for the specific case of currency mismatch associated with FCB by individual firms, greater currency flexibility and large and liquid currency derivative markets, as discussed in Sections 6.1 and 6.2, offer a cleaner and more sustainable long-term solution. Under these broader policy conditions, the chance of systemic risk arising from a large number of large firms undertaking unhedged currency exposure is likely to be low. This view does not contradict the position that a minimum hedging requirement can be a useful transitional policy measure, nor does it contradict the importance of measuring and mitigating potential systemic risks in an overall macroprudential policy framework.

7. Conclusion

In the early years of international financial integration, the simple idea dominating the discourse was that of a "hierarchy of capital flows." It was felt that equity flows are good, while debt flows are not good.

From the late 1990s onwards, this idea has been replaced by a more nuanced one that is grounded in an understanding of the anatomy of market failure. The market failure (that is, externalities) associated with foreign borrowing requires a combination of three things: (a) a pegged exchange rate, (b) currency exposure in the hands of firms who do not have commensurate equity capital to absorb shocks, and (c) a large fraction of the overall corporate sector is made up of these firms.

In order to navigate the policy issues of this field, it is useful to have a normative objective. A sound resource allocation is one where FCB is done by firms with the currency exposure of exporters (even if they do not engage in direct exports), and are able to leave such borrowing unhedged, as it counterbalances their natural hedges. In this allocation, FCB becomes a remarkable low-cost source of funds. A sound policy framework is one which succeeds in giving certain firms this low-cost access to capital, while avoiding systemic risk.

At present in India, the resource allocation does not match up to this normative ideal. A substantial fraction of ECB is taking place in companies which do not have natural hedges. Shifting the resource allocation towards the normative ideal will require significant reforms of the capital controls, and the monetary policy framework. With present capital controls, there are concerns on questions of rule of law and sound public administration.

These need to be addressed by bringing them up to the processes defined by FSLRC.

There is fresh interest in the international discourse in capital controls. This paper thoroughly documents the restrictions and their outcomes for one asset class (foreign currency debt) in one country (India). This paper has shown that there is a large gap between the complexities and the problems of capital controls, in the real world, when compared with an abstract concept of capital controls which is sometimes being advocated in the international discourse.

References

Aghion, Philippe, Philippe Bacchetta, and Abhijit Banerjee. 2001. "Currency crises and monetary policy in an economy with credit constraints," *European Economic Review*, 45 (7): 1121–50.

Céspedes, Luis Felipe, Roberto Chang, and Andrés Velasco. 2002. *IS-LM-BP in the Pampas*. Working Paper No. 9337, Cambridge, Massachusetts: National Bureau of Economic Research (NBER).

Department of Economic Affairs. 2014. *India's External Debt: A Status Report*. Technical Report, Available online at http://finmin.nic.in/the_ministry/dept_eco_affairs/economic_div/India_External_Debt201314E.pdf (accessed on July 7, 2015).

Eichengreen, Barry, Ricardo Hausmann, and Ugo Panizza. 2007. "Currency Mismatches, Debt Intolerance, and the Original Sin: Why They Are Not the Same and Why It Matters," in Sebastian Edwards (ed.), *Capital Controls and Capital Flows in Emerging Economies: Policies, Practices and Consequences* (pp. 121–170). NBER Chapters. National Bureau of Economic Research, Inc., Chicago: University of Chicago Press.

Goedhart, Marc, Tim Koller, and Werner Rehm. 2015. "Getting a Better Handle on Currency Risk," Available online at: https://www.scribd.com/doc/294551723/ (accessed on June 17, 2016).

Jeanne, Olivier. July, 2002. "Monetary Policy and Liability Dollarization," Original Sin Conference, Harvard University, Cambridge, MA.

Krugman, Paul. 1999. "Balance Sheets, the Transfer Problem, and Financial Crises," in *International Tax and Public Finance*, 6(4): 459–72. Springer.

Ministry of Finance. 2015. *Report of the Committee to Review the Framework of Access to Domestic and Overseas Capital Markets. Phase II, Part II: Foreign Currency Borrowing*. Technical Report. New Delhi: Ministry of Finance.

Pandey, Radhika, Gurnain K. Pasricha, Ila Patnaik and Ajay Shah. 2015. "Motivations for Capital Controls and their Effectiveness," Working Papers, Bank of Canada, Available online at http://EconPapers. repec.org/RePEc:bca:bocawp:15-5 (accessed on June 3, 2016).

Patnaik, Ila and Ajay Shah. 2008. *One Way Bets on Pegged Exchange Rates*, Available online at https://macrofinance.nipfp.org.in/PDF/SP2008_onewaybets.pdf (accessed on March 17, 2016).

———. 2010. "Does the Currency Regime Shape Unhedged Currency Exposure?" *Journal of International Money and Finance*, 29(5): 760–69, Available online at http://ideas.repec.org/a/eee/jimfin/v29y2010i5p760-769.html (accessed on June 3, 2016).

Patnaik, Ila, Ajay Shah, and Nirvikar Singh. 2014. "Who Borrows Abroad and What Are the Consequences?" Presented at 12th Research Meeting of NIPFP-DEA Research Program, New Delhi, March 13–14, 2014.

Razin, Assaf and Efraim Sadka. 2001. "Country Risk and Capital Flow Reversals," *Economics Letters*, 72(1): 73–77.

Reserve Bank of India (RBI). 2013. *Foreign Investment in India by SEBI Registered FIIs in Government Securities and Corporate Debt*, Available online at https://www.rbi.org.in/scripts/NotificationUser.aspx?Id=7917&Mode=0 (accessed on January 15, 2016).

———. 2014a. *Reporting of Actual Transactions of External Commercial Borrowings (ECB) under Foreign Exchange Management Act, 1999: ECB—2 Form*, Available online at https://rbidocs.rbi.org.in/rdocs/content/ pdfs/105AP170214_A.pdf. (accessed on January 15, 2016).

———. 2014b. *Capital and Provisioning Requirements for Exposures to Entities with Unhedged Foreign Currency Exposure*, Available online at https://www.rbi.org.in/scripts/NotificationUser.aspx?Id=8694&Mode=0 (accessed on January 15, 2016).

———. 2015a. *External Commercial Borrowings (ECB) Policy Issuance of Rupee Denominated Bonds Overseas*, Available online at https://www.rbi.org.in/scripts/NotificationUser.aspx?Id=10049&Mode=0 (accessed on March 17, 2016).

———. 2015b. *External Commercial Borrowings Policy: Revised Framework*, Available online at https://www.rbi.org.in/scripts/NotificationUser.aspx?Id=10153&Mode=0 (accessed on March 17, 2016).

———. 2015c. *Foreign Investment in India by Foreign Portfolio Investors*, Available online at https://rbi.org.in/Scripts/NotificationUser.aspx?Id=9543&Mode=0 (accessed on March 17, 2016).

Comments and Discussion*

Rajnish Mehra†
Arizona State University, Luxembourg School of Finance, NCAER, and *NBER*

I enjoyed reading this thought-provoking paper. Two of the authors (Patnaik and Shah) played a key role in drafting the Sahoo Committee Report, which pushed for a major liberalization of the complex framework that governs Indian corporations' foreign debt transactions. The report emphasized that the prevailing restrictions on borrowers/lenders, maturity, ceilings, etc., perhaps timely when promulgated, are anachronistic in the current context.

This paper succinctly parses the Sahoo report and explores the market failures arising from corporations in an emerging economy, issuing foreign currency-denominated debt under the restrictive environment of administered currency rates and incomplete markets. I want to use this forum to explore some of the issues raised in the paper.

Figures 1 and 2 given below show the evolution of the Indian and US financial sectors post-1990 relative to GDP.[1] A striking difference is that while the magnitude of the corporate bond market in the USA is approximately equal to the stock market, the corporate bond market in India is insignificant. Figure 3 is a magnified plot of the miniscule corporate bond market in India, which at its peak was about 5 percent of GDP. What I find puzzling is Figure 1 titled "External Corporate Borrowing as a percent of GDP, 1991–2014" in the paper, which quantifies "external corporate borrowing"[2] at 7 percent of GDP. It suggests that external borrowing by Indian firms exceeds domestic borrowing!

* To preserve the sense of the discussions at the IPF, these discussants' comments reflect the views expressed at the IPF and do not take into account revisions to the original conference paper in response to these and other comments, even though the IPF Volume itself contains the revised paper. The original conference version of the paper is available on www.ncaer.org.

† I thank Jamal Mecklai for insightful comments. I am grateful to the participants at the India Policy Forum 2015 for a stimulating discussion.

1. In 2014, India's GDP was approximately US$ 2 trillion. The US GDP was an order of magnitude more.
2. External corporate borrowing is the sum of foreign currency borrowing and trade credit.

FIGURE 1. Evolution of the Financial Sector in India: 1990–2011

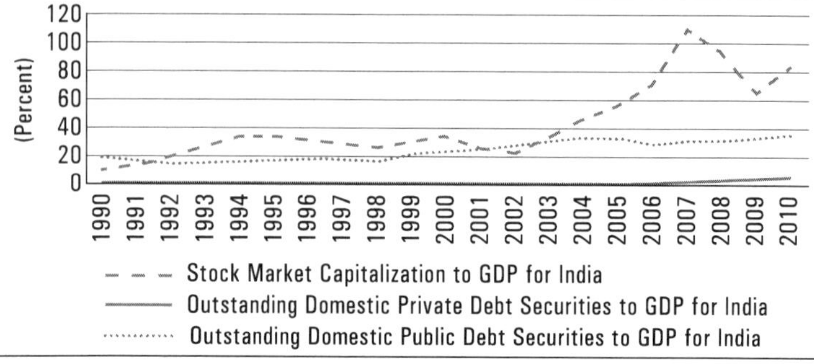

Source: 2015 research.stlouisfed.org.

FIGURE 2. Evolution of the Financial Sector in the USA: 1990–2011

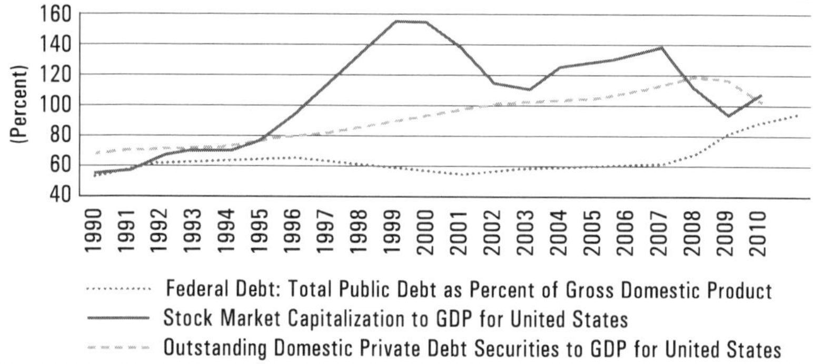

Source: 2015 research.stlouisfed.org.

Private Benefits vs Social Costs

Trade reforms gave Indian firms the ability to compete globally in both factor and product markets. Why not give Indian firms the ability to compete globally for financial capital? This will probably lower the cost of capital, increase investment, and consequently growth. This question cannot be answered in the abstract.

When a firm borrows in a foreign currency, its balance sheet is exposed to exchange rate fluctuations. The optimal response of a value-maximizing firm to this additional source of risk will depend on its perception of how the government will respond to exchange rate movements. The current

FIGURE 3. The Corporate Debt Market in India: 1990–2011

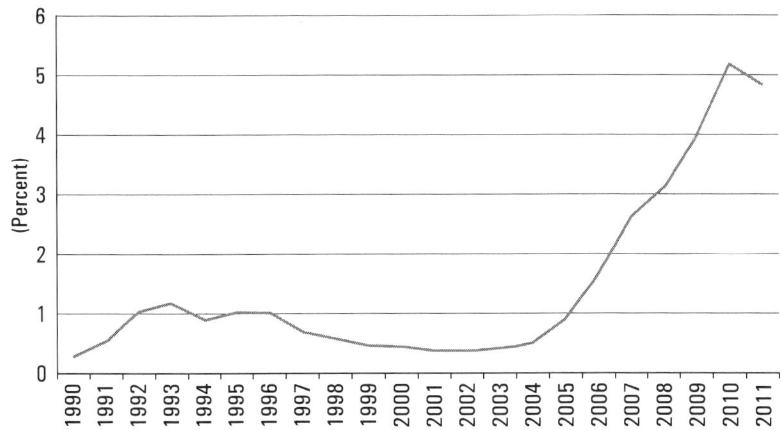

Source: 2015 research.stlouisfed.org.

government policy is an "implicit put," limiting exchange rate movements to a narrow ±5 percent range. This creates an incentive for individual firms to under-hedge their foreign exchange (FX) exposure. If numerous firms borrow internationally and do not optimally hedge their currency exposure, the probability of a correlated default increases in the presence of a large exchange rate movement. Idiosyncratic risk at the firm level manifests as an economy-wide systematic risk. The consequent negative externalities constitute a market failure.

A Suboptimal Response

Hedging FX risk is a component of the overall risk management strategy of a firm. A policy of forcing each firm to fully hedge its exposure is clearly suboptimal. It is isomorphic to costly domestic borrowing. More importantly, as is illustrated in the paper of Patnaik, Shah, and Singh, it does not take into account the FX exposure of an individual firm. A highlight of the paper is an example that shows that a domestic firm—the authors quote the case of an Airline Company—may have implicit FX exposure if import parity pricing holds in factor and product markets. Thus, unhedged international borrowing may actually reduce initial product risk for such a firm, without increasing the risk of contagion.

A Solution?

The authors, echoing the Sahoo Committee Report, propose scrapping the current archaic regulations in favor of a more nuanced, case-by-case approach. Firms would still be required to hedge a part of their currency exposure, net of any implicit hedges in place. The information requirements associated with implementing their proposals are nontrivial. An alternative would be to go beyond the Sahoo Committee recommendations and take steps to eliminate the source of the moral hazard. This will go a long way toward addressing India's fundamental need to access capital at competitive rates.

In April 2015, RBI Governor Raghuram Rajan commented, "We hope to get full capital account convertibility in a short number of years." Full capital account convertibility cannot be wished into being. The first essential step would involve reviving and rejuvenating India's moribund FX market.

In 2007, according to a Mecklai Financial study, the Indian FX market was one of the most liquid markets in the emerging markets. It ranked third out of 15 markets studied.

By 2013, the onshore Over-the-Counter (OTC) USD/INR liquidity had shrunk, relative to trade, by over 50 percent. In absolute terms, while global FX market liquidity increased by around 50 percent, onshore USD/INR trading volumes declined by 12.5 percent. In the global FX market, non-bank financial institutions (NBFCs; mutual funds, hedge funds, insurance companies, primary dealers) generate nearly 52 percent of the market volume. In contrast, in the Indian USD/INR market, non-bank entities make up just 26 percent of the market volume.

As a first step toward increasing liquidity and capital account convertibility, the RBI should permit NBFCs to access the domestic USD/INR market, even if they do not have any underlying FX exposures. This would add about US$ 10 billion to daily turnover, introduce a diversity of players and views, incentivize information-gathering, and lay the foundations for trading transparency and market efficiency. The consequent increase in average volatility would, in turn, motivate firms to endogenously adapt by increasing their hedge ratios to optimally hedge risk.

Concluding Comments

Over the past decade, India's external trade has doubled. However, FX transactions have not kept pace. This is largely because of the absence of non-bank transactions, which typically constitute 50 percent of all FX transactions. This paper is a well-articulated, timely reminder of much-needed reform in this area.

Tarun Ramadorai

Oxford University

Thanks to NCAER for inviting me to discuss this paper. This is yet another thought-provoking paper by Ajay, Ila, and Nirvikar. Looking at the difference between Ila's presentation and the paper as written, I had a sense of cognitive dissonance—her presentation had issues that Ila would probably have liked to have communicated in the paper, but did not.

Let me begin with a quick overview. Foreign currency borrowing has increased hugely, doubling over the last decade to around 8 percent of GDP). Whether or not you think that the "level" is correct, there has been a dramatic "increase" over the past 10 years or so. As usual, given our regulatory environment, there are labyrinthine regulations surrounding who, how, when, how much, from whom, and why it can be borrowed. The authors wade into this complicated issue and, as far as I can see, make three policy prescriptions which seem to roughly correspond to the prescriptions of the Sahoo Committee Report.

First, they recommend doing away with the complex array of controls on foreign currency borrowing in dollars or rupees, once hedging is in place. This is important—note that this applies "once hedging is in place". Second, they recommend eliminating the cap on rupee-denominated borrowing, which is currently lower than the cap on dollar-denominated borrowing. This is because of a design issue—one is a cap on flows, while the other is a cap on the stock of borrowing. This current design does not really make a lot of sense, so it is difficult to disagree with the authors' prescription in this case. Third, and in some sense most controversial part of the Sahoo Committee Report and the authors' prescription, is to compute firm exposure to foreign currency risk and "enforce" hedging by firms.

I will concentrate my discussion on this third prescription, which seems problematic to me for a number of reasons. Let me begin by highlighting some simple logistical complexities before getting into the deeper incentive issues: first, it is clearly difficult to compute exposure correctly; second, we have to decide that some firms are naturally hedged because they have exports offsetting their imports; and third, we have to enforce their putting a synthetic hedge in place. These complications ensure that intrusive inspections and bureaucracy will need to be put in place to enforce this prescription. However, in my view, which I believe Rajnish Mehra shares, this is the least of the worries about this prescription. Enforcing hedging just does not make sense for many other more important reasons, which I will now turn to describing.

One way to begin this discussion is to turn to some of the specifics of the paper. The authors observe in the data that firms' hedging intensity is correlated with foreign exchange rate volatility. This, according to the authors, is evidence that firms have an implicit put option to the government and suggests that there is a moral hazard problem. Let me explain this. The authors' argument is that if firms believe that the government is going to manage the exchange rate when the going gets rough, that is, that there is an implicit cap on the exchange rate when it moves ±5 percent, then firms have a tendency to act as if they have a free ride within those bounds—they can simply forget about hedging at low levels of volatility, since they expect that the government is going to come in and save their bacon if things get any worse on the volatility front. As a result, the authors prescribe mandatory hedging by firms to eliminate this perceived moral hazard problem.

My first issue is that the evidence simply does not support such a proposal. Why? Well, the problem with any empirical analysis of this nature is that it is observationally equivalent with another explanation, which is far simpler—meaning that Occam's razor would lead you to believe it more than the complicated moral hazard alternative. The alternative explanation is that if exchange rate volatility goes up (and we know that volatility is highly persistent), then it changes firms' expectations about future volatility, creating incentives to hedge, and so observed hedging rises. If exchange rate volatility is lower, then firms do not perceive that they need to hedge, ergo they do not hedge and observed hedging falls. According to this simpler explanation, perhaps there is no market failure at all—moral hazard is just illusory, in the absence of more credible identification. My conclusion is that we cannot really say much more about which explanation is true, and we are back to Occam's razor. We can certainly point out that theoretically the implicit put exists, which may lead to some moral hazard issues. But I do not think that we can really prove anything when we look at the data and correlate hedging activity with volatility. My reading of the facts is that firms appear to respond appropriately to the signals that are offered to them by the market.

To my mind, there is another moral hazard here, which is bigger, and which we are completely ignoring in this conversation—this is the question of whether bailouts are available from state-owned banks if things go wrong. That to my mind is one big problem with the Indian banking sector—every time something goes wrong for firms, it looks like domestic banks are willing to step in and provide credit to put it right. That is an important implicit put that exists in the Indian system today—it does not matter if you are truly creditworthy, because if you beg hard enough and apply political pressure, then someone in the state system is going to give you a loan. This is a problem that RBI is fixing, thankfully, and while this is not the problem being referred to in this paper, it is certainly lurking in the background. It might be worthwhile for the authors to see if they can find evidence that foreign exchange losses are "hedged" by cheap credit from the banking system. That would certainly constitute a smoking gun if the authors were looking for one.

Another point the authors make is that they observe that there are not many long-dated derivatives contracts. They suggest that a market may be missing where firms can hedge long term. I should point out a few things in this context. First, the fact that some exchange rate exposures are from very long-term contracts means that firms might not even need the hedge. If purchasing power parity (PPP) holds (we know from plenty of work that the half-life of PPP deviations is about three and a half to five years), then the optimal hedge is not to hedge since real exchange rates are mean-reverting. You just need to wait long enough, and eventually everything is going to be fine. Perhaps firms are not hedging long term because of their long-duration loans or contracts, meaning that it does not make a difference at the end of the day whether they hedge or not. In particular, if transactions costs are high enough, why bother to hedge? It seems to me that the problem lies not in long-term borrowing but in short-term borrowing when PPP does not hold. That is to say, trade credit may well be the issue rather than long-term external commercial borrowing.

In any case, "constraining" firms to hedge is a very inefficient solution, even if you do believe that there is a market failure constraining firms from hedging. An aside—I feel that in India, we have a sense of embarrassment about eliminating regulations. Every time we remove a regulation, we feel the need to add another in its place because we feel a sense of emptiness if we do not have a maze of regulations confronting us! More seriously, if we impose the constraint that firms "must" hedge, then think about the resulting equilibrium.

On one hand, we would have imposed hedging pressure on the market through this constraint. On the other hand, we generally frown upon speculators entering the market. We now have a one-sided market, where we have created enforced hedging demand, with no one on the other side to satisfy it. Let us recall what a hedging contract is—if I take a short position in a currency to hedge a long exposure, then someone has got to step in and provide me with this trade, that is, take the long position on the other side. Who is that entity? Generally, we require speculative capital on the other side. Firms that will be required to hedge generally have very similar hedging requirements (more importantly, on aggregate, we know that there is a trade imbalance on one side of the market or the other). The net result, if speculative capital is not available to step in and fulfill this created need, is severe price pressure on the exchange rate. This, in turn, will create unnatural appreciation or depreciation and artificial exchange rate volatility, since the price mechanism is the only way to achieve equilibrium to clear the hedging market.

This is the classic Keynesian hedging pressure theory of exchange rates—and I suspect that it applies well in this case, meaning that such a policy will simply create additional volatility in the exchange rate. This issue highlights a concern with many of our policies—we tend to think in partial equilibrium, while the world lives in general equilibrium.

Of course, the other problem with the policy prescription of mandatory hedging is that if we push firms to hedge, then there is a potential Frankenstein scenario out there. If we force firms to develop technologies to hedge complex financial derivatives contracts rather than stick to their knitting, then we could end up creating another Enron or Metallgesellschaft, that is, firms that got into hedging, and seemingly stopped doing what they were really good at, to their eventual destruction. I would propose that we do not want firms to develop a capability to engage in financial engineering if they do not already see the need to develop it without a regulatory push.

Let us go back to India's Byzantine regulations for a moment. I would like to commend the authors, who have really been on the frontlines of wanting to scrap regulations and have been at the forefront of the effort to write bright-line laws to eliminate ambiguity. This is much needed, and I fully subscribe to their point of view. While regulations are wonderful for applied economists because they provide lots of identification, and I would personally be quite sad to see them go because it reduces my opportunities to produce research, they are pretty much everyone else's nightmare. So, I fully support the authors' desire to reduce the system of regulations surrounding this issue. However, in the same spirit, I do not believe that the answer is an intrusive system of mandatory hedging. I would propose that the authors explore an intermediate solution—perhaps a disclosure-based solution. In many countries, accounting standards require you to disclose your extent of hedging. My own research using the US data on this issue suggests that firms do not really treat this exercise with the care it might warrant, but, at the very least, one is able to get a sense of what firms are doing. This is helpful—if the information is out there, then it can be used by market participants to assess firms' risk as a result of hedging (or eschewing hedges). If this risk is indeed systematic, then the expected return on firms subject to this risk on account of their hedging policies will change to reflect this in a well-functioning equity market such as we have in India.

I would now like to turn to another issue that the authors highlight in this paper. They point out that foreign currency borrowing stood at US$ 171 billion at end-December 2014, and that rupee borrowing from foreign lenders is capped at US$ 51 billion. I fully agree with the authors that this seems problematic. Short-term foreign currency-denominated borrowing has been highlighted as a form of "bad cholesterol" ever since the time of the Asian crisis. However, with rupee borrowing from foreign institutions, there is one issue that I would like to highlight. We know that there is a parent–subsidiary structure issue here. In particular, foreign parent institutions fund their local subsidiaries to engage in rupee lending. The issue that this raises is whether the parent has the ability to call these rupee loans of the subsidiaries in response to currency fluctuations that they face overseas. If this is the case, then rupee borrowing from foreign institutions is equivalent to foreign currency borrowing, so we are back to the same issue through a different route. My point is that the financing arrangements need to be scrutinized, and as long as there is a contract structure that is robust to this issue, rupee borrowing from foreign lenders should not be any riskier than borrowing from domestic financial institutions in rupees. It just seems to me that we might wish to pay attention to the details to ensure that this is the case.

Overall, I think that this is a great paper, which highlights a really important issue, and which is no surprise coming from these distinguished authors. Thanks for giving me the opportunity to discuss it.

General Discussion

Kenneth Kletzer, commenting on research on the paper, said that the paper references some fairly old ideas about unhedged borrowing and exchange rate stability and a little bit about original sin. He pointed out that a lot more thinking had followed the financial crises occurring before 2000, especially with reference to the development of domestic corporate bond markets. He noted that the corporate bond market in India is much smaller than the corporate borrowing from abroad and that encouraging corporate borrowing signifies a different direction than the lessons learnt from the financial crises of the 1990s and early 2000s. According to him, the problem pertained to underdeveloped domestic bond markets and access to foreign markets wherein the firms would endogenously hedge, with the expectation of potential government guarantees or bailouts in the event of a sharp devaluation or depreciation, as also noted by the authors and the discussants.

Kletzer identified certain interesting questions with reference to the paper, including, firstly, concerning the people assessing the development and reasons for the development and encouragement of domestic corporate bond borrowing and, secondly, the comparison with international bond markets, whereby the Indian market looks really small as compared to not just the US bond market but also the Southeast Asian emerging economies, or even the economies of Malaysia or Chile, for example. He noted that one of the outliers wherein people talk about the reason why the bond market in India is so small and why there is so much foreign borrowing by corporates is by citing the example of Brazil's domestic market, which is grossly bigger than India's, and which presents an interesting agenda from the policy perspective by looking to develop borrowing in the presence of Byzantine regulations and sweeping reforms. He commented that other countries had done this as they had very small domestic borrowings and tight regulations on foreign borrowing, but they swept away these, resulting in severe crises in many parts of the world, including Mexico, East Asia, and Latin America.

Kletzer's next comment had to do with research, as he highlighted the issue of firm-level borrowing. He argued that one of the things that people had done in other countries was to look at bond issues and the choice of whether to issue that bond in domestic currency or foreign currency. This, however, posed a problem in the case of India, which is characterized by a very large percentage of private placements in the domestic market. It would, therefore, be interesting to examine the more recent literature on the development of domestic bond markets as well as the empirical literature on the endogenous choice, which deals with the econometric problem of choosing the currency in which to issue the bond and the currency in which it is issued internationally.

Mihir Desai cited the comment by Tarun Ramadorai on trade credit and wanted to know what the incentives would be. He opined that the incentive is ostensibly to switch toward the shorter duration trade credit. Secondly, he suggested that the large rise in foreign currency borrowing should be documented, but simultaneously, it is important to identify any indication of an associated rise in the natural hedges which would justify that. He said that what was relevant here was the issue of foreign direct investment (FDI). Citing an example, he said that if the company in question is, say, the Jaguar Land Rover (JLR) subsidiary of Tata Motors, the vast majority of cash flows would be in dollars and pounds as JLR is mainly involved in exports. In this case, it would thus be pertinent to have a back of the envelope calculation about the degree to which the rise in foreign currency borrowing is, in some sense, not offset by FDI. These calculations could also be done on a firm by firm basis, as most of the firms involved are large ones, and an analysis of about 30 firms would denote the trend. The information technology sector, which accounts for a significant chunk of foreign currency borrowings, also mainly deals in cash flows in dollars. Finally, he wanted to know if anyone had studied the recent depreciation in currency and traced its effect on firms involved in foreign currency borrowings. He expressed surprise at the fact that this issue had hitherto not been raised by anyone, though there were indications of an unclear borrowing in this area.

Devesh Kapur noted that one of the graphs in the paper showed the recent growth of ECBs by financial firms. He urged the authors to provide a sense of these borrowings, as the ECBs of financial firms could be a big source of worry because of the inherent systemic risk. He questioned if they were public sector banks, private sector banks, or non-banking financial companies, and he also wanted to know who was doing this borrowing. Secondly, he argued that the presentation does not clearly explain the issue of the complexity and Byzantine nature of the regulations it talks of. The authors presenting the paper aver that these are jointly being implemented by a group comprising officials from the Ministry of Finance and the Reserve Bank of India (RBI). Kapoor asserted that since one of the authors is in the Ministry of Finance, they should be able to clarify why the Ministry of Finance agreed to these rules with which the authors obviously seem to disagree sharply. He also wanted to know if this reflects the bargaining power between the Ministry of Finance and RBI.

Anusha Chari raised the question of the systemic risk that is generated by leverage in the system and the fact that firms do not internalize what they are borrowing. This inevitably generates a risk when they are borrowing, which basically arises from the use of debt instruments rather than equity. She stressed that the manner in which capital controls have been implemented in other countries such as Brazil indicates that they have put on Tobin tax type of policies, wherein they add a tax if anybody wants to lend to a Brazilian firm, which introduces a whole set of distortions of its own. Her question, stemming from these issues, was that given that debt is a noncontingent claim, instead of putting on these capital controls, why do the countries not try and limit the leverage in a system by implementing macro prudential regulation? She also claimed that India is seemingly trying to do this, though in a complicated, mindboggling sort of way and asked the authors to express their thoughts on the use of macro prudential versus capital controls.

The authors Ila Patnaik and Nirvikar Singh thanked the participants for their comments and after responding to them on the floor said that they would also incorporate them in the revised version of their paper.

The session was brought to a close by the Chair Dr Shekhar Shah, who thanked the presenters, discussants, and participants in the floor discussion for the interesting session and the significant issues raised during it.

KARTHIK MURALIDHARAN*
University of California, San Diego, NBER, NCAER, and *J-PAL*

New Approach to Public Sector Hiring in India for Improved Service Delivery

ABSTRACT This paper argues that the current structure of the public-sector labor markets in India severely limits the ability of the Indian state to effectively deliver services across a wide variety of core functions including policing, education, health care, and public health. Sources of inefficiency include: too few front-line employees, caused in part by entry-level salaries that are too high; lifetime jobs offered without assessing candidate fit for the position; ineffective training and skilling; inadequate rewards for performance; and spatial mismatch between population needs and employees' preferred work locations. I propose a new approach to hiring front-line service providers to address these issues. The key idea is to introduce three- to five-year-apprenticeships for entry-level service providers, giving priority to local candidates, and interspersing modular training and certification of skills that are consistent with the new National Skills Framework. Hiring into regular full-time positions will be unchanged for the most part, but (performance-linked) credit will be provided for each successful year as an apprentice. One-time exit payments will be made to apprentices who do not get selected for regular positions. I illustrate this approach with several examples, and argue that such an approach can improve the quantity and quality of front-line service providers, in a fiscally feasible way. Additional benefits include reducing youth unemployment, improving their skills, and increasing female labor force participation and empowerment. Since most front-line service delivery responsibilities are under the jurisdiction of state governments, I conclude by noting that the increased fiscal devolution to states under the Fourteenth Finance Commission constitutes an especially promising opportunity for a few states to try out this approach.

Keywords: *Public Sector Labor Markets, Public Expenditure, Public Goods, Service Delivery, Misallocation, Hiring, Training, Personnel Economics, India*

JEL Classification: *H40, H50, J41, J45*

* *kamurali@ucsd.edu*

1. Introduction

Several studies over the past decade have documented that the Indian state does a poor job at effectively delivering basic services to its citizens. These weaknesses are apparent in almost every function of the state, including policing, water and sanitation, public health, and education (Pritchett 2009; World Bank 2003). One strand of explanatory factors for poor service delivery has focused on the weak governance and accountability of front-line service providers—exemplified by high absence rates of teachers and health care workers (Kremer et al. 2005; Muralidharan et al. 2011; Muralidharan et al. 2015). A second strand has focused on the poor training and preparation of front-line service providers (Rao et al. 2011).

While both of these factors are important, a more direct explanation for poor service delivery may simply be the inadequate numbers of front-line staff. The Indian state is remarkably under-staffed in several front-line service delivery functions including police, teaching, and community health. At the same time, fiscal pressures have made it difficult to fill even existing vacancies, let alone create new positions. The standard approach of advocates for any given sector (such as education or health) to address these staffing shortages is to argue for a larger budget—typically, for hiring more staff and launching more programs. For instance, education advocates repeatedly call for 6 percent of gross domestic product (GDP) to be spent on education, and health advocates similarly call for 3 percent of GDP to be spent on health.[1]

However, these calls for increased spending rarely consider the broader fiscal situation (such as the low tax-to-GDP ratio in India of around 17 percent), or the opportunity costs of diverting funds to their preferred sector (within a fixed overall budget). It is then left to the Finance Ministry to juggle the competing demands across a fixed fiscal envelope and in practice most ministries and departments get less than what they seek. The "shortage" of funds then becomes an alibi for poor state capacity and service delivery. However, given the strained nature of public finances as a whole, it should be clear that "more of the same" will simply not work, and that policymakers need to find a way to deliver services more effectively within the same fiscal

1. Understanding the sources of these benchmarks (typically, emanating from international organizations like UNESCO, UNICEF, and the WHO) and the assumptions behind them is an interesting exercise in its own right. Typically, they are based on taking the current structure of costs per user or facility and multiplying them by the extent of additional coverage that is needed to reach universal access. While universal coverage is certainly a laudable goal, what is typically missing from these benchmark calculations is any consideration of the possibility of achieving the same goals in a more cost-effective manner.

envelope, with increased focus on the *quality* of public spending on service delivery and its cost-effectiveness.

I argue in this paper that a fundamental reason for the weak capacity of the Indian state for service delivery is the current structure of public-sector labor markets, which induce several inefficiencies in the productivity and effectiveness of publicly provided services, and also induce distortions in the broader economy. I present evidence to show that the status quo system does not hire enough front-line service delivery staff, does not adequately assess their fit for the roles they are hired for, does not train them the right way, does not allocate them optimally spatially, does not pay them the right way, and does not promote them the right way either. Recognizing these distortions is essential to correctly diagnose the problem. The first goal of this paper is to document the broad range of distortions induced by the current structure of public-sector labor markets, and the ways in which the status quo is sub-optimal.

I then proceed to discuss a possible new approach to hiring front-line service providers that has the potential to mitigate these distortions and improve service delivery without significantly increasing spending. This approach draws on different strands of evidence from India and around the world and it features the following main components: (a) create untenured apprenticeship positions lasting from three to five years in major front-line service delivery departments including police, teaching, community health, and early-childhood care at lower entry-level pay scales than the status quo; (b) give preference to local candidates for these positions; (c) create modular training courses that are taken alongside the apprenticeship and allow the interspersing of theory and practice, and provide certificates of levels of skilling that are compatible with the new National Skills Qualification Framework; (d) retain the current pay scales and process for hiring regular full-time staff (including age limits for entry), but provide extra (performance-based)[2] credit for each year of successful service as an apprentice; (e) provide one-time payments to apprentices (based on years of meritorious service) who do not get hired into regular full-time positions at the end of their eligibility age.

There are several ways in which the proposed approach improves upon the status quo. First, it allows for a fiscally feasible expansion of front-line service providers in areas where they are needed by increasing the hiring of

2. While providing performance-based credit would be ideal, in practice, even an approach that simply provides credit for each year of successful service would enable a considerable improvement over the status quo. See Section 3.1.5 for a more detailed discussion of this issue.

local candidates at a lower pay scale. Second, it improves the effectiveness of training by interspersing credentialing with practice. Further, providing credit for performance on the training modules at the time of regular hiring will improve the extent to which apprentices absorb and apply the training to their jobs. Third, it is likely to improve the match quality of front-line service jobs by allowing candidates to experience the actual job for a few years before getting hired into permanent positions, and by placing more weight on performance on the job before offering permanent positions. Under the status quo, most candidates enter a permanent government job before having any experience of what the job entails in practice. Many of these candidates may be qualified on paper, but they may be a poor fit for the actual job on personal characteristics that are not reflected on a résumé, entrance exam, or interview.[3]

The three main margins on which quality and effectiveness of public employees can be improved are: selection, training, and motivation/rewards for performance. The proposed approach aims to improve the quality of the public-sector workforce on all of these margins. A good way of summarizing this approach is to say that it reduces the barriers to entry into service-delivery positions (since many more apprentices can be hired than regular staff), but it raises the barriers to entry into permanent government positions and it ensures that those selected for permanent positions are more likely to have demonstrated aptitude and competence on the job. The one-time payment to apprentices who do not get selected for regular positions is designed to facilitate their transition to other roles, and the credentials accumulated during the apprenticeship will in turn improve their skills and employability in the private sector.

Beyond these direct benefits to service delivery, there are also likely to be several indirect benefits to the economy. First, educated youth in India waste several years attempting entrance exams to various government jobs without gaining either meaningful skills or work experience. The new approach will be designed to make it more attractive to enter apprentice positions and obtain modular credentials, since it will increase the probability of getting a regular government job. This in turn will reduce youth unemployment and the misallocation of talent by channeling time into more socially productive tasks. Second, a major barrier to increased female labor

3. Teaching is a particularly good example, where qualified candidates who get selected for permanent positions have often not spent much time actually teaching. Many ultimately find that they are simply not ready to deal with the challenges of managing a classroom. The same point also applies to *anganwadi* (early-childhood care) workers.

force participation is the unwillingness (or inability) of young educated rural women who have completed secondary or higher secondary school to travel outside their village to work (this could reflect strong social norms—especially in rural North India). An emphasis on local hiring for new positions as teaching assistants, early childhood caregivers, public health workers, and police personnel can, therefore, significantly improve female labor force participation and empowerment. Third, increased employment opportunities for young women who have completed secondary or higher secondary education will increase both real and perceived returns to education for girls, which will positively affect schooling for younger girls, and delay the age of marriage and fertility (Jensen 2012). These in turn are correlated with better child human development outcomes and are a key step in achieving a demographic transition.[4]

There are several elements of this proposal that are not new and have been tried before with mixed success (such as the use of locally hired contract teachers in lieu of regular civil-service teachers in several states, and the recent program of hiring Youth Brigade police staff in Tamil Nadu to supplement the existing police force). However, I will argue that these initiatives have not delivered to full potential (and in some cases have even failed) because they have been introduced in a piece-meal fashion and have not been implemented as part of a new unified approach to personnel policy in the public sector. These issues will be illustrated with a more detailed discussion of how this new approach can be implemented in the case of education using a model of teaching assistants as the first step in a career ladder (and how it mitigates important professional, legal, and political weaknesses of the contract teacher model). I will also discuss the applicability of this model to other critical sectors such as police and early-childhood care.

Finally, I argue that the current moment is a particularly opportune time to try out this new approach. Most of the front-line service delivery functions discussed in this paper are under the purview of state governments. The sharp increases in devolution of funds to state governments under the Fourteenth Finance Commission and the corresponding reduction in allocations to centrally sponsored (and arguably "strait-jacketed") schemes—especially in the social sector—provide an excellent opportunity for states to use

4. The demographic transition refers to the transition of societies from a "high fertility and high mortality" equilibrium to one of "low fertility and low mortality." The demographic transition is also characterized by families prioritizing the *quality* of their children (in terms of human capital investments) over *quantity*, and it is strongly correlated with societies achieving improved human development outcomes, as well as with achieving higher levels of per capita income.

these additional resources to innovate and experiment with more effective ways of delivering services. The main goal of this paper is to provide an analytical framework and a concrete policy suggestion with which states can potentially experiment to sharply improve service delivery in a fiscally feasible way.

There has been a recent increase in both theoretical and empirical research on the importance of building state capacity for development (Besley and Persson 2010; Persson and Besley 2009; Kapur and Subramanian 2013; Krishnan and Somanathan 2013; Mathew and Moore 2011; Muralidharan et al. Forthcoming). This paper contributes to this literature with a focus on front-line service providers and it is a complement to Krishnan and Somanathan (2005; 2013), who discuss the capacity of the apex civil service in India. It also draws on a growing body of research on personnel economics in the public sector in developing countries, which is summarized well in a recent review by Finan et al. (2015).

The rest of this paper is organized as follows. Section 2 presents the key background facts that motivate this paper and outlines the various distortions and inefficiencies that arise from the current structure of public-sector labor markets. Section 3 outlines the proposed new approach to public-sector hiring and illustrates it with a detailed case study of teaching assistants, followed by briefer discussion of applicability to police and early-childhood care givers. Section 4 discusses a possible implementation roadmap and concludes.

2. Some Key Facts

A large number of facts associated with the weak performance of the Indian state at delivering services to its citizens can be explained by the structure of public-sector labor markets. This section outlines key facts on weak service delivery and then discusses distortions in the broader labor market, which are created by the structure of public-sector labor markets.

2.1. Shortage of Front-line Staff for Key Service Delivery Functions

Aggregate data reveal the striking extent to which the capacity of the Indian state to deliver services to its burgeoning population is constrained by the lack of adequate numbers of front-line staff. India's population has nearly doubled in the last 35 years from 700 million in 1980 to 1.3 billion in 2015. However, during this period, the total number of central and state government employees put together has barely increased (moving from 15.5 million in 1980–81 to 17.6 million in 2011–12).[5] Thus, the number of government employees per capita has fallen sharply in this period and these aggregate statistics are also reflected in the paucity of front-line service delivery staff across a range of sectors in India, with several studies and reports documenting a shortage of staff.

Consider policemen, for instance. Among countries with data, India ranks last in the G20 in terms of police officers per capita. India currently has an average of one policeman per 761 people (DNA 2014), which lags behind even the national benchmark established by the Bureau of Police Research and Development of one policeman per 568 people. The lag relative to international standards is even more pronounced: the United Nations recommends one policeman per 450 people, and these figures depart considerably from the police-to-population ratios in developed nations, such as Italy (one policeman per 181), Canada (one per 191), the United States (one per 224), and Spain (one per 313) (Nandan 2014). Further, as I discuss below, the spatial allocation of policemen is far from uniform, which creates even greater shortages in effective staff in several locations.

India also faces a sharp teacher shortage. Estimates indicate that India's schools fall short of 5.86 lakh primary school teachers and 3.5 lakh upper primary teachers (Pathak 2014). The teacher shortage stems partly from the government's reluctance to fill up permanent posts. At the national level, there are 5.23 lakh vacant posts (Kohli 2015). Instead, states such as Uttar Pradesh, Bihar, and Madhya Pradesh—which have faced acute teacher shortages and fiscal deficits in the past decade—have hired para-teachers (who are typically not well-qualified). The use of locally hired non-civil service teachers by itself may not be a problem (as I illustrate below), but the problem is that the use of para-teachers has typically taken place in a "stop gap" manner, without a strategy to integrate para-teachers into a unified human resource framework. This, in turn, has created several problems, which I discuss further in Section 3.

The teacher shortage will be exacerbated by the Right to Education (RTE) Act, which stipulates a reduction in the pupil–teacher ratio (PTR) in primary schools from 40:1 to 30:1 and proscribes the use of contract teachers or para-teachers. It is estimated that, in addition to filling existing vacancies, the government will need an additional 5.1 lakh teachers to meet the 30:1 PTR norm in classes 1–5. Overall, meeting the PTR norms of the RTE

5. These data were provided by Devesh Kapur in his discussant slides and were obtained from indiastat.com.

is expected to cost over ₹25,000 crores/year. This illustrates the tension between the desire to improve staffing and reduce PTR, on the one hand, and the limited fiscal space, on the other.

Similarly, the ratio of health workers to inhabitants in India is also very low by global standards. The number of allopathic doctors, nurses, and midwives (11.9 per 10,000 people) is about half the WHO benchmark of 25.4 workers per 10,000 people (Rao et al. 2011). When adjusted for qualification, the number falls to about a quarter of the WHO benchmark. Further, there is little indication that the availability of health workers per population is improving over time. In fact, the ratios of health professionals (for example, doctors, dentists, and nurses and midwives) to population have barely budged from 2000 to 2009 (Hazarika 2013).

The problem of lack of staff also extends to the effectiveness of early-childhood health and education programs delivered through the Integrated Child Development Services (ICDS). A recent review of the functioning of the ICDS conducted by NCAER for the Planning Commission concluded that *anganwadi* workers are over-burdened and that *anganwadi* centers are under-staffed relative to the range of functions that they are expected to perform (PEO 2011). These findings were reinforced in recent field visits I made to ICDS centers in Tamil Nadu (in June 2015). Even in a high-performing state like Tamil Nadu, staff shortages were the single most frequently reported concern by workers and supervisors.

The gaps in supervisory staff across sectors are also glaring. For instance, a recent review found that 32 percent of the positions of block- and cluster-level education officers across India were vacant (Government of India 2011). Systematic data is not easily available in other sectors, but interviews on a recent field visit to ICDS centers in Tamil Nadu revealed supervisor-level vacancies of over 40 percent. Overall, the evidence above makes it seem clear that there is a severe shortage of front-line staff and supervisory staff across sectors in India, and that this shortage negatively affects the quality of services delivered to citizens.

2.2. Public-sector Salaries Are (too) High and Not Correlated with Productivity

An important reason for the inability of governments to hire staff to fill the shortages documented above is the limited fiscal and budgetary space to do so. Salary costs account for the majority of public expenditure on services, and the salary costs of additional staff are high. While the total number of government employees barely increased during the period from 1980 to 2010, inflation-adjusted government spending (most of which was spent on employee salaries) in the same period increased more than four times.[6] On the face of it, the large excess demand for every open public-sector job—often exceeding 200 applicants per job opening[7]—may suggest that the pay and benefits of a government job are too high (especially, after accounting for the lifetime job security they provide), and that it may be possible to hire more staff at a lower pay.

But by itself, the fact of high excess demand for government jobs at the existing pay and benefit scale does not show that salaries are too high. If the large applicant pool enables the government to select the very best candidates for permanent employment, then what matters is not the extent of excess demand for public-sector jobs, but rather whether the terms offered are adequate to attract the high-quality candidates who *do* get selected (and may have otherwise opted out of public service).

In other words, establishing whether salaries are too high or low requires a comparison of the marginal cost and marginal productivity of government workers at different levels of pay. This is a non-trivial problem because measuring public-sector productivity is difficult to begin with—let alone mapping productivity to specific workers and levels of pay. However, there is one important government-provided service in which we can measure productivity and attribute it to specific workers. This is the case of teaching, where detailed longitudinal data on the annual learning progress of students, combined with the information on the assignment of students to teachers each year, can be used to estimate the "value added" of each teacher. Since the job description for all teachers is similar (teaching children), teachers mostly work on their own in their classroom, and their output is quantifiable in a meaningful way,[8] education provides a useful setting to compare the productivity of different types of public workers. Specifically, this setting can be used to study the relative effectiveness of regular civil-service teachers and contract teachers (or para-teachers) who are hired through different processes and under very different employment terms.

Muralidharan and Sundararaman (2013) present such evidence based on five years of data collected on primary education in Andhra Pradesh (AP)

6. These data were provided by Devesh Kapur in his discussant slides and were obtained from indiastat.com.

7. Averaging across various categories of central government employees, the "applicant to post ratio" (APR) exceeds 200 (UPSC Annual Report 2010). Data provided by Devesh Kapur in his discussant slides.

8. See Chetty et al. (2014a and 2014b) for evidence that having a "high-value-added" teacher in school (measured by their effectiveness in raising students' test scores) is correlated with positive long-term labor market outcomes.

and report two main findings. First, untrained contract teachers (or para-teachers) are able to significantly improve learning outcomes in primary school. Second, contract teachers are at least as effective as regular civil-service teachers who are more educated, have formal teacher training credentials, and are paid over five times higher salaries.[9] They also find that regular teachers were 50 percent more likely to be absent (with an absence rate of 27 percentage points compared to 18 percentage points for contract teachers). Overall, the results suggest that the contract teachers were able to more than make up for their lower levels of education, training, and experience with higher levels of effort.

Other plausible mechanisms for the positive effects of contract teachers include the lower social distance relative to the communities they served, the greater accountability to the community (due to the renewable nature of their contracts), and the fact that they live in the village closer to the school (reducing the daily cost of attendance). Indeed, Kingdon (2011) argues that the high salaries of regular teachers may *increase* their social distance from the communities they serve and make it more difficult for communities to hold teachers accountable.

Further, analysis of longitudinal data on education from AP finds no correlation between teachers' value added and their salary level. The current pay structure rewards qualifications and experience, but these do *not* appear to be correlated with productivity. Similarly, Bau and Das (2011) also find no correlation between teacher salaries and value added in public schools in Pakistan. Thus, high *levels* of pay seem to be neither necessary nor sufficient to ensure improved public worker performance.

In contrast, Muralidharan and Sundararaman (2011) and Muralidharan (2012) find that even modest amounts of performance-linked pay for public school teachers in AP (equal to an average of 3 percent of annual pay—but within a range of 0–15 percent) led to sharp increases in student learning outcomes that were sustained over five years. Muralidharan (2012) finds that students who completed five years of primary school under a system in which their teachers were paid these small performance-linked bonuses scored 0.54 and 0.34 standard deviations higher on math and language tests, respectively (these are very large effects when compared to those of other education interventions).

9. This does not even account for the additional employer contribution towards pensions (equivalent to 10 percent of salary) that the government pays for regular teachers, but does not for contract teachers.

The idea that the productivity of public-sector workers is much more sensitive to the *structure* of pay than to its levels is further supported by recent experimental evidence from Indonesia. De Ree et al. (2015) evaluate the impact of a landmark teacher law passed in Indonesia that *doubled* teacher pay across the board. They find that the pay increase led to a significant increase in teacher satisfaction with their income, a reduction in the number of teachers holding second jobs (and in the hours spent on these jobs), and a reduction in their self-reported financial stress. Despite these improvements, the doubling of pay had absolutely *zero* impact on improved learning outcomes. While it is possible that the increases in pay may have attracted higher quality candidates over the long run, the results suggest that unconditional salary increases for current workers (that are not linked to performance) are an extremely inefficient use of scarce public funds for improving social-sector outcomes. This lesson is especially relevant for the Seventh Pay Commission in India (and for states considering adopting these norms for their employees).

While the best evidence on comparative productivity across public workers on different pay and employment contracts comes from education, there is also similar evidence from the health sector. Das et al. (Forthcoming) measure the quality of health care across public and private providers in rural Madhya Pradesh using an audit study, where highly trained standardized fake patients presented a common set of symptoms during unannounced visits to health care providers. The symptoms presented were for cases of unstable angina, asthma, and dysentery in a 2-year-old child at home, and the cases were chosen so that the presenting symptoms were consistent with multiple possible diagnoses. The quality of health care provided was evaluated based on the effort expended by the provider to reach a correct diagnosis (measured by the fraction of items completed on an essential checklist of history-taking questions and exams), and the correctness of the treatment provided.[10]

In addition to measuring provider quality, Das et al. (Forthcoming) observe the prices charged for the transaction in the private sector, and

10. The use of standardized patients allows the authors of this study to credibly measure the quality of care provided because they know the underlying ailment that was presented, the corresponding checklist items, and the correct treatment. This would not be possible if they just observed doctors in their clinics with typical patients because the actual ailment presented and the corresponding correct treatment protocol would not be known to the observer. The details of the measurement protocol are important because the fundamental challenge in assessing whether pay is correlated with productivity is to identify the productivity/quality of individual public-sector workers.

collect data on salaries for the public-sector staff. They find that while prices charged in the private sector are positively correlated with effort (time spent and checklist completion) and with the provision of a correct treatment, there is *no correlation* between wages and effort or quality in the public sector.

Thus, while the current structure of entry-level pay and benefits in public-sector jobs may attract more qualified candidates on paper, it is not clear that these qualifications are either necessary (as seen by the evidence on contract teachers) or sufficient to ensure quality service delivery. Overall, the idea that high salaries, benefits, and job security help to attract the most effective public-sector workers does not seem to be supported by the evidence. Further, modifying the structure of pay to include performance-based components is likely to deliver considerably improved outcomes for a given level of spending.

2.3. The Status Quo on Training and Credentialing is Not Working

Another rationale for the current system of public-sector recruitment is to hire qualified service providers. For instance, teacher selection norms prescribe that candidates must have either a diploma or degree in education. While this seems reasonable, it does not seem to produce the expected results. For instance, there is not a single credible study on education in India that finds a significant positive correlation between teachers possessing formal training credentials and their effectiveness in improving student learning—at least in the public sector (see Muralidharan 2013, for a review of the evidence). Why might this be the case? There are three plausible reasons.

First, many of the institutions that provide teacher education certificates are of very poor quality and it is not uncommon for these certificates to even be purchased, in which case it is not surprising that their possession is not correlated with effectiveness. Second, even in cases where the institutions are of reasonable quality and the credentials genuine, a content analysis of the curriculum of teacher training institutions reveals an almost exclusive focus on theoretical issues, including the history, theory, philosophy, and sociology of education, with very little attention paid to effective pedagogy. While the current content may help teachers become more reflective and potentially more effective, it does not adequately prepare them for the practice of managing a classroom full of children and teaching effectively in such a setting. Third, even if the content of the training is useful in making teachers more effective, it may not translate into improvements in classroom effectiveness because there are no career rewards for effective teaching.

The establishment of a Teacher Eligibility Test (TET) as a pre-requisite for entry into the profession is likely to help with the first problem (of low-quality or fake degrees). Yet, it does not address the second or third concerns. In contrast, the global evidence on effective teacher training programs suggests that programs that intersperse classroom instruction with extended periods of teaching practice under the observation of experienced teachers hold some promise (see the next section for the review). This is already common practice in the medical profession, in which residents conduct hospital rounds supervised by senior physicians to diagnose patients and propose a prognosis. I will return to this theme in the next section.

2.4. Mismatch between Selection Criteria and Determinants of Effectiveness on the Job

The results presented above suggest that the current selection criteria (performance on exams and interviews) as well as pay criteria (qualifications and experience) do not predict the performance of employees on the job. At the same time, we also find significant and persistent variation in employee effectiveness when measured directly with performance data (such as teachers' value added). Given that this variation is persistent, it suggests that there *are* characteristics of employees that are correlated with their performance, but that these characteristics are not easily observed at the time of recruitment.

Identifying and quantifying these traits is an active and fascinating area of ongoing research. Some of these include traits such as persistence, grit, discipline, and pro-social behavior that may be correlated with effectiveness on any job, and some are traits that may be relevant for success on specific jobs (such as enjoying working with children for teachers or early-childhood workers).[11] This literature is still nascent, but two broad themes emerge from it.

11. This is an important distinction because sector advocates often argue for policies that will attract higher quality candidates into that specific profession (the most common example is arguing for salary increases across the board—see for instance the UNESCO Education for All Global Monitoring Reports). However, from a social perspective, it is not obvious that this is efficient because attracting high-quality talent into a sector displaces it from other sectors where the social value of the talent could have been higher. On the other hand, identifying the traits that are likely to make candidates more successful in some professions than in others, and using these traits to match candidates to occupations, will likely improve job fit and increase efficiency across the board.

First, there is mounting evidence that employee characteristics that are difficult to observe at the time of recruitment are important for their actual effectiveness. For instance, there is evidence that skills such as leadership, perseverance, and critical thinking are positively correlated with teacher effectiveness (Bastian 2013; Dobbie 2011; Duckworth et al. 2009; Rockoff et al. 2011). There is also suggestive evidence that public employees with higher "socio-emotional" or "character" skills perform better on the job. For example, doctors in Punjab (Pakistan) who scored higher on measures of agreeableness, emotional stability, extroversion, conscientiousness, and openness (collectively known as the "big five" traits), or on a measure of intrinsic motivation for public service, were more likely to attend work and less likely to falsify inspection reports (Callen et al. 2015). Health inspectors who scored higher on these personality measures were also more responsive to increased monitoring. And senior health officials with higher big five scores were more likely to respond to a report of an underperforming facility by compelling better staff attendance.

There is also evidence from teacher interviews conducted in AP that pro-social attitudes and empathy with student conditions is an important predictor of teacher effectiveness (these interviews were conducted as part of the Andhra Pradesh Randomized Evaluation Studies in education). Specifically, interviewing teachers facing similar student populations but who had different levels of effectiveness, we found that low-performing teachers often had a derogatory attitude towards first-generation learners. They claimed that these children would drop out of school anyway and only attended school for the free mid-day meals. On the other hand, high-performing teachers reacted to the same situation with the attitude that *they* were the only hope for a child who was a first-generation learner. The importance of such differences in empathy is almost obvious ex-post, but these are not traits on which teachers are currently selected.

The same theme was repeated during my recent field visits to ICDS centers in Tamil Nadu, where senior field staff mentioned that many candidates simply applied for the job because of the attraction of a government job and often got recruited based on their paper qualifications and interview, but that they were not a good fit for the job because of inadequate empathy with children and inability to keep them engaged in a classroom.

The second important theme from this literature is that while these traits (I shall refer to them as "non-CV" traits) are difficult to measure at the time of recruiting, they *are* observable on the job. In the United States, a number of studies have shown that teachers' performance on classroom observations (Grossman et al. 2013; Kane and Staiger 2012; Kane et al. 2011;

Pianta et al. 2008), student surveys (Kane and Staiger 2011), and principal surveys (Jacob and Lefgren 2008; Rockoff et al. 2012) do a much better job predicting that teachers' capacity to improve student achievement than traditional measures such as graduate degrees or teaching certificates. Again, while the best evidence on these topics comes from education, several qualitative studies from around the world point to the importance of temperament and other "non-CV" traits in the effectiveness of policemen and in their ability to be unbiased in interacting with populations with different demographic characteristics from themselves, which are however easily observable to senior officers and colleagues (Correll et al. 2002; Sim et al. 2013).

2.5. Spatial Mismatch

The average figures on police officers, teachers, and health workers per capita in Section 2.1 may severely understate the extent of staff shortages by masking considerable spatial variation. This is true both across states (with poorer states having worse ratios—partly explained by their lower budgets) and within states (with rural areas having much poorer effective availability per capita of public service providers). Note the use of the term "effective availability" as opposed to "availability." The latter is typically reported in official data on the basis of sanctioned staff, whereas the former accounts for unfilled vacancies and provider absences (which are both higher in poorer states and rural areas).

For instance, the all-India average PTR in primary schools in 2010 was 39.8:1, which was in accordance with the norms at the time (a PTR of 40:1 prior to the passing of the RTE Act). However, this average can be misleading because states like Kerala, Tamil Nadu, Karnataka, AP, and Himachal Pradesh had PTRs of 25:1 or lower; states like UP and MP had PTRs of around 47:1; and states like Bihar had PTRs close to 70:1. Adjusting for teacher absences, the figure is even more striking, with the effective PTR in UP being close to 70:1, in Jharkhand to 80:1, and in Bihar to 100:1 (Muralidharan et al. 2015).

Similar patterns emerge in police to population ratios. The situation is particularly grim in states like UP, where each policeman serves over 1,100 people, which is almost double the national average (DNA 2014). Further, in practice, the spatial allocation of police personnel is controlled by elites and leads to a more than proportionate use of police personnel to address elite concerns as opposed to that of the average population. A striking example is provided by the extent to which police forces are diverted to VIP security relative to general policing. For instance, out of the 83,762 policemen in

New Delhi, the largest police force, only 30 percent work in general policing. The remainder were reserved for personal security details.[12]

Finally, the shortage of health workers differs widely across states. For example, states like Kerala, Tamil Nadu, and Karnataka have 3.46, 3.39, and 3.09 nurses and midwives per 1,000 people, respectively (Hazarika 2013). Others like Uttaranchal, Bihar, and Jharkhand have 0.08, 0.16, and 0.17 nurses and midwives per 1,000 people, respectively. The pattern is similar for doctors and dentists. The number of health workers per 10,000 people ranges from 23.2 in Chandigarh to 2.5 in Meghalaya (Rao et al. 2011). Overall, the combination of fiscal pressures in hiring and weaker governance (which leads to higher absence rates) makes service delivery in large states such as UP, MP, Bihar, and Jharkhand especially challenging.

A further distortion comes from the fact that service providers are typically most needed in rural areas, but qualified providers typically prefer to live in more urban areas closer to better facilities and schools for their children. Indeed, one reason for the high absence rates of regular teachers and health workers compared to contract teachers and community health workers is that the former typically live in the block or even district headquarters and commute to their jobs each day, whereas the latter live in the villages they are serving. Data from AP shows that the typical contract teacher lives one kilometer away from the school, whereas the typical regular teacher lives over 12 kilometers away (Muralidharan and Sundararaman 2013).

Overall, the status quo prioritizes hiring the most qualified candidates at the district or state level, but ignores the spatial mismatch that ensues. Since the most qualified candidates disproportionately come from urban areas or have aspirations to continuously move to larger cities, it is more common to find staff vacancies in rural as opposed to urban areas. This, in turn, leads to lower staff-to-population ratios in rural areas. Even if administrative allocations of staff are equalized spatially, it is impossible to prevent staff from choosing to live far away from their work sites in urban areas and commute to work—which both increases absence rates and reduces their connection to the communities they serve. Further, corruption in transfers and postings is

12. These figures may be particularly extreme because New Delhi is the national capital and has a disproportionate number of VIPs (including diplomatic staff attached to embassies), who may need additional security. Nevertheless, the main point is that data on the average number of police per capita may over-estimate the effective strength of staff for maintaining general purpose law and order, and this is still likely to be true in most parts of India, though systematic data on the spatial allocation of police personnel was not easy to find.

widespread in many states, and again reflects the spatial mismatch between where posts exist and where providers want to live (see Béteille 2009).

Given the earlier results that show no correlation between paper qualifications and effectiveness on the job for front-line service providers, and the evidence from multiple studies of lower absenteeism among locally hired staff with modest amounts of training, there is a strong empirical case for making local hiring a core principle of staff recruitment for service delivery positions. For instance, Bang et al. (1999) and Haines et al. (2007) show that community health workers who receive limited training and are paid much more modest stipends than regular government health workers were able to improve health outcomes in underserved rural areas in India. Further, given that contract teachers and community health workers are effective at a fraction of the cost of regular government employees, using such workers may be a promising avenue to further explore for improving service delivery in a cost-effective way.

2.6. Time Wasted by Educated Youth in Trying to Get a Public-sector Job

Beyond the direct inefficiencies in service provision, the structure of public-sector labor markets also induces important distortions in the overall economy. One unappreciated distortion is the extent to which educated youth spend years attempting to get a government job by taking exams for any government job opening. The most common job aspiration for youth across India is a government job, and millions attempt to get one each year. Many of them spend several years unemployed or under-employed and they are supported by their families and part-time jobs (that do not build skills or certification) while making multiple attempts at passing exams to get a government job. Jeffrey (2010) provides an illuminating ethnography of educated unemployed youth in Meerut, Uttar Pradesh, for whom the phenomenon of "waiting" for a government job is so widespread that the title of his book is *Timepass*.

Analysis of unemployment by age using NSS data finds considerably higher unemployment rates for males below age 30 (which is the age limit for entry into many government jobs).[13] This is also consistent with evidence reported in Krishnan and Somanathan (2013) that the average age of selection into the civil service has been steadily increasing and that the

13. I thank Abhijit Banerjee for sharing these results from his ongoing work on youth employment and skilling in India.

average applicant makes between three and four attempts to get selected. Thus, the average *successful* applicant spends around four years preparing for and attempting these exams. Since the ratio of applicants to positions exceeds 200:1, this implies that hundreds of thousands (if not millions) of youth in their 20s attempt these exams.

The time spent attempting these exams also takes educated youth away from *other* productive parts of the economy. A puzzling fact about youth and skilling in India is the low take-up for training programs, and very high attrition from training programs. There is anecdotal evidence that at least 80 percent of trained candidates leave their jobs within three months of their placement.[14] Anecdotes suggest that a plausible reason for this is that many youth prefer to attempt entrance exams for government jobs rather than getting skilled and entering a competitive and uncertain labor market.

Note that this is perfectly rational on the part of individuals because the returns to winning the "government job lottery" are so large (with above-market wages, pension and benefits, lifetime job security, and the potential to extract rents in several public-sector jobs) that it makes sense to keep trying instead of getting skilled and working in the competitive private economy.[15] However, while it may be individually rational, it is socially inefficient because the probability of winning this lottery is very low, and those who do not make it waste several prime years of youth, which could potentially be used to obtain real skills and be productively employed.[16]

2.7. Corruption in Recruiting

A final manifestation of the distortions induced by the structure of public-sector labor markets is the widely acknowledged prevalence of corruption

14. Interviews with placement managers (conducted by Abhijit Banerjee and his colleagues on an ongoing project) confirm this phenomenon with quotes along the lines of: "Attrition post-placement is one of our larger concerns. While most candidates complete two-to-three-month long trainings, very few of them eventually stick on in the labour market."

15. A particularly striking recent example of this point was the widely reported case of over 2.3 million applicants for 368 posts as a peon in UP, including over 250 applicants with a Ph.D. qualification (Ali 2015; Verma 2015), implying an applicant to post ratio of over 6000. While the story was widely reported in the media as reflecting poor employment opportunities, the data are also consistent with the large "excess returns" over the market wage to a job in the government or public sector.

16. In practice, many of these applicants do combine their exam preparation with various formal and informal jobs and so not all their time is wasted. Nevertheless, obtaining a public sector job and studying for the selection exams is typically the main focus of these youth, as opposed to obtaining skills that are rewarded in the broader economy.

in recruiting for public-sector jobs.[17] Since the present discounted value of winning the "government job lottery" is so large, it is not surprising that candidates are willing to pay to improve their chances or that officials with discretion will be tempted to offer such options. Thus, the potential benefit of paying significantly above-market wages in the hope of attracting the best candidates may be rendered moot if it induces corruption in hiring. Note also that candidates appointed this way are likely to be negatively selected on intrinsic motivation (Schleifer and Vishny 1993) and work less hard since they would have paid for their jobs (Akerlof 1982) and would be more likely to want to recover the upfront cost of their investment through corruption or shirking.

It is of course possible that the status quo benefits political leaders who can either monetize the "excess returns" in government jobs through upfront bribes or offer the promise of a government job as patronage in return for political support. The latter channel may be a particularly important incentive for unemployed youth to work as political party workers, with the government job being offered in return for loyal service. In such a case, there may be limited political incentives for reforming the structure of public-sector hiring. Nevertheless, it is also true that state-level political leaders are under increasing political pressure to deliver better public services. The approach to public-sector hiring laid out in the next section assumes the existence of political will to improve service delivery and offers an approach that would allow this in a fiscally feasible way.

3. A New Approach to Public-sector Hiring

The facts outlined in the previous section point to several distortions in public-sector labor markets, many of which are interrelated. In this section, I outline a proposal for a new approach to public-sector hiring that mitigates several of these weaknesses and can form the basis for a comprehensive human resource strategy for public service delivery. Since the core elements of the idea have been outlined in the Introduction, this section provides a

17. Recruitment scams that have come into public attention recently include the Vyapam scam in MP, the teacher recruitment scam in Haryana (for which a former Chief Minister was convicted), and the recent resignation of a Railway Minister in response to allegations that he was selling positions on the apex Railway Board. However, corruption in public-sector recruitment has long been widespread in India. See Wade (1985) for the classic reference, and see Sukhtankar and Vaishnav (2015) for a fuller set of references.

fully fleshed out example from teaching and then presents brief extensions to police and early-childhood care workers.

3.1. Case Study 1: Teaching Assistants[18]

3.1.1. The Quality Challenge in Primary Education in India

With more than 50 percent of children aged 6–14 not being able to read at a second class level, the quality challenge is the biggest crisis in the Indian education system. Long-term annual data on student learning in primary schools in India shows a sharp flattening of learning trajectories after class 2 (Muralidharan and Zieleniak 2014). The most likely reason for this is that the textbooks and syllabus in class 3 and beyond require children to be able to "read to learn" and children who have not attained reading competencies by class 3 sharply fall behind over time.

The main message from high-quality academic research on the impact of education policies on improving education is that the most expensive components of education spending that have been prioritized in recent years (infrastructure, teacher salaries and training, mid-day meals, and other inputs) have shown very limited impacts on improving learning outcomes. It is extremely unlikely that a "business as usual" expansion of education spending along current patterns will significantly improve learning outcomes (Muralidharan 2013). On the other hand, relatively inexpensive interventions such as using modestly trained and paid community volunteers to provide supplemental instruction to children at their level of learning (as opposed to the level dictated by the curriculum or assumed by the textbook) have proven to be highly effective at improving learning outcomes in multiple settings across India.

The Twelfth Five-Year Plan recognizes the centrality of the quality challenge and has explicitly committed to a target of:

> Improving learning outcomes that are measured, monitored, and reported independently at all levels of school education with a special focus on ensuring that all children master basic reading and numeracy skills by class 2 and skills of critical thinking, expression and problem solving by class 5."

While investing in education quality is clearly one of the most important priorities for the Government of India, the fiscally constrained budgetary

18. This section is adapted from Muralidharan (2013) but has been expanded with more details and references.

environment creates an imperative to implement both cost-effective and scalable policies to address this massive challenge.

3.1.2. Teaching Assistant Proposal Outline

I posit here that changing the structure of public-sector hiring of teachers to include an entry-level apprenticeship position (called a "teaching assistant" or TA) provides one of the most promising and fiscally sustainable ways of achieving the learning objectives of the Twelfth Plan. The fiscal neutrality of the proposal relies on making more efficient use of the ₹25,000 crores per year earmarked for the most expensive stipulation of the RtE Act, which is to reduce PTR from 40:1 to 30:1. This may be especially relevant for states with large effective PTRs like UP, Bihar, and MP.

The proposal suggests maintaining the regular teacher norm at 40:1 (subject to a minimum of two regular teachers per school as per original Sarva Shiksha Abhiyan [SSA] norms) as opposed to 30:1. The same funds that would have been used to achieve the reduction from 40:1 to 30:1 can be used to provide each regular teacher with two TAs from the same village. These TAs shall have an explicit mandate to focus on first-generation and weaker learners and to provide small-group instruction that is tailored to their current level. Such an allocation of TAs to teachers will enable the PTR (defined as the ratio of adults to children in the school) to be reduced to 13.5 (or lower), which will allow for much more individualized attention to children and provide schools with the teaching resources needed to bridge early learning gaps. The main goal of the proposal is to provide the regular teacher with the instructional support needed to ensure that *all children* master basic reading and numeracy skills by class 2 or 3 (to be able to "read to learn") as targeted in the Twelfth Plan, and to hold regular teachers responsible for delivering on this goal.

The proposal allows for a sharp reduction in PTR in a fiscally sustainable way, while also creating employment and skill-building opportunities for educated rural youth (especially young women). The TA position would also be the first step in a career ladder that allows many more candidates to try out teaching and select the best candidates (as revealed partly by their performance on the job) for regular teacher positions.

3.1.3. Qualifications and Appointment Criteria

The appointment criteria for the teaching assistants would be very similar to those used for the appointment of non-regular government employees in several service delivery functions. Examples include the appointment of contract or guest teachers, and *anganwadi* or ASHA workers. While there may be variation across states and sectors in the appointment rules, the following broad principles would apply to prioritize among applicants for the teaching assistant position. Different weights can be assigned to each of the criteria below to come up with a composite score for ranking applicants.

First, in line with the evidence presented earlier, preference will be given to candidates from the same village (or Panchayat if needed). The minimum qualification for this role will be passing 12th standard, though the most qualified applicants in a village will be prioritized for appointments. Current data suggests that around half of the appointees will be college graduates, while half will have passed 12th standard (though in some exceptional cases it is possible that the most educated candidate in a village will only have passed 10th standard). TAs will be appointed for one year at a time with the target duration of total employment being four years. The appointments will be renewed annually, subject to meeting performance and training norms. No formal teacher training credentials will be required to join as a TA, but continuous and ongoing training will be required over four years (see below). Since research suggests that women may be more effective at teaching younger children (especially young girls), each school could target filling 50–75 percent of these positions with women (Muralidharan and Sheth 2016). Reservation policies can be implemented in accordance with current norms.

Note that there is likely to be a surplus of applicants even for these apprentice level jobs and it will be necessary to implement standardized procedures for their hiring at the block or district levels. However, implementing such procedures is within the existing capabilities of the government since the suggested recruiting protocol is similar to ones that are already in place for contract teachers and *anganwadi* workers.

3.1.4. Training and Credentialing

As discussed earlier, a consistent finding in the research on education quality globally over the past four decades, and in India over the past decade, is that there is no association between having a formal teacher training credential and teacher effectiveness in improving student learning outcomes (Hanushek 1971; 1986; 1992; Kane and Staiger 2012; Rivkin et al. 2005). This does not imply that training cannot have an impact on improving teacher effectiveness, but it does suggest that training credentials (as currently generated within the system) are unlikely to be effective markers of teacher quality, and that it is essential to rethink the approach to teacher training.

Some of the most promising innovations in teacher training around the world involve experimenting with different ways of integrating traditional lecture-style teacher training with teaching "practicums" (that is, opportunities for trainees to practice teaching under the supervision of an experienced mentor). There is suggestive evidence that these "practice-based" teacher preparation programs may have multiple benefits, including: (a) broadening the pool of high-talent entrants to the profession; (b) improving the screening of aspiring teachers; (c) accelerating the learning of new teachers; and (d) inducing teachers to work hard at improving their effectiveness in the early stages of their career, when professional habits are formed.

First, these programs may attract high-ability individuals who did not originally study to become teachers. For example, in the United States, there are more than 30 "teacher residency programs" (TRPs), in which college graduates interested in entering teaching simultaneously complete coursework and have a supervised fieldwork experience for at least one year. A study of these programs indicated that TRPs broadened the pool of candidates that entered teaching, attracting candidates who had not initially studied education, and that novice teachers in these programs were as likely to stay in teaching as regular novice teachers (Silva et al. 2014).

Second, practice-based teacher preparation programs may offer an opportunity to assess whether teaching trainees will become effective teachers. For example, a program that recruits college graduates to teach in hard-to-staff schools in New York City requires its applicants to, among other things, deliver a demonstration lesson. A study found that the performance of applicants in this selection process predicted their subsequent effectiveness in the classroom, as measured by student achievement gains (Rockoff and Speroni 2011). Similarly, a "mentoring" program, also in New York City, requires experienced teachers to periodically observe the lessons of new recruits. The same study found that the performance of new teachers on these observations predicted the performance of their students in standardized tests.

Third, practice-based teacher preparation programs may help teachers improve faster. For example, a study of a TRP in Boston, Massachusetts, found that program participants were initially less effective than regular novice teachers at teaching math and equally effective at teaching English (Papay et al. 2012). However, "residents" (as program participants are called) improved faster than regular novice teachers (at least in math), and by their fourth and fifth years they outperformed veteran teachers. Similarly, a small randomized trial of an in-service "coaching" program for teachers in their first four years of service in New Orleans, Louisiana, found that the program improved teachers' performance on classroom observations, principal evaluations, and student surveys (Kraft and Blazar 2014). These effects emerged across subjects and grades, and they persisted beyond the first year.

Finally, practice-based teacher preparation programs may also provide incentives for trainees to try their hardest, if there are consequences for poor and good performance. For example, a randomized evaluation of a high-stakes teacher evaluation system in Cincinnati, Ohio, showed that the system improved the performance of teachers during and after the evaluation process (Taylor and Tyler, 2012). Similarly, a randomized evaluation of another high-stakes teacher evaluation system in Washington, DC, found that low-performing teachers at risk of being dismissed left the district, and that high-performing teachers who received a bonus improved their performance (Dee and Wyckoff 2015).

While all the evidence cited above is from the US, and this literature is still too nascent to make definitive recommendations, there is at least a prima facie case for experimenting with practice-based training. The TA program may be an especially promising opportunity to re-imagine training along these lines. The proposal makes the following suggestions pertaining to TA training.

Selected high-quality accredited teacher training institutes should be invited to create a modular teacher training program that lasts four years and includes three months per year of lecture-based instruction and eight to nine months per year of classroom teaching as an apprenticeship under the guidance of a senior regular teacher. The three-month modules can be implemented during the summer vacation and other school breaks and can also include weekend classes. They should be designed to be sequential so that a new recruit with no teaching experience can function effectively in a classroom as a TA after the first three-month module (that is, the first module will focus mostly on classroom management and instruction skills, with later modules adding more theoretical components).

Thus, a TA who is selected through the recruitment guidelines laid out above can be selected without any teacher training, but then undergoes an initial three-month training module (with tests and grading) before entering the classroom as an apprentice. Over four years, the successful completion of all the training modules combined with evaluations of classroom performance, will lead to a formal education credential issued by the accredited teacher training institute. The TAs will be paid their regular stipend during their training period (subject to passing modular exams), which minimizes financial risk to them. Many of these students would have otherwise paid large amounts of money to enroll in low-quality teacher training programs that do not lead to teaching jobs.

3.1.5. Pay and Integration into Regular Teacher Track

The salary for this position will range from ₹5,000 to ₹10,000 per month, depending on qualification and experience. This is considerably lower than the pay scales of regular government teachers (in the range of ₹20,000–₹40,000 per month), and will roughly be 20–25 percent of a regular teacher's salary, which is what will make it feasible to hire three to four TAs for the same cost as one regular teacher. But as documented in several studies, this pay scale compares very well with the pay offered to similarly qualified candidates in rural India, and it is *higher* than the average salary paid by private schools in rural areas (Muralidharan and Sundararaman 2013). Evidence suggests that there is likely to be an excess supply of qualified candidates at this salary (Kingdon and Sipahimalani-Rao 2010).

After serving four years as TAs, candidates who are college graduates and have obtained the D.Ed or B.Ed equivalent through the modular training program, can apply to be hired as a regular civil-service teacher. They must take the TET and go through the standard selection procedure, but they will receive additional credit for each year of experience as a TA. Ideally, this credit will be performance-based, but I recognize that effective performance evaluation and employee performance rating is rarely done effectively at lower levels of government. But even if fine-grained evaluation is not possible, it may be feasible to have annual ratings of TAs on a forced curve of outstanding (20 percent), average (middle 60 percent), and below average (bottom 20 percent). After four years, applicants can get extra marks on the entrance exam for regular hiring for each year of service based on their ratings (say 4 percent, 2 percent, and 0 percent for each year of service at each rating).

In practice, it is possible that even such a three-tiered forced curve may be difficult to implement in an objective manner. It may, therefore, be prudent to start with simply providing credit for each year of successful service as an apprentice during the process of regular hiring. This way, the high-stakes regularization will still follow the existing protocols, but with extra credit for the apprenticeship period. Over time, with improvements in measurement technology, it may be possible to include more objective performance measures during the apprenticeship period (such as attendance and time on task) and provide additional marks for these.[19] The exact formula can be determined at the state level, but the key idea is to provide credit for experience as a teaching assistant in the regular teacher hiring decision (with a gradual shift over time to performance-based credit).

Thus, top-scoring candidates on the TET may qualify for direct recruitment as regular teachers (without going through the TA experience), but for two candidates with the same exam marks, classroom experience as TAs will enhance their probability of selection as regular teachers. As a result, the TA position will typically be the first step in a career ladder, and the recruiting system will recognize the value of classroom experience in addition to pure theoretical knowledge, as reflected by formal qualifications. Equally importantly, this system will help candidates discover whether they actually enjoy teaching and are good at it before deciding whether teaching should be a life-long career. This will reduce the cases of "mismatches" where candidates train to be a teacher and realize later that they actually do not like the job or are not good at it.

Candidates who complete the modular D.Ed/B.Ed but do not get selected for regular positions through the TET will be eligible for an exit payment of ₹1 lakh after four years of successful service. Some TAs may choose to take this exit payment and attempt other careers. Others may choose to continue working as TAs and make additional attempts to qualify for selection as a regular teacher through the TET (if they are college graduates) until they reach the age limit for selection as a regular teacher.[20] Candidates who complete the modular D.Ed and choose to remain as TAs for the longer run without aiming for selection as regular teachers (because they are not college graduates or they do not want a transferrable job) can be eligible for longer term TA contracts at the village school. There is also likely to be increased demand for these candidates as teachers in private schools, which will increasingly need trained teachers to meet RTE requirements.

The payment of ₹1 lakh as a lump sum at the end of four years of successful service has several attractive features. First, it provides candidates who would not like to continue in teaching with the resources to explore other career options at a young age. Second, it is also likely that many of

19. For instance, the Government of Delhi's pilot initiative to introduce Closed Circuit TV (CCTV) cameras in schools and classrooms may make it possible to obtain objective measures of teacher performance such as attendance and time on task within the classroom, which can then be used at the time of regular hiring.

20. It may be desirable to limit the number of years of credit that can be obtained for successful service as a TA in regular hiring and to cap this at four or five years, but this is a detail that can be worked out later.

the candidates for TA positions will be young women who may only plan to work as teaching assistants when they are 18 to 22 years old, before getting married or starting a family. The lump-sum payment would significantly enhance female independence and empowerment and raise the value placed on girls in patriarchal settings (especially in rural North India). Many state governments already offer lump-sum incentives of around ₹60,000 to girls who complete 12th standard and stay unmarried till then.[21] The suggestion here follows the same approach and extends it to the ages of 18–22, but in this case it provides payments for working in a role that will improve service delivery and can help achieve universal functional literacy and numeracy in the next five years. More broadly, it creates a social contract with educated youth (especially young women) by saying that "you invest in the next generation of school-going children and we (the government) will invest in you."

3.1.6. Summary of Program Benefits

The key benefits of adopting the approach summarized here are the following. First, it provides schools with the additional teaching resources needed to realistically deliver on the Twelfth Plan goal of making sure that all children master basic reading and numeracy skills by class 2. The proposal facilitates the reduction of PTR to below 14:1 and the provision of substantially greater individual (or small-group) attention to children who are not reaching basic competencies in reading and numeracy. Second, it has the potential to make teacher training more effective by integrating lecture-based theoretical training and classroom practice, and it provides a sound foundation for building effective teachers. Third, the modified pathway to teacher recruitment, training, and promotion to "regular teacher" is likely to significantly improve teacher quality over time due to: (a) the better integration of teacher training and practice; and (b) the fact that high-performing TAs will be more likely to obtain regular teacher appointments, and TAs who find themselves to be poorly suited for teaching are less likely to do so. Fourth, it will provide employment to educated youth (especially women) who may be unwilling or unable to work outside their village. Finally, the policy is likely to significantly increase female empowerment—by providing educated young girls with a job, a steady income and greater financial independence, increased respect in the village, and greater control over marriage and fertility decisions. A further benefit is the generation of strong

21. The Ladli Laxmi Yojana in Madhya Pradesh is perhaps the best known such scheme and this has now been replicated in several North Indian states including UP, Bihar, and Jharkhand.

positive role model effects for younger school-going girls. The visibility of these jobs in villages is also likely to increase the perceived "returns to education" and, consequently, increase the demand for education among girls and their parents (Jensen 2012).

3.1.7. Key Differences Between Teaching Assistants and Contract Teachers

As discussed earlier, some parts of this idea are not new. Specifically, many states have hired para-teachers or contract teachers in the past to meet teacher shortages. However, despite the evidence that contract teachers may be less absent and as effective as regular teachers who are paid much higher salaries (which is the empirical finding that underpins the teaching assistant proposal), the contract teacher model was not a practical success for three broad sets of reasons.

First, contract teachers were hired as *substitutes* for regular teachers and not *supplements* (which is what the TA proposal does). Thus, the idea never got support and traction among the education community, which was the policy as driven by short-term fiscal concerns at the expense of long-term education quality. In particular, they were worried about the negative consequences of de-professionalizing teaching in the long run (Kumar et al. 2001). Second, the idea of contract teachers ran into legal trouble for not conforming to the norm of equal pay for equal work. Since contract teachers were working side-by-side with regular teachers and doing the same job, courts often ruled in favor of granting contract teachers regular status, which led to severe fiscal pressures on states (see Robinson and Gauri 2011, for a discussion of contract teacher cases in the Indian courts). Finally, since many cohorts of contract teachers were hired alongside a freeze in regular teacher hiring, it became politically very difficult to resist demands for regularization, which were often granted prior to elections.

The teaching assistant proposal leverages the strengths of community and village-based teachers, while carefully addressing all the three main weaknesses of the contract teacher model described above.

First, as the discussion regarding best practices on training makes clear, the aim of the TA proposal is to *increase* teacher quality and professionalism by: (a) integrating lecture-based theoretical training and classroom practice to create a more effective teacher training program; and (b) regularizing only high-performing TAs. Second, the legal issue of "equal pay for equal work," which has been a challenge under the contract teacher model, is addressed by clearly defining the roles differently. A regular teacher will have much greater responsibility including that of coaching and supporting the TAs and taking overall responsibility for child learning outcomes, while the TA position is an apprenticeship to be completed while undergoing training and obtaining practical experience for a fixed period of time.

Finally, the political challenge of demands for mass "regularization" is addressed by creating a clearly defined pathway for TAs to be promoted to regular teacher status. Note that the process of regular teacher hiring will not be frozen and will mostly stay the same—but TAs will get additional credit for years of successful service. The top-performing TAs are much more likely to get promoted to regular teacher status. Those who do not meet those high standards will receive an exit payment of ₹1 lakh to recognize their contribution as TAs, and to help them make a transition to other jobs.

Here is a different way to see how the TA proposal addresses the legal and political challenges that have limited the effectiveness of contract teachers. No one expects candidates who make multiple unsuccessful attempts to pass public-service exams to be entitled to a government job. Taking the exam multiple times may increase the chances of obtaining the government job, but does not guarantee it or create an entitlement to it. Similarly, completing an apprenticeship successfully for a few years will provide an advantage when competing for public-sector jobs (likely more so than studying and taking the exam multiple times), but does not guarantee selection for the job if the performance on the other components of the selection process (including exams and interviews) are not good enough to get selected (even with the advantage provided by the extra credit for years of apprenticeship).

Overall, the TA proposal is an example of a new approach to public-sector hiring that defines the apprenticeship as a separate step in a career-ladder for employees, and it is part of an integrated human resource strategy for entering permanent government positions. In addition to strengthening the long-term quality of permanent government employees, it also offers the promise of significantly expanding the availability of front-line service delivery staff and thereby improving the overall quality of service delivery—*without* significantly increasing spending. But it is also important to fully spell out this integrated strategy at the outset to ensure clarity on the career path and requisites for success among candidates, as well as broader stakeholders in society including politicians and the judiciary.

3.2. Case Study 2: Police Youth Brigade

While the TA proposal discussed above has been developed in detail, a similar approach is possible in other sectors as well. Perhaps, most relevant is the recent initiative by the Government of Tamil Nadu (GoTN) to recruit a "Special Police Youth Brigade" (SPYB) to support the regular police force. The program was initiated by the Chief Minister and the Tamil Nadu Assembly passed a bill in 2013 to approve the raising of the SPYB. The stated objective for this initiative suggests that GoTN was trying to address the core service delivery challenges caused by a shortage of staff identified earlier in this paper. Specifically, the bill mentions that the police had to be engaged in several peripheral functions that detracted from their core functions of law and order, crime control, and investigation. The functions of the SPYB were defined as including driving police vehicles, delivering mail, entering data, maintaining police quarters, and assisting the police with saving the lives of the victims of accidents (*The Hindu* 2013).

The pay of candidates recruited under the SPYB was ₹7,500 per month, whereas a regular police constable is paid over ₹20,000 per month. Nevertheless, there was still considerable excess demand for these positions: the applicant-to-position ratio was over 10:1. It is clear that GoTN's broader motivation for the SPYB was to improve service delivery (in the field of policing) in a fiscally feasible way. However, there is a risk that this initiative may end up the same way as contract teacher programs because it appears to be a bit of a "stop gap" arrangement without a long-term human resource strategy. In particular, it is possible that once the number of members of the SPYB reaches a critical mass, they will also demand to get regularized, which may be granted under pressure before elections.

On the other hand, this initiative can be a poster-child for the new approach to recruiting outlined in this paper. Consider the following modification. Right now, the training to the SPYB consists of driving heavy and light vehicles, using wireless communications, patrolling during the night, operating computers, and performing basic duties in crime prevention, first aid, and public relations. This could become a "level one" certificate in law enforcement. Once a trainee acquires this certificate, he/she would be deemed qualified to perform this type of function. However, it should be possible under the new National Skills Qualification Framework to introduce packages of training and skills that constitute "level two," "level three," and subsequent skill levels. Passing each of these levels would qualify a candidate to perform more advanced functions and increase the ability of the state to deploy more front-line police to improve law and order and women's security, and prevent and report crimes early. Such a modular approach to training is also an excellent opportunity to train future law-enforcement officers in soft skills such as citizen-centric policing and sensitivity to gender issues, which current police personnel are widely perceived to lack.

SPYB personnel can become apprentices if they are provided with (performance-linked) credit for each year of successful service at the time of regular recruitment.[22] Over time, this will lead to improved match quality between the "non-CV" skills of police recruits and the needs of a citizen-centered police force. Senior officers could observe the performance of potential entrants on the job for a few years and evaluate their prospect for a long-term career in policing. Candidates who do not make the selection cut after four or five years as SPYB staff will receive an exit payment and certificates of training and performance that can aid their transition to other sectors of the economy, including the private security industry.

Overall, an integrated approach along the lines above will lead to the best candidates (as evaluated by on-the-job performance) being selected for permanent government positions. It will also raise the skills of all apprentices (even those who do not make it to permanent positions), thus having a positive spillover effect on skill levels in the rest of the economy. A fundamental market failure in skilling in the status quo is that there is no credible certification of skills. This means that the market will not pay a wage premium for skills, which in turn leads to a lack of demand for skilling. Combining this new approach to public-sector hiring with the new National Skills Framework provides an excellent opportunity to not only define skill levels, but to establish a wage premium for credible demonstration of skills. This could be done using public-sector recruiting as a credible way to deliver a wage premium for skills.

3.3. Case Study 3: Anganwadi Workers

A similar integration of the new National Skills Framework and this new approach to public-sector hiring can be implemented in the case of *anganwadi* workers. Global research on human capital accumulation increasingly points to the critical importance of providing health, nutrition, and mental stimulation to children in the 0–6 age range (Grantham-McGregor et al. 2007; Heckman 2008; Heckman and Masterov 2007; Shonkoff and Phillips 2000). Yet, the ICDS, which is the main policy vehicle for providing this support to infants and young children, is remarkably weak (PEO 2011). In particular, it is severely under-staffed in most states, and it is plausible that augmenting ICDS centers with an additional locally hired worker will

22. A similar forced curve of 20–60–20 percent of staff being rated each year as outstanding, good, and below average can be used for each annual evaluation of the SPYB personnel. Alternately, credit can simply be provided based on years of service.

have large social returns (for instance, if one worker focuses on health and nutrition and the other one on education).

However, this is not being done for the most part for fiscal reasons. Further, training of *anganwadi* workers is ad hoc, and does not lead to any credible signals of skills or achievement. An integrated skilling and recruiting approach that reduces barriers to entry through large-scale apprenticeship/assistantship programs would allow ICDS centers to augment their ability to provide higher quality services by providing additional staff members. Having these apprentices obtain modular training that is mapped into milestones under the National Skilling framework will improve their skills. It would also make later training modules more effective because they will build on extensive practical experience, as well as completion of earlier modules.

Candidates selected for apprenticeship positions can have their modular training programs paid for by the government (just like in the TA proposal). This will increase the attraction of the apprenticeship position (despite its low nominal salary level) and clearly establish a career ladder through which individuals can progress with modular skill acquisition and practical experience. Each step of this ladder will both increase the stipend during the apprenticeship period (providing a direct and immediate return to skills and experience) and increase the probability of being selected as a regular government worker.

4. Implementation Roadmap and Conclusion

The poor quality of service delivery across a range of core government functions is one of the most vexing governance challenges facing India today. One striking indicator of the weakness of the Indian state in service delivery is the large market share of fee-charging private providers in education and health even in the presence of *free* publicly provided education and health.[23] Indeed, one reason for why the crisis in service delivery may not be capturing more policy attention is that elites and middle classes have dealt with failing public services by opting out of them for the most part.

23. Recent estimates suggest that over 30 percent of children in rural India attend fee-charging private primary schools (Pratham 2014) and that the market share of fee-charging private health care providers for primary care in rural Madhya Pradesh was over 80 percent (Das et al. 2015).

Yet, improved public services are perhaps the most direct way for policy and practice to improve the daily lives of hundreds of millions of citizens. There should also be political incentives for democratically elected state governments (under whose jurisdiction most front-line service delivery functions fall) to improve the quality of public services. Yet, state governments appear to be in a near-impossible situation with regard to their ability to improve services because of the fiscal challenges that they face and their resulting inability to hire enough front-line service providers. Previous attempts at using less-trained contractual employees to mitigate this problem have been unsuccessful at a systemic level because of professional, legal, and political limitations of such stop-gap models.

This paper suggests one possible way out of this suboptimal equilibrium where too few providers are hired, partly because salaries are too high, and where the current structure of training and credentialing does not seem to create or identify effective employees. I first document a series of distortions and inefficiencies induced by the current structure of public-sector labor markets. Then, I propose a unified approach to reforming public-sector hiring that can mitigate several of these distortions. The main features of this approach are the following: first, reducing the barriers to entry into service delivery professions by hiring a large number of entry-level staff at the apprentice/assistant level who are locally hired from the areas that they need to serve, and are paid stipends that are competitive by market standards, but substantially below the pay scales of permanent government employees—which allows a fiscally feasible expansion of front-line service-delivery staff; second, modular training and skilling that is integrated with the new National Skills Framework and can be provided by accredited public or private providers; third, performance-based credit given for years served as an apprentice at the time of regular recruitment; fourth, and finally, exit payments to candidates who are not selected into regular government positions, after either a fixed period of time or number of attempts, to help them transition to other professions or similar roles in the private sector.

I also argue that the current point in time is extremely well-suited to implementing such a modified approach to public-sector hiring. The Fourteenth Finance Commission award has significantly increased the fiscal space for states to experiment with new models of service delivery. Of course, the corresponding reduction in central government allocations to centrally sponsored schemes implies that the short-run flexibility may be limited (as state-level funds are used to fund expenditures committed under the assumption of continued central government fund flows).

Yet, the medium-term flexibility is much higher. This provides an opportunity for a willing state to experiment with this new approach.

It should be relatively easy for states like Tamil Nadu, which have already commenced experiments like the TN SPYB, to build on this foundation and make it the first step in an integrated human resource policy for public-sector hiring. Learning from successful state-level (or even district and block-level) experiments with such a new approach can then be deployed across states (including lessons on pitfalls to avoid). It is also important for states to use their newfound fiscal space wisely and avoid committing to irreversible, large expenditures, which may be of limited effectiveness. In particular, the evidence (see De Ree et al. 2015) strongly cautions against implementing across-the-board salary increases for public-sector workers (for which there will no doubt be political pressure and temptation). Modest district-level experiments in a few sectors with this new approach (accompanied by careful, independent impact evaluations) may be a more prudent way forward.

The timing is also excellent with regard to coinciding with the release of the new National Skills Framework. The idea of modular training and credentialing that is interspersed with practical experience is very well suited to an integrated skills framework. Laying down such frameworks and independently testing and accrediting employee skill levels is a public good with economies of scale and scope that is best provided at the national level. This will then allow both public and private providers of training services to develop modular coursework to provide these skills. The government is the largest employer by far, so adopting a human resource strategy for public-sector hiring along the lines outlined in this paper can help catalyze the translation of the skills framework into real impact on the economy. It will help create both supply and demand for skills because these will now be rewarded on the labor market (led by the public-sector labor market).

Service delivery in India is in a crisis and expanding business as usual is unlikely to work. It is also unlikely to be fiscally viable across all the sectors that claim that they need more resources. It is imperative to do "more with the same" rather than do "more of the same," and the approach suggested in this paper offers one way of doing so, which may be of interest to states contemplating ways of improving service delivery in a fiscally feasible manner.

References

Akerlof, G.A. 1982. "Labor Contracts as Partial Gift Exchange," *The Quarterly Journal of Economics*, 97(4): 543–69.

Ali, Mohammad. 2015. "23 Lakh Apply for 368 Peon Posts in Uttar Pradesh," *The Hindu*, Meerut, September 17, Available online at: http://www.thehindu.com/news/national/other-states/23-lakh-apply-for-368-peon-posts-in-uttar-pradesh/article7660341.ece (accessed on May 17, 2016).

Bang, A.T., R.A. Bang, S.B. Baitule, M.H. Reddy, and M.D. Deshmukh. 1999. "Effect of Home-Based Neonatal Care and Management of Sepsis on Neonatal Mortality: Field Trial in Rural India," *The Lancet*, 354(9194): 1955–61.

Bastian, K.C. 2013. *Do Teachers' Non-cognitive Skills and Traits Predict Effectiveness and Evaluation Ratings?* Chapel Hill, NC: University of North Carolina at Chapel Hill.

Bau, N. and J. Das. 2011. *Buy More, Pay Less: Measuring the Performance of Pakistani Contract Teachers*. Cambridge, MA: Harvard University.

Besley, T. and T. Persson. 2010. "State Capacity, Conflict, and Development," *Econometrica*, 78(1): 1–34.

Béteille, T. 2009. *Absenteeism, Transfers and Patronage: The Political Economy of Teacher Labor Markets in India*. Stanford, CA: Stanford Graduate School of Education (SGSE).

Callen, M., S. Gulzar, A. Hasanain, Y. Khan, and A. Rezaee. 2015. *Personalities and Public Sector Performance: Evidence from a Health Experiment in Pakistan*. Cambridge, MA: National Bureau of Economic Research (NBER).

Chetty, R., J. Friedman, and J. Rockoff. 2014a. "Measuring the Impacts of Teachers I: Evaluating Bias in Teacher Value-Added Estimates," *American Economic Review*, 104(9): 2593–632.

———. 2014b. "Measuring the Impacts of Teachers II: Teacher Value-Added and Student Outcomes in Adulthood," *American Economic Review*, 104(9): 2633–79.

Correll, J., B. Park, C.M. Judd, and B. Wittenbrink. 2002. "The Police Officer's Dilemma: Using Ethnicity to Disambiguate Potentially Threatening Individuals," *Journal of Personality and Social Psychology*, 83(6): 1314–29.

Das, J., A. Holla, A. Mohpal, and K. Muralidharan. Forthcoming. "Quality and Accountability in Healthcare Delivery: Audit-Study Evidence from Primary Care in India," *American Economic Review*.

De Ree, J., K. Muralidharan, M. Pradhan, and F.H. Rogers. 2015. *Double for Nothing? Experimental Evidence on the Impact of an Unconditional Teacher Salary Increase on Student Performance in Indonesia*. Washington, DC: The World Bank.

Dee, T. and J. Wyckoff. 2015. "Incentives, Selection, and Teacher Performance: Evidence from Impact," *Journal of Policy Analysis and Management*, 34(2): 267–97.

DNA. 2014. "Police to People Ratio: 3 Cops for Every VIP but Just 1 for 761 Commoners." Zee Media Bureau, New Delhi, 25 August, Available online at: http://www.dnaindia.com/india/report-police-to-people-ratio-3-cops-for-every-vip-but-just-1-for-761-commoners-1879695 (accessed on March 15, 2016).

Dobbie, W. 2011. *Teacher Characteristics and Student Achievement: Evidence from Teach for America*. Cambridge, MA: Harvard University.

Duckworth, A.L., P.D. Quinn, and M.E. Seligman. 2009. "Positive Predictors of Teacher Effectiveness," *The Journal of Positive Psychology*, 4(6): 540–47.

Finan, F., B.A. Olken, and R. Pande. 2015. *Government Workers in Developing Countries*. Berkeley, CA: University of California.

Government of India. 2011. 13th Joint Review Mission (JRM) Monitoring Report, Sarva Shiksha Abhiyan, New Delhi: Ministry of Human Resource Development.

Grantham-McGregor, S., Y.B. Cheung, S. Cueto, P. Glewwe, L. Richer, and B. Trupp. 2007. "Developmental Potential in the First 5 Years for Children in Developing Countries," *The Lancet*, 369(9555): 60–70.

Grossman, P., S. Loeb, J. Cohen, and J. Wyckoff. 2013. "Measure for Measure: The Relationship between Measures of Instructional Practice in Middle School English Language Arts and Teachers' Value-Added Scores," *American Journal of Education*, 119(3): 445–70.

Haines, A., D. Sanders, U. Lehmann, A.K. Rowe, J.E. Lawn, S. Jan, D.G. Walker, and Z. Bhutta. 2007. "Achieving Child Survival Goals: Potential Contribution of Community Health Workers," *The Lancet*, 369(9579): 2121–31.

Hanushek, E.A. 1971. "Teacher Characteristics and Gains in Student Achievement: Estimation Using Micro Data," *The American Economic Review*, 61(2): 280–88.

———. 1986. "The Economics of Schooling: Production and Efficiency in Public Schools," *Journal of Economic Literature*, 24(3): 1141–77.

———. 1992. "The Trade-Off between Child Quantity and Quality," *Journal of Political Economy*, 100(1): 84–117.

Hazarika, I. 2013. "Health Workforce in India: Assessment of Availability, Production and Distribution," *WHO South-East Asia Journal of Public Health*, 2(2): 106–12.

Heckman, J.J. 2008. "Schools, Skills, and Synapses," *Economic Inquiry*, 46(3): 289–324.

Heckman, J.J. and D.V. Masterov. 2007. "The Productivity Argument for Investing in Young Children," *Applied Economic Perspectives and Policy*, 29(3): 446–93.

Jacob, B.A. and L. Lefgren. 2008. "Can Principals Identify Effective Teachers? Evidence on Subjective Performance Evaluation in Education," *Journal of Labor Economics*, 26(1): 101–36.

Jeffrey, C. 2010. *Timepass: Youth, Class, and the Politics of Waiting in India*. Stanford: Stanford University Press.

Jensen, R. 2012. "Do Labor Market Opportunities Affect Young Women's Work and Family Decisions? Experimental Evidence from India," *The Quarterly Journal of Economics*, 127(2): 753–92.

Kane, T.J. and D.O. Staiger. 2011. *Learning about Teaching: Initial Findings from the Measures of Effective Teaching Project*. Seattle, WA: Bill and Melinda Gates Foundation.

———. 2012. *Gathering Feedback for Teachers: Combining High-Quality Observations with Student Surveys and Achievement Gains*. Seattle, WA: Bill and Melinda Gates Foundation.

Kane, T.J., E.S. Taylor, J.H. Tyler, and A.L. Wooten. 2011. "Identifying Effective Classroom Practices Using Student Achievement Data," *Journal of Human Resources*, 46(3): 587–613.

Kapur, D. and A. Subramanian. 2013. "Rebuilding the Indian State." *Business Standard*, September 6, Available online at: http://www.business-standard.com/article/opinion/devesh-kapur-arvind-subramanian-rebuilding-the-indian-state-113090601124_1.html (accessed on March 17, 2016).

Kingdon, G. 2011. "Private Versus Public Schooling in India." Available online at: http://www.india-seminar.com/2011/627/627_geeta_gandhi_kingdon.htm (accessed on April 15, 2016).

Kingdon, G. and V. Sipahimalani-Rao. 2010. "Para-Teachers in India: Status and Impact," *Economic and Political Weekly*, 45(12): 59–67.

Kohli, N. 2015. "Not in the Class: A Story of India's Missing Teachers." *Hindustan Times*, April 6, Available online at http://www.hindustantimes.com/india/not-in-the-class-a-story-of-india-s-missing-teachers/story-8HITtop9bbJbL18cGC5U7H.html (accessed on April 17, 2016).

Kraft, M.A. and D. Blazar. 2014. *Improving Teachers' Practice across Grades and Subjects: Experimental Evidence on Individualized Coaching*. Providence, RI: Brown University.

Kremer, M., K. Muralidharan, N. Chaudhury, F.H. Rogers, and J. Hammer. 2005. "Teacher Absence in India: A Snapshot," *Journal of the European Economic Association*, 3(2–3): 658–67.

Krishnan, K.P. and T.V. Somanathan. 2005. Civil Service: An Institutional Perspective, in D. Kapur and P.B. Mehta, eds, *Public Institutions in India: Performance and Design* (pp. 258–319). New Delhi: Oxford University Press.

———. 2013. *The Civil Service in the 21st Century*. Unpublished paper, New Delhi.

Kumar, K., M. Priyam, and S. Saxena. 2001. "The Trouble with 'Para-Teachers'," *Frontline*, 18 (22): 93–94.

Mathew, S. and M. Moore. 2011. *State Incapacity by Design: Understanding the Bihar Story* (pp. 1–31). London: Institute of Development Studies (IDS).

Muralidharan, K. 2012. *Long-Term Effects of Teacher Performance Pay: Experimental Evidence from India*. San Diego, CA: University of California.

———. 2013. "Priorities for Primary Education Policy in India's 12th Five Year Plan," *India Policy Forum 2012–13*, 9: 1–46.

Muralidharan, K., N. Chaudhury, J. Hammer, M. Kremer, and F.H. Rogers. 2011. *Is There a Doctor in the House? Medical Work Absence in India.* San Diego, CA: University of California.

Muralidharan, K., J. Das, A. Holla, and A. Mohpal. 2015. *The Fiscal Cost of Weak Governance: Evidence from Teacher Absence in India.* Cambridge, MA: National Bureau of Economic Research (NBER).

Muralidharan, K., P. Niehaus, and S. Sukhtankar. Forthcoming. "Building State Capacity: Evidence from Biometric Smartcards in India," *American Economic Review*.

Muralidharan, K. and K. Sheth. 2016. "Bridging Education Gender Gaps in Developing Countries: The Role of Female Teachers," *Journal of Human Resources*, 51(2): 269–97.

Muralidharan, K. and V. Sundararaman. 2011. "Teacher Performance Pay: Experimental Evidence from India," *The Journal of Political Economy*, 119(1): 39–77.

———. 2013. *Contract Teachers: Experimental Evidence from India*. Cambridge, MA: National Bureau of Economic Research (NBER).

Muralidharan, K. and Y. Zieleniak. 2014. *Chasing the Syllabus: Measuring Learning Trajectories in Developing Countries with Longitudinal Data and Item Response Theory*. San Diego, CA: University of California.

Nandan, T. 2014. "With Severe Shortages, India's Security Forces Face Toughest Test with Lesser Men to Guard Citizens." Zee Research Group, New Delhi, July 31, Available online at: http://www.dnaindia.com/india/report-with-severe-shortages-india-s-security-forces-face-toughest-test-with-lesser-men-to-guard-citizens-2006764 (accessed on March 15, 2016).

Papay, J.P., M.R. West, J.B. Fullerton, and T.J. Kane. 2012. "Does an Urban Teacher Residency Increase Student Achievement? Early Evidence from Boston," *Educational Evaluation and Policy Analysis*, 34(4): 413–34.

Pathak, V. 2014. "Acute Shortage of Primary Teachers in India; UP, Bihar Worst-Hit States." *Hindustan Times*, New Delhi, December 14, Available online at: http://www.hindustantimes.com/india/acute-shortage-of-primary-teachers-in-india-up-bihar-worst-hit-states/story-YJE4ttTjG7rtN1hrrw2LAM.html (accessed on May 25, 2016).

PEO. 2011. *Evaluation Report on Integrated Child Development Services*. New Delhi: Programme Evaluation Organisation, Planning Commission, Government of India.

Persson, T. and T. Besley. 2009. "The Origins of State Capacity: Property Rights, Taxation and Policy," *The American Economic Review*, 99: 1218–44.

Pianta, R.C., J. Belsky, N. Vandergrift, R. Houts, and F.J. Morrison. 2008. "Classroom Effects on Children's Achievement Trajectories in Elementary School," *American Educational Research Journal*, 45(2): 365–97.

Pratham. 2014. *Annual Status of Education Report 2013*. New Delhi: ASER Centre.

Pritchett, L. 2009. *Is India a Flailing State? Detours on the Four Lane Highway to Modernization*. Cambridge, MA: Harvard Kennedy School of Government.

Rao, M., K.D. Rao, A.K.S. Kumar, M. Chatterjee, and T. Sundararaman. 2011. "Human Resources for Health in India," *The Lancet*, 377(9765): 587–98.

Rivkin, S.G., E.A. Hanushek, and J.F. Kain. 2005. "Teachers, Schools, and Academic Achievement," *Econometrica*, 73(2): 417–58.

Robinson, N. and V. Gauri. 2011. "Education, Labor Rights, and Incentives: Contract Teacher Cases in the Indian Courts," *Comparative Labor Law and Policy Journal*, 32(4), Available online at: https://works.bepress.com/varun_gauri/8/ (accessed on May 17, 2016).

Rockoff, J.E., B.A. Jacob, T.J. Kane, and D.O. Staiger. 2011. "Can You Recognize an Effective Teacher When You Recruit One?" *Education Finance and Policy*, 6(1): 43–74.

Rockoff, J.E. and C. Speroni. 2011. "Subjective and Objective Evaluations of Teacher Effectiveness: Evidence from New York City," *Labour Economics*, 18(2011): 687–96.

Rockoff, J.E., D.O. Staiger, T.J. Kane, and E.S. Taylor. 2012. "Information and Employee Evaluation: Evidence from a Randomized Intervention in Public Schools," *American Economic Review*, 102(7): 3184–3213.

Schleifer, A. and R.W. Vishny. 1993. "Corruption," *The Quarterly Journal of Economics*, 108(3): 599–617.

Shonkoff, J.P. and D.A. Phillips. 2000. *From Neurons to Neighborhoods: The Science of Early Childhood. Development Committee on Integrating the Science of Early Childhood Development*. Washington, DC: National Academy Press.

Silva, T., A. McKie, V. Knechtel, P. Gleason, and L. Makowsky. 2014. *Teaching Residency Programs: A Multisite Look at a New Model to Prepare Teachers for High-Need Schools*. Princeton, NJ: Mathematica Policy Research.

Sim, J.J., J. Correll, and M.S. Sadler. 2013. "Understanding Police and Expert Performance When Training Attenuates (Vs. Exacerbates) Stereotypic Bias in the Decision to Shoot," *Personality and Social Psychology Bulletin*, 39: 291–304.

Sukhtankar, S. and M. Vaishnav. 2015. "Corruption in India: Bridging Academic Evidence and Policy Options," *India Policy Forum 2014–15*, 11: 193-276.

Taylor, E.S. and J.H. Tyler. 2012. "The Effect of Evaluation on Teacher Performance," *American Economic Review*, 102(7): 3628–51.

The Hindu. 2013. "Bill on Police Youth Brigade Introduced," *The Hindu*, Chennai, Tamil Nadu, Available online at http://www.thehindu.com/news/national/tamil-nadu/bill-on-police-youth-brigade-introduced/article4390333.ece (accessed on May 17, 2016).

Verma, Lalmani. 2015. "Around 250 PhD Holders in Line for Peon's Job in UP," *The Indian Express*, September 17, Available online at: http://indianexpress.com/article/cities/lucknow/around-250-phd-holders-in-line-for-peons-job-in-up/ (accessed on May 17, 2016).

Wade, R. 1985. "The Market for Public Office: Why the Indian State Is Not Better at Development," *World Development*, 13(4): 467–97.

World Bank. 2003. *World Development Report 2004: Making Services Work for Poor People*. Washington, DC: Oxford University Press for the World Bank.

Comments and Discussion*

Devesh Kapur
University of Pennsylvania

The core question that Karthik is trying to address in his paper, namely the Indian State's weak record in public service delivery, is a recurrent thread in the discussions at the IPF over the years. The reasons are complex but rooted in weak state capacity. Karthik argues in his paper that this weakness stems from multiple distortions in public sector recruitment. What are these distortions? (a) There are not enough people; (b) the people who are hired are not the right ones for the job; (c) after they are hired, they are not trained in the right way; (d) even those hired and trained in the right way are not put in the right places or positions; and (e) even when hired and trained in the right way and put in the right places or positions, they are not paid the right way—the structure of payments is not designed to motivate them—and they are not promoted the right way.

This is an important paper because it highlights a critical issue that we really have not discussed much in the IPF, namely the deeply troubling subject of a seriously ailing public administration in India. There have been virtually no attempts at reform, and I would argue that the future of India itself depends on the ability to restructure public administration, which is a tremendously hard and long-term task. So, before getting into Karthik's proposals, one of the upfront things I like about the paper is that it addresses a serious lacuna in the last two decades of social science work on institutions. This literature has been singularly focused on defining institutions as "rules of the game" and has ignored earlier thinking about institutions as organizations and the internal processes of how organizations work, including questions of personnel selection, training, motivation, team building, and career ladders. These issues are fundamental for any private firm, and they expend enormous effort in addressing them. But public sector organizations most often see them as a side issue. Hence, the focus of the paper is a very

* To preserve the sense of the discussions at the IPF, these discussants' comments reflect the views expressed at the IPF and do not take into account revisions to the original conference paper in response to these and other comments, even though the IPF Volume itself contains the revised paper. The original conference version of the paper is available on www.ncaer.org.

important corrective, and Karthik offers a grounded mechanism design to try and address this significant problem.

A central issue—perhaps even an obsession—regarding recruitment in state agencies in India has been social representation, manifested in contentious debates on reservations. I firmly believe that social representation is a necessary condition for the legitimacy of public institutions. But what was a necessary condition has sadly become a sufficient one. In other words, as long as the issue of representation has been addressed, the battle of organizational effectiveness is seen to be won.

The puzzle about recruitment in India's public agencies is that while, at one level, the data appears to show incredible selection—often one out of hundred—we end up with poor outcomes. This raises two basic questions: Who does the selection and at what level? Is it done at the central level, the state level, or at the local level? And what do we know about the appropriateness of the selection mechanisms, for example, the content of examinations, for the position in question?

If one looks at the key selection institutions, the Union Public Service Commission (UPSC) and the State Public Service Commissions (SPSCs), there is not a single worthwhile analysis about their functioning in recent decades. The UPSC only recruits for the central government, while the selection for all frontline staff delivering public services is done by State (and local) level functionaries. There is virtually no SPSC whose members have not been indicted for corruption in recent decades, yet SPSCs continue to be the principal nodal institutions for the recruitment of frontline functionaries for the Indian State. And of course, as Karthik has pointed out, almost all selection is done on the basis of observable characteristics, even though the key predictors of performance are often unobservable characteristics.

So, while the selection questions for the Indian Forest Service examination might test the candidate on specific bodies of knowledge that are mastered through rote learning, a critical characteristic that might have a huge effect on job performance is whether the candidate has a passion for nature. Is the candidate desirous of joining the Forest Service so that he can cut the timber down as fast as he can sell it or so that he can manage it well for the public good? This sort of critical attribute cannot be discerned simply by performing well in an examination. The selection challenges at the entry level are even more acute at higher levels of government, where generalists rule even as India becomes a much more complex economy. There is an acute need for specialists, but the stranglehold of the IAS continues to make lateral entry very difficult.

What is the state of the Indian State? It is an understaffed but a severely overbureaucratized state. Public sector employment has slightly declined over the past quarter century, with a greater recourse to contract labor. Whether it is the size of the tax bureaucracy or the number of judges, by international comparison, the number of employees per unit population in India is amongst the lowest among the G-20 countries. To cite an example: law and order, which is a core function of any state, is a major failing of the Indian State. India has the fewest police officers per million people across G-20 countries. If one goes beyond the size of the police force to the quality of training, the picture is even more dismal. While on the one hand, the police in India are brutal in their use of physical violence, on the other, they are so poorly trained that any mob can overcome them easily. Even in an area—the armed forces—where everyone at least in principle agrees at the political level that adequate staffing is essential, there are notable vacancy rates, and these are most severe among the younger officers who actually lead in battle.

If one compares public expenditures with the number of public sector employees, the latter has been almost flat over the past quarter century, whereas expenditures have been growing enormously, with the gap steadily widening. It is fashionable in some social science circles to call the Indian State a patronage democracy, among other things. The puzzle is not that politicians have been packing the state with their political supporters but the opposite—why have they packed in so few people?

The underlying systemic issues of limited quantity and weak quality plague every aspect of the Indian State. If one looks at the Indian Economic Service and Indian Statistical Service in the past two odd decades, the state has been able to recruit barely two-thirds of the few dozen vacancies annually—this in a country of 1.2 billion and despite a strong belief that good statistical information is the fundamental basis of sound economic policy making. If we look in a very different domain, that of school teachers, only 1 percent of primary teachers (teaching classes 1 to 5) were able to clear their annual evaluation tests in February 2015 in Maharashtra and only 5 percent of upper primary teachers (teaching classes 6 to 8) were able to clear theirs. These are the people whom we entrust the task of teaching the next generation of Indians, and in effect, securing the country's future.

A singular strength of Karthik's paper is its attention to issues of mechanism design for selecting public employees. His key recommendation is to create entry-level jobs, which are untenured paid apprenticeships of three to five years, with a strong preference for "local" hires. In addition, the paper advocates creating modular training courses and providing a ladder for advancement based on performance-based credits. At the end of the apprenticeship, the state either absorbs them fully or terminates them with a lump-sum payment.

There is a range of reasons why these ideas are potentially a singular improvement over what exists currently. First, there would be more time to screen for unobservable characteristics like empathy. Second, there would be more time to train them, especially given the poor quality of education. Third, this mechanism would increase motivation by explicitly linking rewards to performance. Fourth, the proposal would importantly provide a fiscally feasible path for the much-needed expansion of frontline functionaries of the state.

These ideas are creative and a big step forward in thinking creatively about selection issues. Nonetheless, there are questions that need to be fleshed out. First, what is "local"? Is it the local village, the panchayat, or the *Gram Sabha* or is it the local district? Where does one draw the line on what constitutes "local"? Relatedly, how does one address the reservation issue? If reservations are at the state level, how are we to disaggregate them to the village or local level, or if reservations are implemented at the village/local level, how does one aggregate upward?

Second, should policies like reservations matter only during the initial selection, or should they persist subsequently as well, and if so until when? In other words, when, at the end of the three- to five-year apprenticeship period, some are selected to move up the next step of the ladder, will the proportions of Scheduled Castes (SCs)/Scheduled Tribes (STs) be the same as at entry, or will that no longer matter? If not, how will this issue be addressed politically? This will be a very contentious matter.

Also, how does one address issues of social heterogeneity at the local level? If there are two people in the same classroom from very different social groups, we should not assume that they will work together, and the Indian State very rarely thinks about how to make them work together as a team. One group in the Indian public sector that has managed to work well with social heterogeneity is the armed forces. Although they recruit from a wide range of groups, they spend enormous amounts of energy to ensure that the allegiance of the soldiers and the officers is to the unit (whether the brigade or the platoon at the local level), so that while new recruits can come from anywhere, once they join, their allegiances are reshaped toward their unit. This occurs only because of the massive effort that goes into training, which is completely absent in any other part of the Indian public sector.

Gender can be another challenge for the advantages of "local" recruitment proposed in the paper. I will give you an example that illustrates this difficulty. About a decade ago, the then Health Secretary of West Bengal was faced with a problem: when he dispatched doctors and nurses to districts to serve the public, he found that they instead provided proper services only to the ruling party's functionaries and senior district officials, and to get this service, others had to see them in their private practice after office hours. So, the government set up local nursing schools linked to the local hospitals and gave scholarships to local young women who would study for the two- to three-year program and would then get guaranteed jobs in the local hospitals. But then they found that within a few years, these women nurses would move away after marriage, the single largest source of migration in rural India. So, they had to change the design so that they would only hire women who were already married. An important question we would need to answer is how the mechanism design would address the challenges of migration and mobility.

There are key political economy challenges to consider. Who conducts the initial recruitment exams and learning modules? How centralized are these? Perhaps we could create digital learning platforms, similar to what Mr Nandan Nilekani is doing on primary school learning with his *Ek Step* initiative, to provide smartphone-based learning tools. Who decides on contract renewal? How do we know that the proposed system will not replicate at the time of contract renewal of the pathologies that were prevalent at entry, simply shifting the problem somewhere else? If rents are prevalent, why would politicians give them up? Finally, I do not agree with the paper's recommendation to use its proposed approach for recruiting and retaining police, who have the power of extraction in a way in which teachers do not. I would like the author to think about the difference.

T.V. Somanathan

Prime Minister's Office, Government of India

This is a very interesting paper that provides a novel but, prima facie, workable alternative with respect to lower-level public sector recruitment. Unlike many academic papers on these topics, it goes beyond analysis and takes the risk of proposing a very specific reform, thus making it easier to assess. The references to literature, both Indian and international, are relevant and, in some cases, provide new insights. The most impressive aspect of the paper is its understanding of field realities, particularly the legal and administrative issues involved in recruiting for the public sector. This realism is important for the practicality of the proposed new approach.

The idea of an exit payment for those who cannot, for example, clear the Teacher Eligibility Test (TET) after several years of apprenticeship as teaching assistants is an excellent one. In the case of teachers, combined with the requirement to pass the TET, it should effectively address the legal risks with contract employment of the increasing pressure for mass regularization. Those who choose not to take the exit payment and stay on could be required to provide a legally binding undertaking that they are continuing of their own volition and are aware that they may or may not be selected to the post of a regular teacher in future years.

The evaluation of teaching assistants against a "forced curve" and giving them points in the evaluation for their class-room experience is also excellent in concept. However, in the presence of widespread corruption and biases such as those related to caste and gender, there is a big risk that the evaluations would not be merit-based and/or could be done in a corrupt manner. The "forced curve" could become a performance curve enforced by corruption, not merit. Hopefully, the more meritorious apprentices would do better in the TET. Therefore, a simple weight for the number of years of service as an apprentice, with no pretense at qualitative evaluation, may be less pleasing in concept but more robust in practice.

There is one key practical gap in the paper: How do you recruit the apprentices in the first place? The post, while lower-paid than those with regular government scales, still carries two very major attractions: a four-year contract with a guaranteed pay out and an entry track into permanent service. With such major attractions, would this recruitment, to be done locally, be done in a fair manner? I only point this out as a practical difficulty and an aspect not explicitly addressed in the paper. In practice, the system may be able to deliver most of the expected benefits, even if the initial selection is imperfect.

Minor Comments

The following comments do not alter the basic arguments or conclusions, and I suggest them merely to sharpen the facts and analysis.

I find the healthcare example not convincing because of the peculiarities of healthcare as a service. Customer appreciation of healthcare services is sometimes affected by the cost—there is a behavioral issue where more expensive care (even when not strictly necessary) is perceived as better because of asymmetric information. Even among the non-poor, doctors who tell patients that they need no treatment or only simple home remedies are often perceived as not effective. A Primary Health Center (PHC) may have no incentive to provide unnecessary treatments, but a private service provider does. Hence, I am not convinced that the results show what they purport to show, and it is not clear how relevant this is to the larger point of the paper.

The paper uses the example of police deployment on VIP duty in Delhi. The choice of Delhi for this and the reference to only 30 percent of personnel being devoted to general policing and the rest to VIP security is not a good one. Delhi, as the national capital with government and embassies, is definitely an extreme case and not a representative one. This is a strong paper that does not need to quote extreme examples to make its point.

I agree with the basic point that large numbers of young people spend a lot of time on unsuccessful attempts. The paper states that the average successful applicant spends four years preparing and attempting the examinations for a public sector job. This is not necessarily full time: many combine it with a job. Therefore, some nuance in the language is desirable.

There are multiple references to pensions as one of the major benefits of government employment. Since 2004, new central and state governments' employees (except in the armed forces) are operating on a defined contribution system under the National Pension Scheme with significantly lower benefits, a situation that is not better than the organized private sector. Pensions are no longer a major attraction for public sector employment.

Manish Sabharwal

Team Lease Services Pvt. Ltd

Besides wanting to listen to Karthik Muralidharan, my other reason to be in Delhi today is to formally launch our Team Lease Skills University (TLSU) and an apprenticeship program called NETAP, the National Employability through Apprenticeship Program. We sought permission for this from the government some six years back in 2009. Following the amendment of the Apprenticeship Act passed by Parliament a few months ago, NETAP is finally a reality as a public–private partnership between the Confederation of Indian Industry (CII), National Skill Development Corporation (NSDC), Ministry of Skills, Ministry of Human Resource Development (HRD) and TLSU. We faced many challenges in getting this amendment through.

Apprenticeships are not a new concept, but they have received little attention. Apprenticeship was the 20th point in Indira Gandhi's 20-Point Programme in 1975. India only has about 400,000 apprentices, whereas

Germany has 3 million, Japan has 10 million, and China has 20 million. If we had the same percentage of our labor force in apprenticeships as Germany does, we would have 15 million apprentices. So, the upsides are well known. It is a test drive for employers. It creates signaling value much greater than that generated by classrooms for employees because it is learning by doing and there is learning while earning.

There are several reasons why it took us six years to get to this. First, the Ministry of Labour argued that we would have to guarantee 25 percent of the apprentices a job. We said that that was making the best the enemy of the good, since apprentices will not work at their apprenticeship once they are guaranteed a job. Their second argument was that employers would never convert the apprentices into regular workers but would keep rolling them over to save costs. So, we said that we would use Aadhar to authenticate identity and put a cap of two years on the apprenticeships. The ministry then argued that employers would pay exploitation wages. So, all NETAP trainees get the unskilled minimum wage. Finally, they argued that young people would always prefer a formal education degree over vocational training. So, we put NETAP into a university and gave academic credit for it. In India's first academic apprenticeship program, apprentices will get two years of academic credit, after which they can enter a degree or diploma or any other program they wish.

The issues are surely different and more complex for the public sector, though there are commonalities as well. Essentially, the problem is that in public sector jobs, there is no fear of falling and there is no hope of rising. So how does one motivate and ensure performance? The problem goes well beyond ensuring performance at the entry level. Something will also need to be done at exit. I think we can learn an important lesson from the Indian Army, which has a colonel threshold. A colonel who is not shortlisted for brigadier retires at the age of 50 or 52 years, which is why the army is not top-heavy. We need to do this with joint secretaries too. I do not know whether joint secretaries who are not shortlisted should be retired or just told that they are going to stay joint secretaries until retirement.

I think lateral entry and political appointments can create another sort of competition that can help. In the USA, 4,000 people resign in Washington D.C. when a new president is elected, but in New Delhi, only six people resign. I am not saying that the number here too should be 4,000; it is just that six is the wrong number. I think that the intense drama of appointing or transferring, say, a foreign secretary or a defense secretary has to stop. The permanent civil service should not have a monopoly on these roles, and various measures such as the colonel threshold, lateral entry, political appointments, and performance management will need to be used to address the problem in conjunction with entry-level measures.

I would have a million public employees if the civil servants, particularly in health and education, used their skills and did their jobs well. But, if the large majority have performance management issues, and we do not give the top jobs to good people when they are 45 rather than when they are 58, then just working on the entry level will not suffice. The apprenticeship idea for public sector job entry is obviously a very important one, but we should combine it with the other in-service measures, and this could make a huge difference.

General Discussion

Sudipto Mundle appreciated the paper but pointed out that there would be considerable political pressure to retain those who had failed to make it to regular employment. To overcome this, the exit payment would have to be very attractive. The financial pros and cons of a large exit payment would have to be worked out.

Dilip Mookherjee noted that the paper was proposing to create a US-style tenure system for Indian primary schools. Publications and teaching evaluations make this relatively easy in the USA. But, that will not work here. So, who would make the decisions at the retention stage? Who would make the subtle judgments of the interplay of intrinsic motivation and skills? Probably some senior teacher would have to do that. So, this would take us right back to politics and corruption, albeit at a different level. This could be solved if the exit payment were large enough, but then the cost effectiveness of such a scheme would be doubtful.

Down the line, there would be another problem of how to make the regular teacher exit if performance falls. Some variant of the colonel threshold will be needed. There were two other problems. If apprenticeship was the only way to secure a public sector job, then young people would spend years trying to get in. How do we solve that? On training modules, this would require a completely revamped approach to the practicum of teaching rather than to the current focus on the philosophy and history of teaching. Given all these difficulties, would it not make sense to focus on education vouchers that would allow parents to choose whatever school they wanted to send their children to, with the school being evaluated so that they meet standards, though we know that is also quite hard to do? But it is, at least, conceivable and has been tried elsewhere, whereas the paper's proposal may not work.

Jeffrey Hammer liked the paper and said that he would like to try out its ideas, except that they are systemic and would cost a lot to experiment with. He felt that there is a prior step to what the paper is proposing that needs attention. How could one change norms so that teachers and doctors are real professions with accountability to both peers and clients? In health, he often just fell back on saying that the doctors have to act like doctors, they have to care. They have to go beyond asking the first question of *kya hai* (what is wrong?) to their patients, just as teachers have to care whether their students are learning or not. Karthik's proposals seem to be designed to make them care, but he was not sure they would work. Teachers and doctors have to care what their peers think of them, of their image, and their performance. With police, it is even harder. In practical terms, who will mind the monitors and the screeners, because they also have to undergo a change in norms? In public service delivery, they will need to care as much as the writers of the Indian Constitution! How does one get these public servants to adopt different professional norms?

The problem Hammer thought was that in the rich countries, these professions came about before there was any public provision of such services. Doctors were acting like doctors, even before they had anything serious to contribute in the form of useful medicines or proven procedures. Here, we were dealing with a situation where they were all public servants already, and we now need to change their professional norms and make them care. He did not think that a clever mechanism design would do it.

Nirvikar Singh worried that adding a closely integrated training and certification program to a dysfunctional system may not work. It is more than likely that an apprentice teacher working with senior teachers would eventually be trained to be a part of the same system. An equilibrium exit payment that could change this would have to be equal to the present discounted value of future rents, which could be huge. The paper was attempting to overcome the difficulties in the contract teacher arrangement that has been tried in India for some years now. Apprenticeship and training were critical, but we should also think about other ways of doing this that are not tied to the existing systems or the existing bureaucracy. Examples include the various Teach for India or Teach for America programs.

Rajnish Mehra felt that one way of insulating the system from political pressure and corruption was to build in a mandatory separation after the apprenticeship, with candidates not allowed to take a job at their school but encouraged to apply elsewhere. He gave the example of the habilitation program in German universities: after completing a PhD, the person cannot be hired by his university. Otherwise, apprenticeships would simply push corruption by three-four years out at the time of retention, rather than preventing it. Only mandatory separation and having to compete in the job market would solve the problem.

Premila Nazareth differed with Nirvikar Singh and thought that the apprenticeship idea had a lot of merit. However, she felt that there was no need for an exit payment, and instead the money saved should be spent on building the capacity of the trainees and developing better training modules. She pointed out that a large number of private schools would be desperate to recruit the apprenticed teachers, so that the apprenticeships would create a market for skilled teachers. A key to its success would lie in ensuring that the certification was credible and portable, particularly in rural areas. She agreed that however it is done, there would be intense political pressure and potential corruption in any such certification, even if school management committees were involved—the *Pradhan* would still want his people favored. She also worried about what would happen to the regular teacher who may shirk work with two effective teaching assistants now available.

Vijay Joshi suggested that the author may want to take a look at the work of George Akerlof on identity economics, which might have important ideas on how to ensure that public hires providing public services actually internalize the public objectives of their organization.

Anupam Khanna wanted to know if the paper's proposal could be taken beyond highly decentralized services in healthcare and education to other government services such as in infrastructure, for example, in road repair, railways, airline services, and airports, where the solution being pursued seemed to be either outsourcing or PPPs.

Devesh Kapur went back to the West Bengal example in his discussant's comments and cited the clever way they had tried to overcome corruption in selection of the local trainees. They decided to take only those candidates who ranked high in their high school board examination at the district level, and this information was posted at the district level. The selection process was, thus, more transparent and fairer than otherwise, even though it had its limitations.